# The Gospel
# Within Us

**The Gospel Within Us** brings you on a complete verse by verse tour of *The Gospel According to Mark* and shows how this first Gospel can be seen as a workbook that provides a complete program of spiritual learning and growth, from the first stirrings of conscience to the final transformation, as Christ within us guides us into a life led by The Holy Spirit.

*Through this new, updated, refreshing look at the Gospel of Mark, Jan Kuniholm guides you and then suggests that you experience what it means to become your own spiritual Self. He has taken on the task of deciphering difficult passages into the everyday language of life. He puts into words what we are all searching for: the ability to reach God within us.*
 — Shamai Currim, PhD, Psychotherapist,
  Lachine, Quebec

Most of us read Matthew before we read Mark, and then we consider Mark in the light of what is presented in the other three Gospels. I suspect that most of us "fill in" the gaps that seem to be missing in Mark with information we get from other New Testament books, but this not only fills in "information," it also colors our reading of Mark and injects interpretations that do not belong in Mark.

What if Mark is *the* original Gospel, perhaps written by an aide to Peter as the tradition suggests—what if the original Gospel is intended to be sparing of details so that the Gospel *process* would take hold in the lives of readers and students?

If we take the Gospel of Mark by itself and read it without filling in the "blanks" by reference to other New Testament writings, but take Mark entirely by itself, we arrive at a startlingly different view of Jesus, his words, life and death. — from the *Afterword*

**The Gospel Within Us** will show you this view. Seeing it and working with it may deepen your faith and change your life.

# The Gospel Within Us

The Gospel According to Mark As a Handbook for Healing and Personal Transformation

Jan Kuniholm

Copyright © 2012 by Jan L. Kuniholm and Barbara D. Kuniholm

All rights reserved. No part of this publication may be reproduced, distributed, or transmitted in any form or by any means, including photocopying, recording, or other electronic or mechanical methods, without the prior written permission of the publisher, except in the case of brief quotations embodied in reviews and certain non-commercial uses permitted by the U.S. Copyright Act of 1976.

Published by Cheshire Cat Books
P.O. Box 599
Cheshire, MA 01225-0599
www.Cheshire-Cat-Books.com

Book and Cover Design
    by Jan Kuniholm
Drawings, Crochet Doilies and Pressed Flower Arrangements
    by Bonney Kuniholm
Final Drawing "Take My Joy"
    by Virginia Flint Kuniholm

The material in this book is intended for educational purposes only. No expressed or implied warranty is given or liability taken as to the use of this material. Users of this book are advised to seek professional assistance, guidance or support should they encounter any difficulty in applying the material herein.

Library of Congress Control Number:   2012915724
                         ISBN   978-0-9882024-0-5

Website: www.GospelWithinUs.com

For Bonney,
without whom this would not have been written

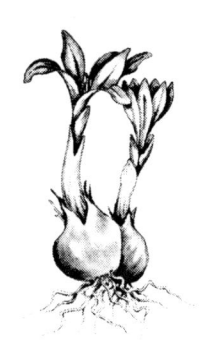

Contents:

Preface　　　　　　　　　　　　　　　　　　　　　xviii

PART I　　　　　　　　　　　　　　　　　　　　　　1

A Different Kind of Book　　　　　　　　　　　　　　2
The Teacher　　　　　　　　　　　　　　　　　　　11
A Unique Teaching Tool　　　　　　　　　　　　　　13
How to Use This Book　　　　　　　　　　　　　　18
About the English version of Mark
　and the Organization of this Book　　　　　　　　　21

PART II　　　　　　　　　　　　　　　　　　　　　26

The Gospel According to Mark

A: PREPARATION　　　　　　　　　　　　　　　27

1) Change: Conscience and the Presence of the Spirit　28
　a) The awakening of conscience:
　　　hearing its voice, response to its call
　b) The choice to change
　c) The presence of the Spirit of God
2) Negative Voices, The Adversary,　　　　　　　　36
　　　and the Spiritual Process
　a) Distinguishing negative voices: conscience,
　　　the inner critic, the adversary
　b) The adversary is always present.
　c) Testing by the adversary
　d) Qualities that help when we are tested
　e) What testing does to our goals and desires
3) The Gathering: Spiritual Qualities　　　　　　　　44
　a) Awareness of inner subpersonalities
　b) Inner disciples
　c) Balance and extremes of qualities
　d) "I am"
　Table A — Spiritually Helpful (Disciple)
　Qualities: Balanced Qualities Between Opposites　52

4) The Work Begins 57
   a) Awareness of how testing pressures balanced qualities into extremes
   b) Balancing qualities
   c) The "inner Simon"
   d) The "inner mother-in-law"
   e) What parts of us need to be healed?
5) Healing, Forgiveness and Faith 68
   a) Awareness of what parts of us need to be healed
   b) Spiritual gatekeepers
   c) Getting past the spiritual gatekeepers
   d) Listening
   e) The "inner tax collector"
   f) "Inner scribes and Pharisees"
   g) Ideals that inhibit learning
6) A New Spiritual Pathway 84
   a) Spiritual disciples
   b) Spiritual greed
   c) Relief and Healing
   d) Inner qualities, suffering, inner progress

**B: FOCUS** 96

7) Mobilization for Service: The Twelve 97
   a) Inner qualities that serve the Spirit
   **Table B** — More Spiritually Helpful (Disciple) Qualities: Qualities Associates with the Twelve 104
8) Identity and Spirit: Who is This, *Really?* 109
   a) The Holy Spirit
   b) Consistency
   c) Binding "the strong man"
   d) Inner resistance to change
   e) Strategies to overcome inner resistance
   f) Giving and receiving unconditional forgiveness
   g) Forgiveness of all
9) The Family of Habit and the Family of Spirit 117
   a) The "inner family" we grew up with
   b) The "inner spiritual family"
10) Parables: The Kingdom of God 120
    a) First principles of the Kingdom of God
    b) Inner voices

    c) Paying attention
    d) Attitudes of "having" and "not having"
    e) Changing an inner community
11) Into the Depths     131
    a) Inner storms and inner calm
    b) Finding the inner "man in the tombs"
    c) The "economy" of being unhealed
    d) Deep healing and spiritual truth
12) The Work of Faith: Life and Healing     139
    a) Inner parents and inner children
    b) Inner "infertility"
    c) Inner "dead" ones
    d) What is faith?
13) History, Knowledge and Faith     146
    a) Familiarity and faith
    b) Knowledge and faith

## C: PRACTICE     153

14) Action and Reaction     154
    a) The active work of the inner disciples
    b) The "inner Herod"
    c) The "inner dancing princess"
    d) Sabotage of growth by the needs of inner children
    e) The stifling on conscience
15) Spiritual Resources     163
    a) Inner "bread and fish"
    b) Bringing inner resources to the Spirit
    c) The multiplication of resources
16) Crossing Boundaries: Reality and the Mind     169
    a) Spiritual discernment: vision and interpretation
    b) Recognizing inner events
    c) Recognizing "the other side"
    d) Receiving the Spirit
17) Things of the Heart     176
    a) "All who touched him were healed"
    b) The false conflict between "the practical" and "the spiritual"
    c) Inner exposure and outer exposure

    d) What comes out of the heart,
       and what comes into the heart
18) Loving "The Other," the Alien                     184
    a) Acknowledging the inner "alien" or foreigner
    b) Overcoming the "victim" mentality
19) Healing is a Beginning                                188
20) Spiritual Resources, Part 2                       191
    a) Water in the desert
    b) Crossing ordinary boundaries
    c) The power of faith is action, not a "sign"
    d) Validation from our own experience
    e) The spiritual walk is about practical faith,
       not about doing "right" or doing "well"
    f) Some lessons need repeated effort

## D: REALIZATION                                                201

21) Who is This, *Really?*                                202
    a) Real attention, real awareness, real presence
    b) What or who moves us toward healing,
       peace, wholeness?
    c) Who is the Christ?
    d) Who am I?
    e) To picture the Christ is
       to picture one who must die
    f) The death of the man-Christ allows
       the birth of the Spirit of God in us
    g) The life of the Spirit in us is a
       reciprocal relationship
22) Listening for Meaning                                214
    a) Our first task in the spiritual life is to listen
    b) The life of the Spirit in us is the completion
       of our spiritual traditions
    c) Our task is to discern meaning
       from stories, from events, from life
23) Faith                                                          218
    a) Spiritual "high points" are often followed
       by challenges
    b) "Facts" do not provide a channel for inner
       power
    c) Faith is to be applied to facts

- d) Faith is a response to the will of God
- e) Faith must be learned
- f) Power comes to the one who has faith

24) A Private Teaching — 223
   - a) The meaning of "Death and resurrection of the Christ" must be learned from experience

25) Leadership — 227
   - a) When we do not have spiritual guidance, our egos want to lead us, choosing the part of us that is "the greatest"
   - b) Real leadership arises out of service, both within us and outside ourselves
   - c) One must become as a little child to receive spiritual guidance from the Spirit

26) The Temptations of the Chosen — 231
   - a) Disciples tend to want to "protect the message" and close it off from "corruption"
   - b) Real spiritual action cannot be counterfeited
   - c) God does not need us to defend him
   - d) Real healing cannot be counterfeited
   - e) One who exercises the power of the Spirit has the Spirit
   - f) The authority of the Spirit is in the healing Power
   - g) Our ideals can become an obstacle to faith and healing, in ourselves or others
   - h) If we realize that we have such an obstacle, we will feel like a piece of burning trash
   - i) Removing the source of the obstacle
   - j) Experience will both "cure" and "season" us, and this will sometimes be painful
   - k) External and internal "seasoning"

27) Wholeness — 239
   - a) Which inner characteristics are essential or not essential to our being
   - b) The vital native characteristics within us must be cherished, "married" and maintained
   - c) "Divorcing" any of our own essential characteristics is a self-violation
   - d) Non-native, non-essential characteristics may be kept or released

    e)  Essential characteristics are those through which we exercise our will
    f)  Non-essential parts of us are only attachments through which we react
    g)  Essential characteristics may be expressed in seemingly opposite ways
    h)  Wholeness involves the marriage, or synthesis of seemingly opposite essential parts of us
    i)  Wholeness involves our embrace and acceptance of all parts of our essential being

**Table C** — Balanced Qualities from a "Synthesis or Marriage of Opposites" — 246
**Table D** — Expanded Qualities from a "Synthesis or Marriage of Opposites" — 248

28) Spiritual Power — 249
    a)  Spiritual life is not something one can "get" like a commodity or position
    b)  Spiritual life is an orientation to a relationship with God
    c)  Spiritual power is not a "transaction;" it flows one way: outward from God
    d)  The order and priorities of things of the world are no indication of spiritual order
    e)  The relationship of each person to the Spirit is unique, and there are no comparisons

29) Spiritual Power, Part 2 — 258
    a)  Spiritual life and power is about giving power and giving life
    b)  The most common earthly manifestation of this giving is called "service"
    c)  The Spirit of God serves All

30) Faith, Part 2 — 263
    a)  One model of faith in action

## E: CONFRONTATION — 268

31) Confrontation — 269
    a)  The Spirit within us will confront the dominant ego that controls our lives
    b)  The goal of the Spirit is to rule in peace and end strife

- c) The Spirit will withdraw power from empty gestures and "signs"
- d) The Spirit will end any "transactions" that masquerade as "spirituality"

32) Spiritual Power, Part 3     275
- a) Four steps of faith

33) Authority and Power     280
- a) Our inner gatekeepers will resist the rise of the Spirit to rule our lives
- b) The gatekeepers within us are unable to conceive power that is not coercive
- c) The ego will pretend ignorance in order to avoid facing the reality of the Spirit
- d) We all run our lives by a "system" or a "program" of some sort
- e) Our inner systems are often based upon opposition to something
- f) We do not really understand what it is like to be ruled by the Spirit

34) Recognition     287
- a) The Spirit recognizes that our resistance to it may become violent
- b) A greater One will remove power from the parts of us that resist the Spirit

35) Polarities and Conflicts     291
- a) There is no conflict between what is practical and what is spiritual
- b) In the spiritual life the bases for conflict are removed
- c) Polarity is built into the outlook of our ego-centered life

36) Three Responses to Scribes     296
- a) The commandments to love God and to love others as ourselves
- b) All issues of "right" and "wrong" must follow after these commandments
- c) The Christ is within, and was available to King David as much as he is to us
- d) The scriptures were made for mankind, not mankind for the scriptures
- e) The priorities of those who "keep the book" are not the priorities of God

**F: TRANSFORMATION** 303

37) Spiritual Power, Part 4 304
   a) The level of personal commitment is of greatest importance
   b) The Source and direction of spiritual Power
38) The Great Transformation 307
   a) The edifice of our self-serving ego must come down
   b) It dissolution will be accompanied by struggle, conflict, and temptation
   c) The one who follows this process through may be hated and betrayed
   d) We must trust the process
   e) The greatest temptation will be to try to force the process
   f) The process is a new birth, like that of a butterfly from the chrysalis of a caterpillar
   g) Those who do not recognize it for what it is may try to stop it
   h) The one who endures this process to the end will be delivered
   i) Stay awake, be prepared, for this process comes to all of us in one way or another
39) The Anointing 319
   a) Our disciple parts may have only a very limited understanding of the process
   b) An unknown, unnamed part of us does recognize what is happening
   c) The Spirit will acknowledge that recognition in some way
   d) A misguided inner disciple responds by initiating spiritual warfare
40) Spiritual Warfare: The Beginning of the Betrayal 322
   a) One of our "inner disciples" provokes a confrontation between the Spirit and the ego
   b) This provocation takes a form that appears to be betrayal to our inner disciples
   c) Life pressures move us away from inner balance to inner extremes and polarities

41) Love and Betrayal — 327
   a) Our inner qualities can be moved to an extreme polarity
   b) We may try with all our ability to prevent it, nevertheless it may happen
   c) In the Spirit, there is no failure and no betrayal
   d) Our task is to completely absorb the teaching and presence of the Spirit
   e) Our work is to surrender the man-image of God
42) Surrender — 336
   a) We need support in order to undergo the great transformation
   b) We may not be able to remain consciously aware of the process as it unfolds
   c) This inability is something that we must accept
43) Capture and Condemnation — 341
   a) Even our "better" parts may respond violently, but the Spirit will not take part in conflict
   b) The image of the Spirit of God will always fail to satisfy the ego's demands
   c) The Spirit will not allow itself to be drawn into conflict with its adversary
   d) In the end the ego is enraged by the reality that it encounters
44) Love and Betrayal, Part 2 — 348
   a) Even our most devoted "inner disciple" will betray the Spirit and deny it
45) Good and Evil — 351
   a) The practical, "power-oriented" side of us will kill off "spiritual" aspects of us if it can
46) The Death of Jesus — 355
   a) The strain of our spiritual transformation may show in unexpected ways
   b) The human representation of the Spirit of God within us must die
   c) This "death" will remove the barriers between ordinary awareness and spiritual awareness

47) Beyond Death     361
    a) The "inner death and resurrection" is now witnessed by the "inner mothers"
    b) The resurrected Spirit of God will lead the way back to ordinary life
    a) The Spirit of God now lives within us and within our awareness, present and available

48) Summary: The Process in The Gospel Story     368

Appendix A— The Fruits of The Spirit     371

Index of Study Question Issues     374

## PART III     383

**Walking Out the Gospel: Exercises in Spiritual Psychology**

**Introduction and Preparation for the Exercises**     384

| | | |
|---|---|---|
| **Exercise 1a:** | Repentance (for one person) | 388 |
| **Exercise 1b:** | Repentance (for two people) | 389 |
| **Exercise 2:** | Presence (for one person) | 391 |
| **Exercise 3:** | Immediacy (for one person) | 392 |
| **Exercise 4a:** | Qualities (for one person) | 394 |
| **Exercise 4b:** | Qualities (for two or three people) | 396 |
| **Exercise 5a:** | Qualities of a Subpersonality (for one person) | 397 |
| **Exercise 5b:** | Witnessing (for one person) | 401 |
| **Exercise 5c:** | The Quality that is Witnessed (for two people) | 403 |
| **Exercise 6:** | Discerning the Inner Parts of Us that Need Healing (for one person) | 405 |
| **Exercise 7:** | Silence (for one person) | 407 |
| **Exercise 8:** | Eating with "Them" (for one person) | 408 |
| **Exercise 9:** | Gathering Our Twelve (for one person) | 410 |
| **Exercise 10:** | Recognition and Choice (for one person) | 412 |
| **Exercise 11:** | Inner Child (for two people) | 415 |
| **Exercise 12:** | Becoming Aware of Blessings (for one or two people) | 417 |
| **Exercise 13:** | Trust and Awareness (for two people) | 418 |

**Exercise 14a:** Inner Marriage (for one person)     419
**Exercise 14b:** Building Inner Marriage
                 (for one person)     420
**Exercise 15:**   Asking (for two people)     422
**Exercise 16:**   Prayer (for one person)     423

**Afterward:**   The Author and the Work:
               A Believer in Search of a Faith     425
**Take My Joy**     435

# Preface

This is a book to help you discover ways the Gospel of Mark may be used personally and practically to fulfill the Gospel's purpose in your own life.

In the Gospel's own language, its purpose it to help prepare you, when you are ready, to live "in the kingdom of God." The Gospel's purpose, as I see it, is to be an aid in transforming you from someone subject to habits, passions, and the prevailing influences that blow us all this way and that, into a spiritually mature person who lives in responsive awareness of the larger context of life— of the reality that includes the spiritual and the physical— and whose being and action manifest a higher (or deeper, or *greater*) purpose. The Gospel's purpose is to move you from the *awareness* of spiritual life, through some of the pitfalls and questions, toward the *reality* of spiritual life.

This book, like the Gospel itself, may not appeal to everyone but is addressed to those who have "ears to hear" this particular message. I hope that the material presented in Part I may help you to decide whether this is a book that you wish to work with.

Nevertheless I want to alert those who may expect to find a "self-help" or "self-improvement" book between these covers. While I do address myself a great deal to what we can or may do with respect to the Gospel, I also want to emphasize my deep conviction that each of us is part of a Network, and the Power coming through the Network also moves us. In the larger context I see this book as something like "Bartimaeus' helper"— something that helps the blind man get to the road where Jesus comes walking.

I hope to present a new way of looking at this particular Gospel that may complement or enrich other ways of looking at it. In our modern Bibles the Gospel of Mark is sandwiched between longer and more "detailed" gospels, and the fact that Mark follows Matthew in our books leads many of us to read Mark in the light of Matthew. But if we remove the interpretive filters we have acquired from reading the stories, interpretations and theology in the other books of the New Testament and subsequent teachings, we can discover something new in the special perspective Mark offers us. This way of approaching the Gospel of Mark is a secret that has been hidden in plain sight for 2000 years.

Mark, taken by itself, is remarkably free of some of the elements of exclusivity, judgment and condemnation that are found in some other New Testament books. This freedom leads us in a different direction than what we find in, say, Matthew. It is also what makes Mark more accessible and useful for many modern students, for I believe that Mark's Gospel provides us with an inclusive approach to spiritual life that recognizes all aspects of the person, and that teaches a way that involves body and soul, mind and Spirit.

I have produced a work that on occasion moves freely between fact and metaphor, thought and feeling, and this may be difficult for those who require "rigorous" thought and precise definitions of terms. My observation is that life is sometimes too large and complex to be contained in cleanly defined terms, so I ask you to be prepared to allow some of the words in this book to be "warm and fuzzy" rather than "sharp and clear," to allow some words to be evocative rather than definitive, to allow these words to ask you something rather than tell you. Our focus is not on words or terms, but on the locus of living that crosses over between word and feeling, thought and action, body and Spirit, so my use of words does some crossing over, too. The purpose of the book is to stimulate and to guide rather than to inform, for I trust that there is a sufficient wealth of *information* about Mark's Gospel available from other sources. I hope to stimulate your ability and willingness to take the Gospel right into your inmost thoughts, your emotions and actions, into your way of being yourself. The Gospel itself will guide you once you take it in.

I am grateful to Dorothy Firman, John Coan, Claire Goodwin and all the people connected with The Synthesis Center in Amherst Massachusetts, for the training in psychosynthesis that not only helped me to become more balanced as a person, but also enabled me to open up more fully to the spiritual life. That new openness enabled me to go back to the Gospel with a new mind, and this book is one of the results.

I am grateful to Penney Oedel and Karen Pesavento, who read the manuscript and made many helpful suggestions; to Walter Polt, who helped me make some vital connections on how I express my thoughts, and especially to Bill Schillaci, who helped me reshape the organization of the manuscript and clarify what I was trying to say, and challenged me to say it well. Bill's questions also stimulated me to think harder about what I am presenting, and I have learned a lot in my efforts to respond to them. I thank Anne Yeomans and Wendy Webber, whose encouragement and support have helped me persevere with this project.

Like all work, this book has its limitations, and responsibility for its failings is mine alone.

My deep love and gratitude to my wife, Bonney, for being with me and encouraging me through this time, simply cannot be expressed in words. She has contributed much to the content of the text as well as all the artwork, and without her I would not be on this path at all.

*Cheshire, Mass.*
*September 2012*

# PART 1

## A Different Kind of Book

Suppose that a pair of men show up in a little Mediterranean town some time around the year 60. They say they are disciples of Jesus of Nazareth, the Christ, and they have a "joyous message" for those "with ears to hear." They invite all who are interested to listen. They find some people who respond to what they say, and they stay in the town some time, working with and teaching all those who respond to their message. While they are in the town, they invite one of the new students to memorize a handbook to keep and to help them remember the lessons, work out the teachings and practice them. That handbook might have been what is now called The Gospel According to Mark—a workbook for students, to be kept as a reference for people who are engaging with the teaching over a period of time.

Of course, we do not live in the year 60 and cannot approach the Gospel of Mark with the same outlook as those who taught it or heard it nearly 2000 years ago. We are not intimately acquainted with events in the first century—we can only attempt to reconstruct some of them from the sketchy evidence that can be gleaned from archeological digs and the New Testament books and other documents. The archeological evidence suggests possible answers to questions but cannot offer definitive explanations, and the record shows that arguments over how to interpret the evidence have gone on for extended periods. And there is a major problem with our relying on other documents—there is no way to determine whether any of them are unbiased observations or complete, accurate reports. There are a lot of discrepancies in the documents we have—for example, even different ancient manuscripts of the same book contain discrepancies in important details such as the names of Jesus' disciples.[1]

Between Mark's time and ours, three other gospels have been written along with the rest of the New Testament and innumerable commentaries and other writings that build on the foundation of the story of the life, death and teaching of Jesus of Nazareth. It is widely

---

[1] Robert Price, quoted in Michael Turton, *Historical Commentary on the Gospel of Mark,* Chapter 3 page 7. See Note 3 next page.

held that the writers of the other three gospels either knew of Mark or used Mark as a source. With the possible exception of some of the genuine letters of Paul, which may be earlier than or contemporary with Mark's Gospel, all of these other documents are at successively greater distances from the life and ministry of Jesus. The extant manuscripts and later references to the Gospel of Mark that we have do not go back further than early second century, so there is reason to suppose that the "original" Gospel According to Mark is irretrievably lost, but that it (or its original core) may have been of an earlier date than any other New Testament document. Some studies of Mark try to connect not only its source but also its meaning to historical events. An examination and comparison of Mark with the other gospels and with other New Testament documents reveals significant differences in historical details as well as in teachings.[2] Some studies such as Michael Turton's *Historical Commentary of the Gospel of Mark*[3] argue that Mark used a little history and a great deal of Old Testament as source material to construct a brilliant work of fiction. Many observers note that works of fiction are often able to communicate truth more incisively than works of history. Regardless of whether the Gospel is history or fiction, my observation is that historical, literary and critical studies of Mark do not look closely at what the Gospel itself, *taken just as it is*, can do to change the inner and outer life of a person.

---

[2] A brief overview of Markan scholarship can be found online at the Wikipedia article http://en.wikipedia.org/wiki/Gospel_of_Mark. A history of the currents and cross-currents of early Christian beliefs, practices and documents can be found in Helmut Koester's *Introduction to the New Testament,* Philadelphia, Fortress Press, 1982 and 2nd edition 2000. See especially Volume 2, "History and Literature of Early Christianity." Koester's work also contains an extensive bibliography.

[3] At http://www.michaelturton.com/Mark/GMark_index.html, which is an interesting verse by verse commentary focusing on the historicity of people, places, events, and sayings in the world of the Gospel of Mark. Turton is a skeptic whose arguments may not appeal to some believers, (especially his flat rejection of the historicity of miracles) but he provides a wealth of fascinating analysis of Gospel scholarship and the discussions concerning its historicity. Turton also provides a lengthy bibliography of books on the Gospel of Mark and related topics at http://www.michaelturton.com/Mark/GMarkrefs.html.

I suggest that there is a personal meaning embedded in the Gospel of Mark—something that can be found within the Gospel itself without reference to other documents, and that this meaning is the most important aspect of this Gospel. This meaning can be seen in the Gospel regardless of whether it is a historically accurate document or not, for the meaning derives not from the Gospel's sources but rather from its application. I believe that the Gospel was written with application in mind, and that the basic direction that the Gospel's application takes is not dependent on its historicity or its literary sources.

How would we apply the Gospel of Mark to our own lives if it were presented to us as a fresh new document by a traveling apostle today? Such an apostle would not be a scholar or a archeologist; he would be working to change peoples' lives one person at a time, or one group at a time, much as many contemporary preachers do. But it seems that few if any contemporary preachers are able to affect the kind of radical change in people that the earliest apostles facilitated. Early Christians were *different* from other people—they believed, thought, behaved in ways that were unlike their contemporaries. They lived—and died—in ways that baffled others of their time, and that would baffle many modern people. They were sharers, truth-tellers, forgivers, lovers, healers. I believe that they *received* something from—or through—the Gospel that cannot be recovered in comparative studies or critical analysis, something that *can* be recovered by reading the Gospel with an eye to its original purpose. Of course we cannot read the mind of the original author, but we can try to hear what the Gospel says to us in and about our inmost selves—to our hearts—for it is here that we find the difference that marked off the early Christians, and it is here that we will see the difference in ourselves.

But we do not live in the year 60. In our culture the relationship between men and women is vastly different from what was found in the ancient Near East. We go to physicians and hospitals when we have diseases, and we believe that most diseases are caused by stress or viruses or nutritional deficiencies, not demons. We do not eat by breaking loaves of bread as the ancients did, and most of us buy our fish already filleted from markets, not whole and fresh caught from the boat. Few of us actually have visions of Elijah or Jesus, and fewer still have seen anyone raised from the dead. So how can we relate directly and personally to the events that are portrayed in the Gospel? How could we possibly respond as the early Christians responded?

I think that for many of us the short answer to that question is, "We cannot." Any attempt to reconstruct exactly how an early Christian would have responded to the Gospel is more useful as a historical exercise than as a way for us to experience what the early Christians experienced. We are just too different and our lives are too different. But while the details of life as related in the Gospel are separated from us by place as well as two millennia of human and social change, I believe that there is an underlying human condition that is essentially the same now as it was then, and is the same in all people at all times. If we look at the surface of the Gospel, all we may see is how its people and times differ from ours; but beneath the surface there is a wealth of common ground, and it is here that the Gospel can speak to us most directly. I believe that the underlying spiritual and human realities the Gospel addresses were transmitted to ancient people through the characters and events in the Gospel story—people related the events and people in the Gospel story to themselves and their own lives, and when that association went deep enough, radical change resulted.

These underlying realities can be translated into terms that can speak to anyone today, provided of course that we have "ears to hear," a condition that was also needed for people to understand the Gospel in ancient times. That condition cannot be defined because it is a unique receptivity that can be identified in an individual only after the transmission has taken place, as happened to the woman in Chapter 5 of Mark. The "translation" needed for us to be able hear the Gospel's message is not from one language to another, but from a set of ancient symbols and experiences to modern ones that can have a similar effect.

It would be fruitful, then, to construct an analogous way that we modern people could respond to the Gospel so that the *difference* it made in early Christians could be available to us. This book attempts to provide an interpretation of the Gospel of Mark that is analogous *in its effects* to what the early Christians received from the original Gospel.

At the core of this interpretation of Mark is the view that the Gospel is an extended "teaching story" that contains wisdom from which learning and benefits are derived only when a student applies her or his own personal experience to the teaching, and approaches and uses the teaching with openness, humility, and a willingness to be transformed as persons.

This book starts from the premise that the teaching that can be found in Mark is a flexible tool, an instrument of personal transformation that is available to those "with ears to hear." For those who are able to follow the way of the teaching, its results are that the student lives in "the kingdom of God"—that is, the person is transformed into one in whom the divine manifests consciously. The transformation the Gospel aims to facilitate is a change in life orientation, not a change only in thought or behavior. This transformation is the central purpose of the Gospel, and this purpose underlies everything in Mark, from the first line to the last.

The Gospel does not by itself *make* anything happen, for tools do nothing by themselves. Memorizing or quoting the book will not give anyone "The Answer." Its power lies entirely in its use—its application. Allowing the Gospel to speak to you at certain critical moments in your life can help to open you to your own spiritual path, to quicken your relationship with God, to bring to life something you need, to reveal something you must become aware of, in your walk with God. This makes things happen in your life.

The Gospel of Mark, then, is not merely a story to read—for as a story, it is a relatively bare-bones tale compared with the other gospels. Many readers both ancient and modern prefer other gospels to Mark because the others have more details, more words of Jesus, more deep theology. Compared with the other three gospels, Mark seems to have a lot missing. But this impression relies on the assumption that the Gospel is essentially the *story* of Jesus. I believe that this assumption is not valid for the Gospel According to Mark. Whether or not Mark contains the recollections of Peter or another eyewitness, I think that if this Gospel had been intended as a history it would have contained much more detail, such as are contained in the other gospels. If, on the other hand, the purpose of the Gospel of Mark is not to relate history but rather to change the lives of the people who hear and learn the story—and change them in a specific way—then the content of what is presented needs to be different from the content of a history.

I believe that Mark *uses* the story of Jesus as a platform to affect personal change that can be so profound it may be referred to as transformation. That this level of radical change was the intent of the early Christian apostles is attested elsewhere in the New Testament, especially in some letters of Paul, who writes explicitly of our being transformed, and of our taking on the mind of Christ.[4]

Whereas Paul more often wrote about issues that were of concern to groups of people as they formed churches, this book proceeds on the assumption that the Gospel According to Mark is concerned with the transformation of individuals, without which the changes in groups are mere reorganizations. Paul wrote some letters to groups of people concerning problems in their beliefs and behavior, suggesting that perhaps the desired transformation (also called regeneration) had not occurred in some individuals. When the Gospel was preached or proclaimed as something to be heard and confessed rather than presented as a work to be practiced over a lifetime, the result may have been "Paul's problems," such as those he addressed in letters to the congregations in Galatia and Corinth. Similarly in our time, preaching the Gospel to multitudes only begins to convey the depth of the transformation in which the Gospel invites us to participate.

I believe that Mark's Gospel is intended to be a more interactive document than other New Testament documents, and it is addressed to the individual. The elements that for some people seem to be "missing" in this Gospel have the same function as blanks in a modern interactive questionnaire. Instead of a text such as the Gospel of Matthew that says, "Jesus said *such and such*," Mark's Gospel presents us with something analogous to a questionnaire that reads, "Jesus says_____ (listen within yourself and fill in based upon your own experience)." Filling in that blank, so to speak, is not a matter of learning the "right answers" and giving them back, as a modern student would be required to do in a test, and it is not even a matter of searching our thoughts and feelings and responding with answers from our heart and mind. The Gospel of Mark guides us to learn to *hear* responses from within ourselves and to *see* meaning in our experience, and takes us through some transforming experiences that allow a new kind of response to emerge from within us.

In Mark's Gospel the story frames a series of teachings, each of which is to be applied when the right circumstance arises—a series

---
[4] See 1 Cor.2, Rom.12:2, for examples.

of lessons aimed at bringing the spiritual learner to successively greater stages of spiritual maturity and receptivity—not only of thinking, but of living. The good news— the "joyous message" is how I translate it from the original Greek— is that these lessons are available for all of us and the *end* (or ultimate purpose) of the lessons is available to all of us. In applying them, we become persons in whom God lives and breathes and loves—something that does not happen by merely saying the "right" words, thinking the "right" thoughts, or even doing the "right" deeds. One who lives "in the kingdom of God" lives in conscious relationship with God, and is someone who can teach the way by *being* the way.

The Gospel According to Mark was written by such a person, one who had walked the way and knew the bends in the road. The Gospel is there for you to learn from *when* you reach certain bends in the road. It is a guide book with suggestions for those who travel the spiritual way. It is not an answer book, but more a book to raise questions and to help us learn to be open to genuine spiritual guidance as it emerges in our lives. As you walk the spiritual path you will come to realize *which* questions are directed at you, and *when* they are relevant—some will have little or no significance until you arrive at a certain point in your life. In this way the Gospel is analogous to a tour guide, in which the descriptions of what to look for in the view of the mountain are not practically helpful *until* you have walked up the trail far enough to come to the outlook where the mountain is visible. Once we see the mountain, the guide helps us look, to really see what is there, and to respond to it. What "answers" are given to us, then, are given to us *after* we have looked and responded.

When I speak of "successively greater stages of spiritual maturity" the reader may get the impression that the process that the Gospel leads us through is a clear road leading in a straight line from "less maturity" to "more maturity." But the process of spiritual maturation is in fact not a "straight line" affair, but more like a spiral that winds forward and back, up and down, in an uneven movement toward a goal that is unclear to us as we go. Sometimes the way seems to be leading away from the goal, much as a road up a mountain may wind around and switch back before continuing upward. There is a reason why the word for "spirit" was the same word used for "wind" in many ancient languages, and our way toward spiritual maturity is a process that is no more regular than the flow of the wind. The Gospel itself is no more "regular" than the wind, and we find that it flows this way and that, often coming back to a point like the wind swirling, only to do something new. This apparent repetition is deliberate, I believe, because the process of spiritual growth that is being nurtured by the Gospel is one that requires us to revisit lessons, which are often learned one aspect at a time and which are then augmented by successive experience. The augmented experience allows us to return to the lesson to learn another aspect of it, continuing until we have it complete—we hope! And then, we have the *rest* of the good news: there is more than our learning to this process, for our learning is just the means to move us, like Bartimaeus, into the "road where Jesus is coming."

This experience is perhaps a little like learning to drive a car—one learns the function of brake, gas pedal, and steering wheel, one at a time, and then practices this learning by coordinating the individual functions in driving in a straight line and stopping. But then one must revisit these functions as one encounters different driving experiences such as coming to a stop on a hill, or parallel parking. Only after applying the basic skills in an increasing variety of circumstances, polishing our abilities and learning how to respond appropriately to situations, do we develop an "inner driver" who can use these skills in a coordinated way in every circumstance and respond appropriately without our having to stop and think about the individual functions of acceleration, braking, steering and so on. After we have developed our "inner driver" we no longer *think* about the mechanical functions of driving the car—rather we get in the car and just go somewhere, responding on the way to whatever occurs.

The purpose of the Gospel of Mark is to allow us to develop within us a spiritual "inner driver" who coordinates all the functions of our lives in a spiritual context and allows us to open ourselves to truly Spiritual guidance.[5] It proceeds with lessons about faith and power, attitudes and responses, leading us toward a greater realization of the life in the spirit. Just as a book about driving a car is no substitute for the actual practice of driving, the Gospel is not a substitute for living, but rather it is a guide book to show us some of the essential lessons in the process of spiritual maturation.

---

[5] Over time we may discover that our inner spiritual "driver" is not the same as "me."

The Gospel According to Mark, then, is a guide book written for people who lived two thousand years ago in the Middle East, in a style that was more familiar to them than it is to us. Early users of such a guide book were not scholars or theologians, but people who wanted to live spiritual *lives*. Western culture and churches have presented ways to interpret this Gospel that may not allow it to do for us what it did for early readers. While I recognize that there is no single "correct" way to read this Gospel, I do think that there are ways to read Mark that unlock it for us personally in a manner that historical, literary or critical approaches do not. In this book I present one such way.

This book, then, is a "guidebook to the guidebook." It is a line by line interpretation of the entire Gospel from Chapter 1 Verse 1 to Chapter 16 Verse 8, and presents a way to look at this Gospel and work with it that may allow you, the reader, to use the Gospel to learn to live a life similar to what early Christians lived. This book, like the Gospel itself, is not intended to be simply read and digested as one would learn from a history book. Rather, it is a handbook that is meant to guide thought and spiritual practice, alone or in groups, and to help those who are more mature to help those coming with them to learn and live. It may help you by stimulating a new reflection or understanding, prompting new self-awareness and awareness of others, suggesting new interpretations of experience and new ways to respond to experience, and a new way to understand the flow of your life in a larger context that may lead to a profound life change—yet this book will only be as useful as you make it, and as Jesus suggests in the Gospel, nothing is guaranteed, for the first may be last and the last first.

This book is designed to be read in small bites rather than all at once, so that you can take in what is being presented and work with it a little at a time. Some people who try to take it in all at once may feel overwhelmed—or miss what it has to say as a result of going too fast. I invite you to read the Gospel as if it is about *you*—for on one level *it is*—and this book is designed to help you unlock how it relates to you. I suggest that you allow the images and words of the story to flow into your awareness and try to prevent them from settling into "answers." The stories, sayings and events of the Gospel are designed to evoke something *from* you. The response they evoke must be something that is *yours*, something unique, for your relationship with God is unique. If you have more than one response, allow each to emerge, for your relationship with God is a multifaceted, evolving relationship. Your responses may evolve, too, and this is good. Grow with God.

If the Spirit of God calms a storm within you, then the Gospel has something to say to you. If you *want* the Spirit of God to calm a storm within you, then the Gospel has something to say to you. In this book I hope to provide some opportunities for you to explore how the Gospel may speak to you about your own life, here and now, and also about how it might lead you into healing and wholeness. When you are led into healing and wholeness, the process never stops with you but overflows into others, in your life and beyond.

### The Teacher

Most often, people who speak to Jesus in the Gospel of Mark call him "Teacher." Teaching was an essential part of his ministry and life; at one point the Gospel says that, whatever else he may have done at any given place, it was his *custom* to teach people.[6] At any given time his followers may have numbered dozens, hundreds, or even thousands. Many people came to him to be healed, but they *stayed* to hear what he taught. They jammed rooms and crowded around doorways, traveled into deserts and filled the land to hear him. At more than one point he has to get into a boat to avoid being crushed by the crowd, and then he sits in the boat, teaching those on the land. Jesus teaches people from the first day of his ministry to the last. Teaching is the most constant and consistent aspect of his ministry.

The Gospel says explicitly that he taught each according to her or his ability to hear and understand. The general public was taught mostly with parables— teaching stories that have an amazing quality. They reveal meanings according to the interest and effort of the listener or reader. To the casual listener, they may say little, offering perhaps a wise or catchy saying. To a serious student, however, the same story opens up more and more as the student engages with the

---
[6] Mark 10:1

story and searches out the life experience to which the story is addressed to find practical spiritual applications.

Jesus chose twelve people out of all his disciples.[7] The twelve formed a learning group in which Jesus' teaching would reach maximum effect. They became, as it were, professional students for three years, devoting their lives to hearing, absorbing and living the teachings of Jesus to the best of their ability. Many experienced teachers will recognize why Jesus' inner circle of students numbered twelve— a group this size is ideal for "life teaching" that addresses both "theory" and "practice" on a personal and interpersonal level. A group of twelve is small enough that close personal relationships can blossom and develop, as these are necessary for spiritual and personal learning. Yet such a group is also large enough to contain a wide diversity, enough to include differences of experience, temperament, approach and thought that are necessary for the development of respect, compassion, and the variations in individual application that stimulate growth for the group. The twelve are an ideal community, and each is necessary for the learning of every other member of the group.

The twelve began by hearing the same parables that were given to the public, which they then discussed, tested, questioned, explored, and lived until the meaning of the teaching became part of the fabric of their experience. They also had many chances to watch each other miss the point, misinterpret the parables, misapply the teachings, and misunderstand Jesus on their way to finally seeing, hearing, and receiving what he had to give them. In the end, the disciples had much more than a body of theoretical knowledge at their disposal. They had seen and experienced the teaching *through* the thought, emotions and experience of twelve different people, under the guidance of their teacher, so they had learning that was absorbed on many levels and applicable to diverse populations. The disciples themselves were a group with diverse backgrounds and included at least two pairs of brothers. Notice the Greek names mixed in with the Hebrew names. The humble were mixed in with the professionals, fishermen with tax collectors, married men and single people.

What did these students devote three solid years, day and night—more intensive than any modern professional program—to

---

[7] "Disciple" is a translation of the Greek word for "student" or "learner."

learn? The disciples were *not* studying scripture or becoming scholars. Jesus' teaching only occasionally quotes Hebrew scripture directly, and is not devoted to helping students learn theology, philosophy, psychology, or any other academic discipline. His students are never tested for their theoretical knowledge. They are repeatedly challenged to *interpret*—to extract meaning from parables, stories, experiences and to relate these meanings to the overall goal of the teaching.

In this book one of the ways that we translate from ancient symbols and experiences to modern ones that can have a similar effect is to view the Twelve as representations of our inner qualities that are to be mobilized to serve the purpose of the Gospel in our lives, just as the Twelve in the Gospel story were taught and mobilized to carry out Jesus' mission in the world. His mission to save the world begins with the Gospel's mission to transform each of us who engages with it. The purpose of Gospel's teaching today is analogous to the practical work that Jesus did to teach his disciples many years ago: not only to change us, but to transform us into people who embodied the life of the Spirit of God on earth and who would then be capable of becoming teachers of others. The primary way this book approaches Jesus' teaching is to look for its applications *within ourselves*—not only in its ethical application in our behavior toward others, but for its psychological application in our "inner behavior," in ways that inner disharmony and conflict can be healed. When inner healing occurs, the resulting personal peace can then make peace outside of ourselves possible.

## A Unique Teaching Tool

Let's return to our two disciples in the year 60. They are not carrying around a modern Bible. Their own learning may have been crystallized during the ministry of Jesus, and their handbook is the story of Jesus' ministry. The life and ministry of Jesus is like that of other prophets and teachers of the ancient middle east in one important respect—he lived and embodied the things he taught. For example, just as the prophet Hosea actually married a prostitute to live and embody his teaching that God loved the nation even though its people had "prostituted" themselves to alien gods, so Jesus' entire life during his ministry was a living embodiment of his teaching. For this reason, the story of his ministry contains all the essential elements of the teaching that the disciples took part in, and became the basic "text" for the teaching that the disciples then passed on to their students. This story may have been enriched by references to events related in the Book of Kings and several prophetic works, events which would have enabled readers to understand better the objectives of the Gospel by putting them in a larger context.

Our disciples in the year 60 who used this Gospel to teach would not arrive in town with a library—they would likely carry this book and no other, for at the time Mark was written, there probably was no other.[8] The disciple's purpose could be served by this book, and it is that purpose I wish to explore. Therefore, I suggest that in order to unlock the purpose of these early disciples of Christ, it is best to read the Gospel of Mark completely by itself, with little or no reference to the other gospels or the rest of the New Testament and other documents or evidence. It is often tempting to "fill in" the meaning of the brief accounts in the Gospel of Mark by referring to the more elaborate, detailed accounts of the other gospels, but I suggest that this is the easiest way to lose the original message and purpose of the Gospel of Mark, which is unlike the others in scope and purpose. I see Mark as a unique document, not as one gospel among many.

I do not approach the Gospel of Mark in complete isolation, for it arose in a context that cannot be ignored. The context that I recognize is that of a work written by an early Christian some time after the death of Jesus, who either witnessed or was aware of Jesus' living ministry, who was aware of the oral traditions about Jesus, who probably had access to some of the earliest writings or oral traditions about Jesus when he wrote it. Beyond this, it seems evident to me that that context was manipulated and took on political overtones at a fairly early date, as the quest to establish an orthodoxy of belief and practice took on a life of its own.[9] We know that in the

---

[8] It is widely held by scholars that Mark was written before the other gospels; so it seems fruitful for our purposes here to view the text as if it were the only Gospel, for when it was written it was a unique document.

[9] See Helmut Koester's *Introduction to the New Testament,* op.cit. Note 2, for some of the history.

early days the "Greek Christians" argued with the "Jewish Christians," and each argued with the "Gnostic Christians," and then there were Romans, Syrians and other groups, each with their own agendas, who worked to spread their own versions of Jesus' teachings, life and death. I think it likely that the priorities of church organization fueled the growing politicization of Christianity and obscured, distorted, and in some ways obliterated the original Gospel, the "joyous message" of Jesus himself. The Gospel According to Mark represents one of the earliest statements of the Gospel message, probably the earliest that is available to the modern reader. It is probably less encumbered with the agendas of various competing Christian factions than other early writings, and therefore retains more of its original purpose than others. This book will contain some references to outside scholarship or to general conditions of the ancient middle east, but primarily I wish to look at this Gospel by itself as much as possible, before the manipulation of the context began to change the message. I would like to emphasize that I do not attempt to present *"the truth"* about this Gospel or about Jesus. I do not accept the proposition that there *is* a single such "truth," and I regard any attempt to find or establish a single monolithic, "catholic" or "orthodox" body of spiritual truth to be legalism of the kind that has historically resulted in persecutions of those regarded as "in error." I wish to stay out of "doctrinal controversies." I see Jesus with open arms, as free and as accepting as the Holy Spirit, and offer this work as both an attempt to walk into those arms and as an invitation to you to do likewise, in your own time and in the manner that the Spirit leads you.

 I hope to present this book to two audiences. To non-Christians who thirst for spiritual truth, I hope that this interpretation of the Gospel According to Mark may give you an indication of the depth, profundity and breadth of the spiritual practice that can arise from the guidance that is in the Gospel. To Christians, I hope that this interpretation may open up new vistas in familiar territory, and suggest a way that the Gospel of Mark may be used as direct guidance in your spiritual life.

 By "direct guidance" I do not mean you will necessarily find answers, solutions, fixes, or revelation. A guide *shows* the way; a traveler *walks* the way. The Gospel of Mark provides guidance, and is best learned so that the Gospel's lessons are ready in the mind for the time when one's experience in living calls for the guidance. It is a tool for a spiritual traveler. Most travelers do best when they go with companions, and I suggest that, if possible, you share this guidebook and your work in it with one or more companions on the way for maximum benefit. Walking and working together often open up opportunities that are not available to us when we travel alone.

The Gospel of Mark has been the subject of numerous commentaries over the millennia, including a host of modern studies. To the best of my knowledge, these commentaries and studies approach the Gospel as a document that is addressed *to* the reader, portraying the Gospel story *about* Jesus and the disciples as an inspiration to be learned from or followed. The studies and commentaries may use criticism, analogy or other tools to provide a bridge between the Gospel and the reader.

I interpret Mark's Gospel as if it is essentially *about* the reader. I believe that the most powerful guidance is gained when the narrative is read so as to take the entire Gospel *personally*; that is, I interpret the Gospel in such a way that each person, place and event in the Gospel is pointing toward an *inner event*, or a possible inner event, and the context for the Gospel story and its lessons is our own personal lives. I call this the "inner interpretation" of the Gospel. I see the life and ministry of Jesus as the embodiment, the incarnation, of what he taught; that is, his life and ministry are themselves the first example of what he teaches—the medium contains the message, and *how* Jesus teaches is an example of *what* he teaches. Many people accept Jesus' teachings as merely a stepping-stone toward their belief in the person of Jesus. I *begin* with a belief in the person of Jesus, and follow his own words when he says, "Let us go to other towns, that I may preach there also, for that is what I came for." I take Jesus at his word—his purpose was to preach and to teach, so that people could enter the Kingdom of God by following his teachings—by themselves living the Word and thus being the Word, bringing it into the world by actions that emerge from inner learning and transformation. The "inner interpretation" of the Gospel is a guide to translate the people and events in the gospel story into lessons that come alive within us, and from us they become a gift to the world.

Jesus offers a unique teaching—an inner orientation to events that is to be taken into us so completely, so thoroughly, that his life becomes our flesh and blood. The work begins with the awakening of the Spirit of God within us— the Christ— by the action of conscience. It proceeds with the healing, reconciling work of the Spirit within us on many levels as we become awakened as persons, and it ends with the "death" of the limited, earthly, personal religious incarnation of the Spirit, which dies in the same way that a seed is planted in the ground. Once the seed (Jesus) has been planted in good soil within us, a new growth emerges and frees us to be guided by the Spirit at all times and in all things. The Gospel is a guide to the spiritual planting process.

The Gospel is a distilled teaching that makes sense only in the light of appropriate experience. Its meaning is neither theoretical nor theological, but personal and spiritual, and I believe this is the reason the Gospel is presented in the form of a story. This Gospel was written by a person who had a profound personal acquaintance and intimacy with the processes of spiritual planting and growth, with all their joy and pain, frustrations and triumphs.

I believe this Gospel was never intended to *be* "the teaching" by itself, or to stand on its own. It is a handbook to be used by an experienced spiritual teacher, or by someone who has dedicated herself or himself to walking the path of spiritual and personal transformation. It provides guideposts and reminders to help the student keep well oriented when the challenges of the spiritual path might be confusing; to keep the goal in sight when we might be led astray.

The "inner interpretation" can itself be challenging—it is a direct application of the Gospel story to the inner life of the *reader,* the student—the modern disciple. It is designed for the reader to use in direct reference to the events of one's own life. The difficulty is to refrain to filling in the "gaps" in the Gospel by referring to other works or by going outside ones own experience. I believe that the "gaps" in Mark are left there deliberately, for the gaps must be filled in by the student out of his or her own experience. Another challenge is to resist reading the Gospel of Mark in the light of history, for again the purpose of the Gospel is to draw the light *out of the student.* Biblical history can be a fascinating study, but it is not helpful *in this context.* In the Gospel Jesus repeatedly focuses our attention on "what comes out of a person"—out of our hearts, our minds, our mouths, our hands—and this is where learning takes place. If we introduce biblical history as a tool for interpreting the Gospel, then the focus of study shifts to what comes *into* the student, and then the power of this Gospel is lost. History is useful *after* the spiritual lessons are absorbed.

Some readers will notice that my interpretation and my use of terms do not conform with many widely accepted Christian beliefs and teachings. Even though my approach to the Gospel has led me in some directions that are not shared by others, I am not presenting this work as a challenge to the beliefs of others and I hope that differences of belief will not prevent you from taking something of value from this work. It may be difficult for some readers to consider some of what is presented here in the face of what they already believe about Jesus and the Gospel, yet it may be possible for you to enrich your faith by following the direction of this book without compromising your own beliefs, for the interpretations in this book may show you additional facets of your faith. Nonetheless, it may be a challenge for some readers not to argue with what is presented here, but to look for ways that this interpretation can be a constructive addition to your spiritual life.

A last challenge is to resist the urge to take the Gospel as a whole with the assumption that it *all* applies to us *now*. Some of the lessons may apply to us now, but some will not be relevant until some time later in our lives when an appropriate experience occurs. We do not know when that experience will happen, which is why Jesus exhorted us to "Keep awake! Watch!"

## How to Use This Book

The Gospel According to Mark resembles a compressed or "zipped" computer file that cannot be read the way we would read a text file. The meaning must be extracted before we can work with it, and its meaning and significance will not be unlocked only by reading, because reading is an activity of the intellect. The Gospel According to Mark needs to be worked with over time. Even in writing this book I have had to come back to various passages again and again over years to understand them, for their meaning has emerged only in the crucible of experience.

This book follows Mark's Gospel in the order it was written from Mark 1:1 to 16.8. The English version[10] presented here is not intended to be a "definitive" scholarly version of the Gospel. I have chosen to use some words in English that reflect what I believe to be the potential of the Greek original to stimulate inner growth and healing, rather than words that seem smooth, poetic or more grammatical than the original. If this English version of the Gospel does not work for you, then I suggest that you read existing published translations to gather a sense of what different people have seen in the Gospel as they attempt to render it into English.[11] An interlinear version (which presents the Greek above the English, word by word, with lexical references) may be particularly helpful. I recommend that you bear in mind that a translator tends to choose English words that conform with his or her beliefs, or that conform with certain teachings about Jesus. Some people think that certain translations are inspired, but I suggest that all inspirations (including mine, of course) are filtered through the prism of an individual mind. So I suggest that you "watch!" and "keep awake!" to all possibilities as you read the Gospel.

The interpretation that follows each section of the Gospel in this book is intended to highlight some aspects of the Gospel that I believe are essential to our understanding of Jesus' life and ministry, and to our ability to receive the gifts that he bestowed. I cannot and do not intend to try to explore every aspect or possibility that the Gospel contains or suggests. I focus on certain aspects that form a unified whole teaching for a particular work in a spiritual life.

I have drawn my interpretation from the words in the text as they speak in a common sense way, or as they speak to my own understanding and experience. I have followed no "rules" for interpreting the text, but rather have engaged in a personal, spiritual dialogue with the text and present to the reader the results of that dialogue in the form of observations, analogies, insights and questions that my experience has shown to be helpful, or that my intuition leads me to share. The work is informed primarily by my own

---

[10] See the following section, "About the English Version of Mark, and the Layout of this Book."

[11] In my opinion, some of the existing translations in English alter the sense and meaning of the original text. I suggest that you consult several translations.

practical and spiritual experience and learning over the years, of which I share some pieces in the Afterword. While the experience of my life in sixty-four years has included teaching, care-giving and counseling, I present this material as the reflections and suggestions of a fellow student rather than as the precepts of a teacher. I encourage you to approach this book in a similar way, allowing a dialogue to develop between you and the Gospel.

The questions or exercises that appear throughout the book are for reflection, for experiment, for "working out" salvation in the crucible of your own experience. They are not intended as rigid methods, but as suggestions, questions, actions and reflections that may be helpful to you or to someone you are helping. Many of these questions are asked in a general way and you will have to make them specific for yourself to make the question useful to you. They are not "test questions;" there are *no* "correct" answers to the questions—the objective is not to get "the answers" but to see, to listen and hear, and to act—and to allow God's will to work in your life. Many of the questions *cannot* be answered when you read them—they are meant to stimulate your awareness over time. I recommend that you put the book down for some time after each question to allow the words to percolate down into various levels of your awareness, and find an appropriate way to respond to the question (or pass it by) before reading the next section of the Gospel. You might find it helpful to express your responses to the questions, such as writing or discussing them and exploring similar work with others. Some questions are intended to stimulate awareness and action in your everyday life, some are aimed more at thoughts and attitudes. Specific exercises could be developed to take these questions further in personal or group experience and learning. Some of the questions may not be appropriate for you—or not appropriate for you *now*. Feel free to leave them and move on if you feel that the questions don't speak to you.

The process that I offer you in this book is also the process I used to write it. My experience has been that one reading did not begin to open up what the Gospel has to offer. I have worked on this book and with the Gospel for years, and have discovered that I could return to sections after a period of time and discover new things, as changes in my life and perspective enabled me to see things in the Gospel that I had missed before. The more I explored the Gospel the more

I found it offered; so the words that you read here reflect where I have walked with the Gospel so far, and are not even my own final words on the subject, as I continue to learn. I hope that this book may provide a way for this Gospel to be personally helpful in your journey also.

## About the English Version of Mark, and the Layout of This Book

I have constructed a reading of the Gospel using the Greek text (see the first reference below in this section) and multiple published English translations as references. No published version has been quoted in its entirety, although I have found that in some verses the reading I present uses the same words as a single published translation, while in other verses the English words I have chosen for a single verse may be the same as one translation for some words and the same as another translation for other words. In some cases I have offered my own original translation of words where I thought that none of the published ones rendered what I perceive to be the meaning or intention of the writer. I have not chosen readings for their elegance or poetic power in English, and I have deliberately left in some of the roughness and the repetition that I found in the Greek (that is usually omitted or changed in most English translations), so this version may seem a little awkward to some people. For example, a large number of Mark's sentences in Greek begin with "And . . ." and proceed to convey events in the nearly breathless style (in the present tense)[12] of a neighbor relating the events of the day. I have retained this style in English wherever possible, because I think it conveys the immediacy of Mark's Gospel—which is very much in line with the Gospel's purpose. I am not a Greek scholar and I do

---

[12] There are many instances in which the majority of English translations change the tense of verbs in Mark from present to past, presumably for grammatical and temporal consistency. It is my belief that that present tense is often used deliberately in Mark, even in the midst of paragraphs whose other verbs are in the past tense; I have therefore kept the original tenses, even when such usage appears at first glance to be awkward or even "incorrect."

not put this reading forth as "definitive," and many readers may find that they prefer other versions. My intention is to present the Gospel in a way that highlights what I believe to be the intent of the Gospel writer and to allow for interpretation and application. I have presented the Gospel as a continuous narrative, with chapter and verse headings only at the beginning of each passage, so that the reader may focus on the meaning of the sections as a whole.

I have not included or considered the portion the Gospel of Mark beyond Chapter 16 verse 8, because the verses handed down as Chapter 16 verses 9-20 are considered additions that are widely recognized as not part of the original Gospel. Many ancient texts of Mark end at verse 8 and the original ending of the Gospel (if there was one beyond 16:8) is unknown, and probably lost. From the inner perspective it is clear to me that the content of verses 9-20 do not belong with the original, because the spirit of these verses is polarizing, divisive, exclusive and condemning (especially verse 16)—not the same spirit that pervades the rest of the text, and not serving its original purpose.

I have used the following works as references:

1. **Word Study Greek-English New Testament**: a literal, interlinear word study of the *Greek New Testament* United Bible Societies' Third Corrected Edition with New Revised Standard Version, New Testament, edited by Paul R. McReynolds, Carol Stream IL, Tyndale House Publishers, Inc. 1999.
2. **The New Oxford Annotated Bible with the Apocrypha**, Revised Standard Version, edited by Herbert G. May and Bruce M. Metzger; New York, Oxford University Press, 1973 and 1977.
3. **Young's Literal Translation of the Bible**, by Robert Young: Revised Edition reprinted 1995 by Baker Books, Grand Rapids MI from the 1898 Edinburgh edition.
4. **The Word: The Bible from 26 Translations**, edited by Curtis Vaughan, Th.D., Gulfport MS, Mathis Publishers, Inc. 1993.
5. **Strong's New Exhaustive Concordance of the Bible**, by James Strong, S.T.D., LL.D., Iowa Falls, IA, World Bible Publishers, 1994.

6. **Thayer's Greek-English Lexicon of the New Testament, coded with Strong's Concordance Numbers**, by Joseph H. Thayer, Peabody, MA, Hendricks Publishers, Inc. 2005 (reprinted from the fourth edition published by T. T. Clark, Edinburgh, 1896, with Strong's numbers added by Hendrickson Publishers)

7. **Numerous on-line bibles and references have been helpful, including BlueLetterBible.org, BibleStudyTools.com and Biblos.com. I also consulted The New American Bible's online notes at usccb.org and other sources.**

**I do not necessarily agree with or endorse the opinions or content at any site or source, nor do I assert that any other person or source necessarily agrees with or endorses the opinions or content in this book.**

Part II of this book has been designed with three distinct sections that are interwoven. The Gospel of Mark is printed in a large font and is set off in a box:

---

1:2 As it is written in Isaiah the prophet, "Look! I send my messenger before your face, who will prepare your way, a voice shouting in the desert, 'Prepare the way of the Lord, make his paths straight—'"

---

The Gospel is annotated by chapter and verse only at the beginning of the section that we are focusing on.

Each section of the Gospel is followed by my interpretation and commentary on the Gospel, printed in a different font:

Repentance means simply to turn. The baptism of John is a way to

This interpretation and commentary are intended to show how the Gospel can be used on a personal level, how outer events may have real inner significance, how physical events may also at the same time be symbols and signs for inner events that carry real meaning.

Questions for the reader are then printed in a third, darker, font, in a shaded box and marked with circular "bullets:"

> o **Who are our inner disciples? They are parts of us**

These are questions with which to start your own reflection on, and work with, the Gospel. They are drawn from the interpretation and are presented as examples of how one might "walk out" the Gospel. There are no "correct" answers to these questions—if they do not help you to explore your own life in the light of the Gospel, then they aren't the right questions for you – or they are not the right questions for you *at this time*. In that case, feel free to develop other questions or practices that you can use to walk out the Gospel's joyous message, or come back to the question at a later date, when it may evoke something meaningful for you.

I recommend that you take some time with this work and not read it all at once. After you have read one section and worked with the questions, set the book aside for a time—until the next day, perhaps—before reading on. This will allow the Gospel and your response to it to flow into deeper parts of your being and to reach parts of you that do not respond as quickly as your intellect,[13] but which may enable understanding when they are given time.

The symbol ♦ ♦ ♦ in the text is placed where I suggest a pause in the reading to allow the work to "percolate" before going on.

---

[13] I know of at least two people who read the entire text of this book in a relatively short time, who then put it down for a year or more, who were then inspired to read it again. The second time each person read more slowly and sporadically, and worked with the text more. Both commented to me that it was as if they had not read it at all the first time: the second reading was a revelation that began to change their whole understanding of the Gospel.

Periodically you will see an invitation to do an exercise, such as this:

## *WALKING OUT THE GOSPEL: TO EXPLORE THIS FURTHER, DO EXERCISE 1A OR EXERCISE 1B IN PART III, PAGES 388-389*

The Exercises in Spiritual Psychology are found in Part III beginning on Page 383. They are designed to be done by one or two people to enhance your own experience of exploring the Gospel within yourself and your experience.

This is not intended to be a book of ideas or beliefs so much as a book to practice with, and you yourself must discover what practice and how much is right for you, to open you to the Life of the Spirit.

This reading of the Gospel According to Mark has arisen after a long study, and after much reflection on the Gospel's relationship to events of my own life and that of many people I have known or known of. I hope that it may speak to you personally in some way. If it does, may it be a blessing to you and to the people in your life.

# PART 2

## The Gospel Within Us

# PREPARATION

The first part of the Gospel process is preparation. We discover that the Gospel begins with a call to change and we see quickly how that call may provoke a negative response. We see a gathering of resources to support the process as the work of the Gospel begins. We discover the qualities needed to go forward and see that healing, forgiveness and faith are the core of the Gospel. As the Gospel begins to work in our lives we discover that there is resistance, but we also discover that there are qualities within us that are called upon to support the Gospel's work in our lives.

The Gospel process begins within ourselves in a growing awareness, and a commitment to change. We discover quickly that the spiritual journey is no "cakewalk," but a challenging process that engages us to the utmost. The qualities that we bring to support the Gospel process are tested and tempted and we experience pressures that try to push us off track. We may bring old habits, thoughts and beliefs in to support us, but we may also discover that these may inhibit the process as much as they support it.

Sections 1-6 that follow will bring us from the beginning of the Gospel According to Mark at Mark 1:1 as far as Mark 3:12. These sections will introduce us to the "inner interpretation" of the Gospel and help us get oriented to how the Gospel provides us with cues to learn the inner awareness that is needed to support change. The work will begin, the forces of resistance will be identified, and a new spiritual pathway will open up.

# 1. CHANGE:

## CONSCIENCE AND THE PRESENCE OF THE SPIRIT

PREPARATION

> 1:1 The beginning of the joyous message of Jesus Christ.

The Gospel—the joyous message—begins with John the Baptist. This "Gospel Within Us" is a reading of the book that receives it as a personal teaching for those "with ears to hear." In this "inner interpretation" I understand the Gospel as a story in which all the people and events have been chosen for the purpose of eliciting spiritual understanding, and the purpose of this understanding is to facilitate the spiritual transformation[1] of the reader. This Gospel is not "the story of the life of Jesus," but a story *that uses the life of Jesus* to give birth to the Christ, the Spirit of God, *in us.* The beginning of this transformation occurs when the voice of conscience appears in our lives and cries out for repentance.

> 1:2 As it is written in Isaiah the prophet, "Look! I send my messenger before your face, who will prepare your way, a voice shouting in the desert, 'Prepare the way of the Lord, make his paths straight—'"
>
> John the Baptist appeared in the desert, proclaiming baptism of repentance for forgiveness of sins. And people from the Judean country and all the people of Jerusalem were traveling out to him, and were being baptized by him in the river Jordan, confessing their sins. And John was clothed with camel's hair and a leather belt around his waist, and ate locusts and wild honey.

Repentance means simply to turn. The baptism of John is a way to turn away from aspects of our lives that we need to leave behind. A baptism is one way of physically acting out our intent—in this

---
[1] See Part I for a discussion of "transformation"

CHANGE

case, to "wash away" the behaviors, the memories, the attachments, the ideas, the allegiances, idols, ambitions, addictions, the mental or physical habits and preferences that are not right for us. John is the conscience[2] that draws us away from what is not right for us, and in the story people confess their sins— meaning that they recognize what they have been doing, and in being baptized they renounce it. They make the decision to change and they act upon their decision.

> 1:7 And he was preaching, saying, "One more powerful than I comes after me, the strap of whose sandals I am not worthy to bend down and untie. I baptized you in water, but he will baptize you in the Holy Spirit."

John's baptism is a way of disconnecting us from what is wrong for us. But he announces that he is only the forerunner for another, who will connect us with what is right for us. John's job is to lead us away from error, the one who follows him is to lead us toward truth. John has announced in advance the work of the one who is to follow him—to immerse us in the Holy Spirit as part of a radical transformation in our lives. We each have a conscience, whose function is to discern right from wrong in our lives. For some of us, conscience is a voice within us that moves us in the direction we need to follow; but for many of us, there seems to be an accuser within us, a harpy, a voice that finds fault and tears down, even though its intent may be to move us away from what is harmful. It is important that we understand that our inner John—our real conscience—does *not* find fault or tear us down. Its call is for repentance, for change. When it says "NO!" it is intent upon building us up by moving us away from what is harmful.

---

[2] While I treat John as symbolizing conscience, this is clearly not the only significance John may have in the Gospel or in our lives. Any of the characters or events in the Gospel may lead us in many directions, and the discussion in this book points to only one of those directions.

PREPARATION

Later in the story, the Gospel personifies the negative voice within as "the adversary" ("the satan" in Greek)[3]—and who of us has not experienced an inner voice that accuses us and tears us down no matter what we do? There are also other accusing voices in our lives, which have their sources in the voices of parents, teachers, friends, family, books, or the popular media. These inner accusers arise from our experience, and often have a hidden agenda which is promoted as they eventually become voices within us instead of the voices we learned from. The Gospel also personifies these learned accusations as "scribes" and "Pharisees"—people who have learned the ways of church, synagogue, mosque, government, school, media, tradition, and who believe that the ways of the world are right and should be upheld. The scribes and Pharisees, then, represent all we have ever learned, all of our training and education, which moves us to conform to what we have learned, and "do the right thing."

John, on the other hand, represents a deeper conscience within us—one that has not learned by study, training or social interaction. John appears in the wilderness as a kind of wild man, a natural man dressed in skins and eating uncultured foods—not one to teach what was studied or trained. John is outside polite society, and equally apart from those who rebel against society. In this Gospel he does not pick or enumerate specific errors. Why not? Because the purpose of this Gospel is to provide space for us, the readers, to listen for our own inner John, who will tell us, show us, what we need to hear and see. The work of our own inner deep conscience is to call out to us, "Something is wrong here! Give up the wrongness, move on! Stop doing what is harmful, what is unprofitable, what is *missing the mark* (what the Gospel calls "sin").

In this "inner interpretation" of the Gospel, everything and everyone signifies or refers to some aspect of our own persons and lives, at least approximately. So when John calls people to repent, people from all over respond, and this is the beginning of the Gospel

---

[3] "In biblical sources the Hebrew term the *satan* describes an adversarial role. It is not the name of a particular character. Although Hebrew storytellers as early as the sixth century B.C.E. occasionally introduced a supernatural character whom they called the *satan*, what they meant was any one of the angels sent by God for the specific purpose of blocking or obstructing human activity." Elaine Pagels, *The Origin of Satan*, 1995

CHANGE

Within Us. Before the "greater one" arrives in our lives there is a deep and broad response within us to the call of conscience to change our lives. This tells us *who* will have "ears to hear:" this Gospel is addressed to us only after we have already experienced a deep response to conscience, not when we are thinking about spiritual things for the first time.

♦ ♦ ♦

- Whenever you feel an inner voice or prompting, a feeling that calls on you to change or to stop doing what you are doing, you may be experiencing what this passage in the Gospel is talking about. Some people hear a voice talking in their minds— usually their own voice, but sometimes another voice. Some people feel an inner prompting or urge. Others hear nothing inside but notice that the words of others take on a personal significance. How do you experience it?
- (I will refer to the "inner voice" often in the text. When I do, please refer to your own way of inner experiencing.)
- John calls us to change, to repent, to turn away from something. Feel your own "inner John" (you may have a different name for it, or no name).
- What does your conscience call you to turn away from?
- I invite you to make a choice to respond to this inner leading and voice, when you are ready

PREPARATION

> and able to do so.[4] When you make this choice, do something— an action of some sort, literal or symbolic— to act out your choice. Notice what happens within you when you make this choice. Reflect on this awareness. Notice your responses to this choice on several levels—mental, emotional, physical, behavioral. If you notice specific responses, make a note of them. If you do not see any specific responses, this is all right too. Either way, you may simply move on.

## WALKING OUT THE GOSPEL: TO EXPLORE THIS FURTHER, DO EXERCISE 1A OR EXERCISE 1B IN PART III, PAGES 388-389

> 1:9 And it happened in those days that Jesus came from Nazareth in Galilee and was baptized in the Jordan by John. And immediately, coming up out of the water, he saw the heavens split and the spirit descending upon him like a dove; and a voice came from the heavens, "You are my beloved son,[5] in you I delight."

---

[4] You may have already made such a choice, maybe more than once. If so, reflect on your memory of your responses for the following questions. If you are not ready to make such a choice or have not made it, this is all right. As you read on, bear in mind that the Gospel and its work actually begin with the choice to change.

[5] The meaning of the word "son" may seem straightforward to us: "male child of a parent." But this is not necessarily the meaning that is intended here. Smith's Bible Dictionary says, "The term 'son' is used in Scripture language to imply almost any kind of descent or succession, as *ben shanah*, 'son of a year,' i.e. a year old; *ben kesheth*, 'son of a bow,' i.e. an arrow." It may be fruitful to contemplate how the voice of the Spirit uses this term here, and what richness of meaning may be contained in the word "son" in this context.

## CHANGE

The conscience that leads us away from what is harmful to us is not what leads us into the path that is helpful, life-affirming, productive, fulfilling. Something greater than conscience is needed here, but this greater one does not appear in our lives until the conscience has made a sincere call for change, and there has been a response within us. In this Gospel, nobody knows Jesus, not even John. But this passage is written to tell *us* who this is. Why?

When we, in our pain or poverty or trouble or perplexity, decide to change our lives, our cry for help and change *attracts* the response of one greater than ourselves, greater than our conscience—and it happens that we may easily fail to recognize his[6] presence, let alone discern his identity.

The story means to show us that when we repent—that is, when we decide from deep conscience that we need to change—this action evokes a response that is much greater than our minds, greater than our consciences, a response that we may or may not be aware of. The presence that joins us is "from heaven," even the Son of God, who will be included in our process. If we do not recognize this presence, we may try to change on our own—an attempt which often takes the form of resolving *not* to continue in our bad habits, or perhaps responding to conscience with a general resolve to "be good:" share with others, do your job honestly, be content with your lot in life.

But the Spirit is present in our desire for change, and if we recognize it, there is something greater in store for us than avoiding our errors or "trying to be good," for "trying" inevitably leads us back to the river of repentance when we fail the next time.[7]

We are interpreting the Gospel as an inner guide, as a handbook for spiritual growth. From this point of view, who is the Son of God? We are at the beginning of the Gospel, not at the end. Our work is

---

[6] The Gospel was written using mostly male pronouns, following the conventions of the time. I often follow the Gospel's usage for convenience, while acknowledging that God and The Christ include both genders, and also transcend gender. I encourage the reader to listen to the Spirit within and not to be bound by conventions: use the pronouns through which the Spirit speaks to you. I urge you to allow some poetic freedom in the Gospel's language and also in your own, and focus on the *meaning* more than on specific words.

[7] I am not minimizing the value of trying to do things. But when we need real change, "trying" can actually be one of the ways that we may remain stuck where we are. The Gospel shows us something deeper.

PREPARATION

barely started, and no "answers" are possible here. But the story is announcing that the person of Jesus plays a special role, even though at this point in the story, *we do not know him;* but the story makes it clear that when we take action to change, he is present.

The process of spiritual growth is begun in ignorance, but our will to change and our commitment to change, followed by actions to fulfill the commitment, open up the heavens, so that a deeper process is also initiated, if we respond to it.

---

- Return to your awareness, to your choice to change, to repent.
- Ask the Spirit of God to come to you, to be present in your awareness.
- Use language or other means that are appropriate, that speak to you personally.
- Notice what happens; do not interpret, for now—just notice. Stay with this awareness for some time, allow it to move you if it seems to be doing so.
- Notice what else comes into your awareness— thoughts, feelings, impulses, intuitions, sensations. Hold these in your awareness.
- Again, ask the Spirit of God to just be with you.
- You may notice something, or nothing. Either way, it is all right.
- Do not expect or judge, but allow.

---

***WALKING OUT THE GOSPEL: TO EXPLORE THIS FURTHER, DO EXERCISE 2 IN PART III, PAGE 391.***

# 2. NEGATIVE VOICES, THE ADVERSARY, AND THE SPIRITUAL PROCESS

PREPARATION

Voices within us that say "NO!" or "Stop Doing That!" in one way or another may have different sources and different agendas, whether they are voices within you or the voices of others speaking to you.

One inner voice that says "no!" is simply the voice of Love that says "no" to whatever is harmful to you or to others. This voice may be gentle or forceful, but it is not critical, blaming or attacking—this is often experienced as the voice of conscience.

Another voice may back up its "No!" with arguments, criticism, guilt, blame, or attacks upon you or others. This is a critic, and if it is in the mind we call it an "inner critic." An inner critic may have good motives, but it is bound by a focus on the negative and as a result its positive intentions often have a negative result.

A third voice that we may hear within us has no such good intent—when negative results accumulate and grow, negative focus may grow into hatred, fear, vengefulness or violence of some kind. We are now dealing with a spiritual adversary: "the one who is against"—"the accuser"— either within us or outside of us. So long as we live in this world, there is always an inner adversary present in our lives, whether its presence is seen and acknowledged or not. It is very helpful for us to be aware of it without underestimating or overestimating either its significance or its power.

It is also helpful and important to be able to distinguish between these three negative voices that may appear in our lives, for our responses must be different for each. The negative voice of conscience commands an affirmative response—we repent of error or harmfulness, we change and move on to life-affirming behavior. The inner critic, on the other hand, is a part of ourselves that needs to be healed. It arises out of the mixture of good intentions with harmful experience, and its good intentions are sidetracked into negative behavior. It can be particularly challenging for us to respond affirmatively to a call for change while not accepting an inner critic's blame or attack. It is important to know that the need for change may include changing the inner critic. Healing our inner critic can be a tough task, for negative life patterns are often not easy to change.

The adversary, however, is not open to real change, even though it may appear to change a great deal. The adversary is a force of negation in our lives (whether an inner force or something outside ourselves) that may arise from (or through) a variety of sources. It is vital that we become aware of such a force if it is present in our lives, and it is equally important that we avoid cooperating with it—but also avoid *actively* fighting it, for fighting is just one way to surrender to it. The only way that we can successfully resist the adversary is by a conscious non-engagement with it; but non-engagement with the adversary is not the same as non-engagement with parts of ourselves or with other people whose ideas, attitudes or behaviors are influenced by the adversary. Jesus will give a good example of the difference when he confronts Peter later in the Gospel.

A "NO!" that originally arises out of conscience may get picked up by an inner critic, which adds a negative charge and some baggage to it. If the inner critic's good intentions are not strongly affirmed and maintained, the adversary may enter the process and turn the original "NO!" into a powerful destructive force that may be inimical to ourselves as well as to others.

We will have occasion to see all the negative voices in the Gospel story—John, the scribes and Pharisees, Judas, the council and Pilate.

> 1:12 And immediately the Spirit casts him into the desert. And he was in the desert forty days being tested by the adversary, and he was with the wild animals, and the angels were serving him.

The story tells us that when the greater power is awakened—perhaps a better, more accurate expression would be "when we are awakened to the greater power"—something else is also awakened, and makes it presence felt "immediately."

> o  **Take some time to reflect on a time when a negative voice or influence entered your life.**

PREPARATION

> o  Can you distinguish whether this voice or influence was that of conscience, an inner critic, or the adversary?
> o  Have all three types of negative voice been present in *your* life? Recall one occasion when you heard each one. How are they alike? How are they different?
> o  How have they affected you? Are they still present in your life?

◆◆◆

We notice that often, as in verse 1:12 above, the Gospel speaks in the present tense—"the spirit *casts* him into the desert." It sometimes feels as if the writer of the Gospel is telling us something that he is still watching—something that is happening *now*. Many people have remarked on Mark's repeated use of the word "immediately." If the Gospel is viewed as a historical narrative, the word makes little sense in most contexts. But with our focus on what the Gospel may be teaching us about an internal, personal process, the word takes on great power. In our external lives, everything takes time; whereas within ourselves, in our minds and spirits, events can occur with an "immediacy" that is impossible in our outer life. In real inner life, things happen *now,* and the Gospel guides us to focus on the present with its repeated used of the word "immediately." In our interpretation of the Gospel, then, the word "immediately" often signifies that something of importance may happen within us at a given time. This does not signify that the inner event actually happens "immediately" in physical time as we read or think about it; rather, the word "immediately" is used as a special connector in the story, to indicate an inner relationship that is immediate, intimate and important. The "now" is not a present moment in physical time, but a "present connection" in inner time. The compression of time in the story is a way to express a spiritual connection between what happens before and what comes "immediately" afterward *in the story*. In our lives, such a connection may actually involve a lot of physical time. *When* we experience this connection, our focus is to be in our own

## NEGATIVE VOICES

"now," not looking forward or backward into past or future. A good example is this passage about Jesus being cast into the desert in verse 1:12. There is an "immediate" spiritual connection between the scene at the river and the casting into the desert, and we need to have an awareness at any given time of what such a connection may produce in our lives. The reaction of being cast "into the desert" to be tested may actually happen much later in physical time than our response to conscience, but when we decide to act on our awareness, we must respond *now*.

♦♦♦

**WALKING OUT THE GOSPEL: TO EXPLORE THIS FURTHER, DO EXERCISE 3 IN PART III, PAGE 392.**

♦♦♦

When the Spirit of God is awakened in us, a negative power is also "immediately" awakened—an inner adversary—a voice that tempts us to go another way, one that may tempt us to override the voice of conscience, to become inflated with our lofty intentions, to question the validity of our experience, or some other inappropriate response to the call of conscience. Or it may infect one of our inner critics and assault us with guilt, blame or some other self-destructive response. Mark shows us the polarity—Jesus was with the wild beasts, yet the angels ministered to him. Mark does not specify the nature of the testing, because for each of us it will be different.

With the awakening of a great power within us comes the awakening of the possibility of that power going awry—of its being thwarted, twisted or diverted. There is a need for heightened awareness at this time, to know what calls us and what pulls at us. The story is telling us that when we are awakened spiritually, we may *immediately* find ourselves alone amidst wild beasts, tempted to go wrong one way or another.

It may happen so fast that the actual awakening is not even noticed, for the trials can be like wild beasts, barking and roaring and completely dominating our awareness.

PREPARATION

♦ ♦ ♦

> o  Can you recall a time when you resolved to change your life, and instead of your life just turning around, you found yourself assaulted by doubts or skepticism, or you heard an inner voice that told you something like, "no, you can't really do that," or "you talk a good line but nothing will really happen?"
> o  Can you recall a time when you resolved to change your life, and instead of your life improving, nothing improved, or "all hell broke loose," and things seemed to get *much* worse?
> o  Recall one such time now, but see if you can stop the flow of your memories at a point before things became difficult.
> o  Look for the awakening that quietly may have occurred before the "beasts" began to roar. Recall the thoughts, feelings, events that preceded your decision to change.
> o  What comes into your awareness? Just hold this awareness for some moments before you go on.

When we have completed a period of trial (forty days signifies a time of completion, which for us may be days or years), during which we are to receive the help and ministry of those who are sent to us ("angels" means messengers, "those who are sent"), then we are ready to begin.

♦ ♦ ♦

# NEGATIVE VOICES

> ○ Recall a difficult time in your life, when you felt alone but got unexpected help. When you are tried, tested or tempted, who or what has been "sent" to you? A friend, a counselor, a doctor, a priest or minister, or a family member? a pet, a poem, a flower, a sunrise? a quotation, a memory, a thought, a vision?
> ○ What inner aspects of you rise and become visible when you are tested?

***WALKING OUT THE GOSPEL: TO EXPLORE THIS FURTHER, DO EXERCISES 4A OR 4B IN PART III, PAGES 394 & 396.***

♦ ♦ ♦

Getting past testing, temptation and wild beasts is just the beginning. The Gospel describes a process, not an "event," and this is *not* a one-time process. For most of us, it happens again and again throughout our lives. Any time conscience calls us out of the path we have been walking, crying "Change!" and we respond deeply to this call, two things happen: Christ, the Spirit of God within us, is there with presence and power; and also there is temptation and conflict that may be experienced as being tested by an inner adversary, or being in the midst of wild beasts. For us to go forward it is necessary for us to confront these conflicts and temptations, again and again, as often as we need to. Many observers of the spiritual life have noticed that as the student learns and "evolves," so do the temptations. They do not necessarily leave us.

> ○ Recall your choice to change, on page 33.
> ○ Notice where your awareness goes, as you reflect on your choice to repent and change.

PREPARATION

- Notice whether there are goals, desires that are the outcome of your choice.
- What does temptation or testing do to the desires and goals that you have chosen?
- Come back to this section and to these questions whenever you go through a difficult time in your life, whenever you feel tested or tempted.

# 3. THE GATHERING: SPIRITUAL QUALITIES

PREPARATION

> **1:14** After John was delivered up,[1] Jesus came into Galilee, proclaiming the joyous message from God and saying, "The time is ripe, and the Kingdom of God is at hand. Repent and trust the joyous message."

Jesus adds on to the message of John. Instead of "Repent!" Jesus calls us to "Repent—*and trust.*"[2] The process has two aspects: an active renunciation of ways that do not work, and an active commitment to a way that involves more than our own decision making.

We do not necessarily resolve our conflicts right away, but in the Gospel story Jesus meets his adversary, which (or who) tests him in the wilderness. He *goes on,* for this testing shows him who his adversary is and what negative forces confront him. Our own recognition of our inner adversaries is equally necessary for us to go on, and this passage of the Gospel is meant to bring this to our attention.

Only when the conflicts or resistance have been confronted is the time fulfilled, and a great birth is ready to begin. The Gospel is a *joyous message*—be glad and joyful, repent of error, and believe in the "good news," which is that the Kingdom of God is *at hand,* present and available, here and now. We are speaking of going forward on a path of life, and here are presented the ingredients we need for an attitude that will sustain us on our way—repent of our errors and leave them behind as we go on our new way; choose new goals; be joyful and believe in what we are doing; be aware of God's presence; trust that something greater is at work than our own conscious intention, for we are not alone on the path. Be aware of what stands in our way as we prepare to go on.

---

[1] John is arrested—an event that is not addressed in Mark's Gospel until Chapter 6, which is the subject of Section 14 of this book.
[2] The Greek word used here (Πιστευω) is probably the most important word in the Gospel. It may be translated as "trust," "have faith," "believe," "be committed," or "accept." Later sections in the Gospel focus on different aspects of its meaning.

# THE GATHERING

> <sup>1:16</sup> And going along by the Sea of Galilee he saw Simon, and Andrew, Simon's brother, casting a net into the sea, for they were fishermen. And Jesus said to them, "Come after me, and I will make you become fishers of men." And immediately they left their nets and followed him. And going on a little farther he saw James, the son of Zebedee, and John, his brother, in their boat mending the nets. And immediately he called them, and they left their father Zebedee in the boat with the hired help, and went after him.

The Christ (the Spirit of God in us) does not work alone. The Kingdom of God within us is just that—an entire kingdom, with a rich and varied population, which has previously been a loose assortment of impulses, thoughts, feelings, images, desires, intuitions, and sensations that have interacted in random ways, perhaps in conflict. The Kingdom of God is not a "place." It is a way of being a person. Jesus tells people that it is "at hand" because we get "to" it not by traveling over space and time, but by changing who we are, and how we are, right here and now. We "get into" the Kingdom of God by living in a certain *way*. "The Kingdom of God"[3] implies relationship and order, and we can be in it only by a profound change in who we are and how we are. To begin this process of change, the Spirit gathers together certain qualities within us that support its goals. The gathering begins only after "John is arrested," that is, after the provocations of conscience have done their work and ceased. At this time in one's life there is a marshalling of forces, so to speak, as the resolution for change reaches out into the various aspects of the person to find resources. In Mark's Gospel, Jesus finds four fishermen, Andrew and Simon, James and

---

[3] In his *History and Literature of Early Christianity* (op.cit, p.79) Helmut Koester points out that the meaning of the Greek is more like "the rule of God," or "the rulership of God." The term points toward relationship more than condition or location, and a "kingdom" is thus "where God rules." Jesus explains how rulers behave later in the gospel (see Section 29, page 258).

PREPARATION

John. Fishermen are seekers, casting their nets into the water for food.

The symbolism of water is of central importance throughout the Gospel story—water is used to represent life in various ways, as well as consciousness. Also of central importance is the symbolism of food, which is meant to represent spiritual nourishment. We will see these two symbols used repeatedly as the Gospel story unfolds.

As we look at the Gospel story with an eye for its inner significance, we view everything and everyone in the story as representing something within us. The disciples, then, are qualities that together form a "subpersonality" within us—an inner "person" who follows Christ, who seeks the Kingdom of God, who works for spiritual life and light and growth. There are parts clearly present within each of us called subpersonalities that we can easily identify— aspects we might call a "playful self," or "my inner child," or "my professional personality," "an inner critic," and so on. This is perfectly normal. I play a different kind of "role" when I am at work than the "role" I play as a husband at home, and I draw on different abilities and qualities in each situation. I played different "roles" in life as a child than I do now. "Subpersonality" is a term that recognizes the different "selves" within us, which respond differently to different situations and may even be in conflict with each other.[4] We are most concerned with a "disciple" subpersonality in this work, and we see the disciples in the Gospel According to Mark as representing the qualities that collectively make up this disciple subpersonality within us. At the beginning of our journey we feel the need to change our lives because various aspects of our lives are out of control, or responding badly, or suffering, or are in need of help or healing in one way or another.

---

[4] This term is taken from the work of Roberto Assagioli, M.D. who discusses the concept of subpersonalities in *Psychosynthesis: A Collection of Basic Writings*: The Synthesis Center, Inc. Amherst MA, 2000. The concept has been elaborated by other writers on psychosynthesis, such as James Vargiu, whose monograph *Subpersonalities* is available at www.aap-psychosynthesis.org for those who wish to explore a technical discussion of this topic, but a technical understanding is not necessary for us to see how disciple qualities work in our lives and how they are represented in the Gospel.

## THE GATHERING

♦ ♦ ♦

The Gospel story so far has shown us how the call of conscience brings forth our awareness of the presence of the Spirit of God, which we may or may not recognize. This Spirit's presence is accompanied by the presence of temptations to use inner power in ways that are futile, destructive, self-serving—in which the goals are sidetracked, undermined, or our pursuit of them becomes unbalanced. Some form of inner struggle takes place in which the narrow, futile or destructive impulses are confronted, and a resolve emerges within us to move forward on the path of change. We achieve enough balance to go on, left foot-right foot, with a working equilibrium. But does this mean we have become balanced, or that we have learned to work with our imbalances? This will become important later in the story.

♦ ♦ ♦

The qualities most likely to get us going along the path are those aspects of us that are already seeking in one way or another. These are our "inner disciples," who may or may not be easily recognizable to us. In the story, Jesus seeks them out and invites them to follow him. On the inner level, the Spirit seeks out qualities within us, personal aspects that most desire growth, positive change, peace, healing, wholeness, relatedness—qualities that can coalesce into a disciple subpersonality.

In "real life" it does not seem likely that a professional worker would drop his work in the middle of a task (even jumping out of a boat!) and follow the call of a stranger. But within ourselves, everything is different—the Spirit that beckons us is no stranger, and when we are called out by the Spirit there is an unexpected recognition on one level, and a surprising awareness that we are known, and that in some indefinable way we know who is calling us. A part of us responds to the call, and that part is represented in the story by one or more of the disciples. In the Gospel, Mark says "*immediately* they left their nets and followed him."

Who are our "inner disciples?" They are qualities in us through which the Spirit will act in some way to bring all the parts of us into

PREPARATION

alignment and harmony. There are particular qualities that are most helpful at given times, and that usually lead the way in most of us. Some qualities will be of more significance in our spiritual journey at different times in our lives, and the relationship between the qualities will change as we go along. At one time humility will be most important; at another time a sense of daring will help us to break through barriers. A questioning attitude will keep us from being arrogant or dogmatic, while at another time the quality of deep faith and trust will lead us. But "qualities" are not the same as "interests"—qualities are *how* we live, not *what* we live for.

"Disciple qualities" are learning qualities, and they are also learned qualities. For most qualities there is an ideal balance point between extremes of excess and deficiency. In Table A below we share some thoughts about spiritually helpful qualities, along with their polar opposites.

♦ ♦ ♦

The qualities that we see expressed or manifested in our lives tell us where we are in life. These qualities are not rigorously defined or quantifiable phenomena, but they are human conditions that most of us can easily identify in ourselves or in others. The basic impulses of our lives are often expressed along a continuum, so that like Goldilocks (and Aristotle) we discover what is too much, what is too little, and what is "just right" for us. The "middle way" that is ideal for one person may often not be the "middle way" for someone else, and the "location" of the balanced point may change for us as time goes by. Nevertheless it is worth our while to search out what is the balanced point for us in many of the qualities of life, for like Goldilocks' porridge, chair and bed that were "just right," the balanced qualities can feed us, support us, and give us peace. More importantly for our purpose here, they also further the work of the Spirit.

But we are looking at inner qualities, not porridge, and inner qualities have a way of shifting dramatically as our lives change. The "testing" of our lives will often move us from balance to one extreme to another, but finding or returning to balance allows us to move forward in spiritual life. One way to view finding spiritual balance is to see it somewhat like learning to ride a bicycle—we learn not to lean too far to the left or to the right, but balancing in the middle allows us to go forward. This "narrow gate" through which we must pass is not one of exclusion, but one of learning how the quality can be manifested in a life-supporting way. Using these qualities in working with the questions you find in the text may help you in your own spiritual maturing, and in your ability to help others in their walk in life.

In Table A below are samples of spiritually helpful qualities, which manifest along a continuum (more or less) from deficiency to excess. The "balanced quality" is not necessarily half-way between the extremes, but rather a psychological location in which constructive aspects of our lives are well balanced. You may notice that something seems to be added to or taken from the balanced quality when the extreme manifests; for example in the first line when hope is removed from interest, cynicism may be the result; but when narrow-mindedness is added to interest, the result is fanaticism. The following list is simplified, as any such list must be; but it may be a starting place for you to examine you own inner qualities. I have structured the list so that there is an essential quality (or in some cases more than one quality) hidden "underneath" the qualities that are listed, that can change things in a significant ways when life's vicissitudes or pressures blow us one way or the other. For example in the first line a hidden quality is optimism. If our interest in someone or something lacks optimism we may be cynical, but if our optimism is extreme it may become unrealistic and make us fanatical. This table is meant as a starting place, not as a "definitive" list.

PREPARATION

## Table A:
## Spiritually Helpful (Disciple) Qualities:
## Balancing Between Polar Opposites

| Deficiency | Balanced Quality | Excess |
|---|---|---|
| Cynical | Interested | Fanatical |
| Timid, fearful | Courageous | Foolhardy |
| Uncaring | Caring | Worrying |
| Heedless | Alert, awake | Hypersensitive, paranoid |
| | | |
| Stingy, greedy | Generous | Profligate |
| Unthinking, Thoughtless | Thoughtful | Over-analytical |
| | | |
| Lethargic, depressed | Aspiring | Ambitious |
| Deceitful | Honest | Naïve |
| Boastful | Humble | Self-abasing |
| Self-hating | Self-respecting | Egotistical |
| Self-neglecting | Prudent, self-caring | Greedy, self-centered |
| | | |
| Skeptical | Trusting | Gullible |
| Impatient | Patient | Indifferent |
| Unreliable | Trustworthy | Compulsive |
| Indecisive | Decisive | Inflexible |
| Passive | Engaged | Manipulative |
| Careless | Conscientious | Perfectionist |
| Inferior | Self-assured | Superior |
| Apathetic | Committed | Jealous |
| Submissive | Respectful | Dominating |
| Habitual, automatic | Free, with decision and choice | Coercive, with "will-power" |
| | | |
| Trivial | Joyful in play and work | Bound by "the shoulds" |

| Mechanical | Inspired | Impulsive |
| Rigid | Flexible | Indiscriminate |
| Inactive | Purposefully working | Productive for its own sake |

| Insensitive | Empathic, Discerning | Oversensitive |
| Passive | Receptive | Driven |
| Condemning | Merciful | Permissive |
| Cruel | Kind | Patronizing |
| Critical | Encouraging | Flattering |
| Indifferent | Involved | Obsessive |
| Choleric | Content | Complacent |
| Unaware | Mindful | Distracted |
| Uncontrolled | Self-controlled | Controlled by others |

| Angry or resisting | Accepting | Acquiescing |
| Uninvolved | Persistent | Over-attached |
| Uncaring | Compassionate | Oversympathizing |

---

What "hidden" qualities unite the qualities on each line? How do they apply to you?

You can probably think of other qualities that are meaningful to you to add to this list, or you may find it helpful to rearrange these categories. The balanced quality is not merely the middle between extremes, of course. There is something else that allows us to live in the balanced quality. We may work and practice to become balanced, but when balance is experienced it is not only an achievement, but a gift—it is grace that comes from beyond ourselves.

The balanced qualities keep the inner disciple on the spiritual path. The tests, temptations and pressures of life tend to move our disciple qualities into the extremes, where the disciple qualities are scattered and fall away—or, in extreme cases, even work against or betray the Spirit. The Good News is that we have help.

PREPARATION

- Which qualities or combination of qualities do you see in yourself?
- Where along the spectrum of extreme or balance are your qualities at this time?
- Which pressures in life move your qualities toward one extreme or another?
- Are there times when you choose to move your qualities to an extreme? Why?
- What or who helps you to move into balance in each area? How?
- Each line in Table A has three parts—notice the relationship between the qualities of deficiency, excess and balance. See what they have in common.
- I invite you to take one set of qualities in Table A that speak to your own life in some way, and become aware of the ways that these qualities can manifest—balanced and unbalanced:

Example: Critical—Encouraging—Flattering
Visualize yourself riding a bicycle—tipping to the left is your quality of deficiency (critical), tipping to the right is your quality of excess (flattering), and staying in the center is being balanced (encouraging), so that as you ride forward in life you can feel what pulls you toward one quality or another, and how you can stay in the position that allows you to actually "ride your bike." Feel the similarities and the differences in these qualities.

Example: Critical—Encouraging—Flattering
There is awareness in both the critical and the encouraging qualities, but being critical uses awareness to arrive at a negative conclusion while being encouraging uses awareness for a positive action. There is positive feedback in both the encouraging and the flattering

53

qualities, but the positive feedback in encouraging is for the benefit of someone else, while the feedback in flattery is used to promote an ulterior motive of one's own.
- When you are under pressure, being tested, which of your balanced qualities might get pressured into excess or deficiency, or both (as you may find that you sometimes bounce from excess to deficiency, unable to keep your balance)?
  <u>Example:</u> I might be encouraging to my subordinate when business is really good, but maybe I will get more critical if I am afraid of losing my job and afraid that my subordinate will get my position. I may be encouraging to my boss under normal circumstances, but will maybe start unconsciously to flatter him if I am afraid of losing my job.
- How does this pressure effect your ability to deal with a given situation?
- Recall a time when you have felt tested, and reflect on the qualities in you that came to the surface to help you get through. Are these the balanced qualities in Table A, or some others?
- Are these qualities available to you now? What else helps you get through a time of pressure or testing?
- When the time is right, feel free to return to this section and review other qualities in your life, looking for balance and imbalance.

◆ ◆ ◆

You may realize that certain qualities combine in your life to form parts of yourself that we can call your subpersonalities, and

PREPARATION

that not all of those qualities are balanced. My "worker" self, for example, is hard-working, conscientious, reliable, and honest, but that part of me is also worrisome, over-analytical, skeptical and a little stingy! My "husband" self is generous, tolerant, loving, patient, thoughtful. My "student-seeker" self is aspiring, eager, but also thoughtless and gullible. I have an "inner child" who is exuberant and playful, but also selfish, impatient and demanding and easily angered.

Each of us can be seen as having many parts, or subpersonalities, each of which may exhibit a different set of qualities. Some may even have opposite extreme qualities—my "worker" self is stingy, my "playful" self is profligate, while my "husband" self is generous in a more balanced way.

- Can you identify some of your subpersonalities, or parts of yourself?
- I invite you to take some time to do so. You may find it helpful to ask someone who knows you well to help you identify the parts of yourself.
- See if you can identify all of the qualities that emerge in each subpersonality, and how aspects of yourself differ from each other; whether they interact well or whether they conflict.
- Which parts of yourself or subpersonalities are most interested in and supportive of your spiritual life at this time?
- Do you have inner disciples?
- If you do, what qualities do you observe in them?
- Are they all balanced qualities, or are some of them more extreme?
- If you do not have an "inner disciple," which qualities within yourself do you feel are your "best" qualities, and which qualities tend to make you a better person?

# THE GATHERING

- How might circumstances pressure or tempt your balanced qualities into becoming one of the extreme polarities of excess or deficiency?
- How might your best qualities be "turned" into liabilities?
- Can you sense a deeper identity, an "I am" who lies within and beneath all of the qualities and subpersonalities, who observes them?
- How might the "I am" within you work to keep you in balance?
- Who is this "I am?"
- Come back to this section and these questions to assist you in learning about the depths of your own life, or when you sense that you are approaching a major change in your life.

♦♦♦

***WALKING OUT THE GOSPEL: TO EXPLORE THIS FURTHER, DO EXERCISES 5A, 5B OR 5C IN PART III, PAGES 397-404.***

♦♦♦

The qualities we have seen in ourselves are those we will want to be aware of as we go forward in the work of the Gospel.

# 4. THE WORK BEGINS

# THE WORK BEGINS

> **1:21** And they go into Capernaum, and immediately on the Sabbath he entered the synagogue, and was teaching. And they were astonished at his teaching, for he taught as one having authority, and not as the scribes [do]. And immediately there was in their synagogue a man with an unclean spirit, and he shouted out, "What is between us and you, Jesus the Nazarene? Have you come to destroy us? I know who you are—the holy one of God!" And Jesus rebuked him, saying, "Be silent and come out of him." And the unclean spirit, convulsing him and crying out in a loud voice, came out of him.

When there is a first conscious contact between the Spirit and one or more aspects of ourselves, we experience—from the point of view of our subpersonalities—a deep learning that is unlike anything we have learned from experience or from other people. "He taught as one having authority," does not mean that he was self-assured and did not need to quote scripture. Rather there is a sense that when the Spirit of God teaches us, we *experience* the teaching as a self-evident truth, rather than as an empirical learning. We notice that Mark does not tell us *what* Jesus taught, for that is not important here—we are learning the Gospel *process*. If we view this personally, we see that a synagogue symbolizes a context for worship, a gathering place for seekers of truth and of the presence of God, and it is here that the Spirit of God within us, the Christ, connects with us. The teaching is not something universally the same for all, but will be a specific application of truth and love that is designed to meet the person's needs. But again, the presence of the Spirit of God evokes a contrary spirit, just as occurred at the Jordan. This "unclean" spirit feels threatened by Jesus. We notice the juxtaposition of the phrases, "Have you come to destroy us?" and "I know who you are—the holy one of God!" Here is a hallmark of inner fragmentation and disharmony—the feeling of being threatened by what is actually holy and healing.

◆ ◆ ◆

PREPARATION

Viewed personally, what is the meaning of "unclean spirit?" To understand this, I believe it is helpful to look at the things that influence us, for influences live within us in a real and palpable way. We are subject to innumerable outside influences, everything from the overt influence of someone's words and actions to the subtler influences of someone's attitudes. The words of our parents on our first day at school may have shaped our responses to teachers for the rest of our lives; an event in our great-grandmother's life may have created an attitude that was taught by parent to child through the generations. Influences such as these exert strong or subtle forces on our lives all the time. Some are as obvious as a slap on the back, unmistakable and immediate. Some are as invisible as the gravitational pull of the moon, which affects our individual biology as surely as it does the tides. The influences on us range from conscious and deliberate, to unconscious and automatic, and they are often felt in combination. The sources of some of the influences on us are inanimate, like forces of nature, and others arise from the actions of people. Some influences seem mechanical, like the heat of the sun, whereas other influences seem to be more active and variable, even exhibiting what seems like purpose. When a combination of influences has what seems and feels like purpose, intent or direction, we may call it a spirit.[1]

For an example, let me suggest the difference between anger and "the spirit of anger." I may feel anger at someone or something when someone has deliberately hurt me, for example, or when something breaks unexpectedly at a critical moment that spoils my plans, bringing all my effort to nothing. The emotions of anger, of fear or hatred, etc. are responses to specific persons, things or events. What

---

[1] I do not mean to suggest that "spirit" is no more than "influence." Ultimately, "spirit" cannot be defined any more than "life" can be defined. A virus cannot survive without a living host; do we deny that it is "alive?" Similarly, an "unclean spirit" cannot survive without a host. It is not a physical being, any more than "hatred" or "revenge" or "self-loathing" are physical; but such a "spirit" is nevertheless real, and can exert influence, and it arises usually out of like influences. In the gospel the being of an "unclean spirit" is not on the same level of reality as the Holy Spirit, yet the gospel uses the word "spirit" to refer to both, so I follow the gospel and leave the larger discussion about the nature of "spirit" for another occasion.

I call "the spirit of anger," on the other hand, does not arise in response to someone or something specific, but seems to reside within our psyche, awaiting something to activate it—anger, waiting for something to get angry about; or fear, waiting for something to be afraid of. It seems to have the intent of feeding off circumstances to increase itself.

Mark's language makes a neat distinction between actions, attitudes, persons or spirits that are helpful, edifying, healthy, life-giving, sacred, and in accord with God's will—which are usually called "clean"—and those that are unhealthy, threatening, unhelpful, degrading, destructive, not to be shared, out of accord with God's will—which are usually called "unclean."[2] This language may not fit with our contemporary use of terms, but at the time the Gospel was written the meanings were accepted. Still, people even in that time used the terms differently—some people labeled whatever they disapproved of or disagreed with as "unclean," just as today some people may call what they do not like "evil" or "bad."

We can adapt these terms to our inner perspective on the text. The "unclean spirit," then, can be any influence within us that tends toward what is unhealthy, etc. that comes from outside of us and seems to have some coherence and direction. It is similar to a virus. It will look for an opportunity to express and increase itself, and it will recognize and evade any force that limits it.[3] The Spirit of God acts within us to edify, to correct, to heal, to integrate us as people, and its presence always ultimately works to "eject" whatever influences limit its work, in a way that is similar to the way that light eliminates a shadow. An "unclean spirit" may be a way of designating the unhealthy attitudes within us, acquired from outside influences, around which one of our subpersonalities may be focused.

Here is an example from my own life. I have a subpersonality I call "Little Jan." He is a part of me that is at the six year-old level. When I was that age I was angry without knowing why, sensitive to

---

[2] This usage is not the same as the strict ancient Hebrew usage, but the terms I am using provide an approximation that may be helpful to those of us who are not biblical scholars, and this usage may be more helpful from the inner perspective.

[3] Among modern teachers, Eckhart Tolle has coined the term "pain body" to refer to a similar phenomenon, and others may use different terms.

teasing, and I attacked other kids when provoked. This "Little Jan" subpersonality is a piece of myself who for a long time was stuck emotionally in the first grade, where he was ostracized and teased, felt abandoned by his parents and out of place in school. He covered his inner wounds with a shell of toughness and aggressiveness, and was slowly, over decades, moved beneath the surface of my personality because his behavior was unacceptable. The anger he felt may have seemed justified when I was six years old, but over the years the anger found additional justifications for its existence, blended with the anger of my grandparents and parents and others, and was fed by an "inner critic" who absorbed all the angry voices from outside. It eventually acquired more socially "acceptable" ways of expressing itself (such as in verbal sarcasm), and established itself as a relatively permanent part of my life, like a spiritual herpes virus that would break out in angry outbursts at times. It could then be seen as a "spirit of anger." I felt a part of myself that contained anger with no object, that lay in wait for some event or person in my life that it could use as an excuse to vent. My "Little Jan" subpersonality is the one who carried this "unclean spirit," for it dominated him.

What the Gospel calls an "unclean spirit" is more than psychologically repressed emotion. It is at least partly acquired from outside the person, an influence that seems to have intent and direction that becomes quasi-independent of conscious awareness. Like a dangerous virus that has a person for its host, it destructively feeds off the energy of another being—either its host, or someone else, or both. It can be transmitted from one person to another and is often passed down through generations of family members.

To return to the example above, at a certain point in my life, a different influence entered my life—a Spirit that looks over all of my attitudes, thoughts, feelings, actions, with an intent to heal, to integrate, to help, to edify, to "cleanse" me. The presence of this Spirit *immediately* provoked the spirit that dominated my "Little Jan," because the two spirits are incompatible. The old influence tried to protect its "turf:" Our attitudes will not change easily, and they are often reinforced by habits, thoughts, perceptions, and the unknowing collusion of other people. Healing does not take place without effort.

In the Gospel story, the unclean spirit convulses the man and cries out as it comes out of him. But from the man's perspective, it

## THE WORK BEGINS

seems that it is he himself who is shaken and it is he who cries out. The nature of having an "unclean spirit" or negative influence within us is that we experience the spirit or the influence as "me," or part of "me," which is why so many of us have such difficulty separating ourselves from such influences. The first step in such healing, then, is the realization that "I" and the unwanted influence are not the same, even though we seem to be joined. The separation may be experienced as a difficult and painful process. For some of us, it may so painful that we would not willingly endure it without help.

A spirit of healing, to be successfully introduced into our lives, must be supported by the love, strength and understanding of other people, as well as by practices and processes within the person. The Gospel is full of tools and techniques and teachings to help reinforce and strengthen a newly introduced "clean" Spirit.

If the spirit of healing, the "clean" spirit within us, is the Holy Spirit of God, it works to drive out the contrary spirit, just as Jesus said, "Be silent and come out of him." That new Spirit does not simply come in and take the ascendancy within us—if spiritual healing and transformation were that simple, it could all be done without our cooperation. But we are composite beings, with families, with pasts, with psychological functions, influences, subpersonalities and so on. We are *communities* within ourselves, and often our inner communities are marked by differences or conflicts on many levels. One part of us may be a "disciple" who fervently desires God, peace and love; another part of us may be a lover of pleasure who thinks only of herself; another part may be a stern taskmaster who inflicts guilt or punishment on the part of us who "slacks off" or "doesn't measure up." One part of us may invite the Spirit into our lives while another may not—one part of us may actively resist it.

It may not be a simple thing for us to be present to the Spirit of God. One day we may be open and responsive, the Spirit moves in us and we are aware and know it. The next day a crisis occurs in our lives and another inner aspect may "take over" control of our conscious awareness, and suddenly our priorities seem to change. This may happen without our being aware of it at all, for within us it just feels like "me," even though my "moods" seem to change. Such a change may be much more obvious to other people, who may also just mark it off as a change of "mood."

PREPARATION

> - Think back to the disciple qualities we looked at earlier, and remember your response to the question of how you may be tested or tempted, as balanced qualities get pressured to move toward one of their extreme polarities.
> - Where does such pressure come from in *your* life? From within you or from outside—or from both?
> - What can you do to keep your qualities balanced?
> - How do you respond to outside influences that work to upset your balance? Think of an example from your own experience, and observe your responses as you recall. Do not judge, only observe.

♦♦♦

> 1:27 And all were astonished and asked each other, saying, "What is this? A new teaching, with authority! And he commands the unclean spirits and they obey him!" And immediately the report of him spread to all of the whole country around Galilee.

In the Gospel story Jesus entered the synagogue and taught, and cast out an unclean spirit. Jesus enters the synagogue with the assent of the people, not against their will. They only begin to discover who he is and what he does *after* he is there. We do not know who the man was or what kind of unclean spirit he had, because these are not important. In our interpretation this is not history. This is a story to illustrate what happens when we invite the Spirit into our lives—it heals and teaches us, and it arouses the spirits of contrary forces, which recognize it. The power of the Spirit in our lives is not like any other experience, and its action will amaze and astonish the other parts of ourselves. It will shake us up, and the result may be something uncanny, unusual. We may mark the result off to coincidence, or luck, or the like, but it will not go unnoticed.

> 1:29 And having left the synagogue, immediately they entered the house of Simon and Andrew, with James and John, but Simon's mother-in-law lay sick with a fever, and immediately they tell him of her. And going to her and taking her by the hand he lifted her up, and the fever left her, and she was serving them.

In the synagogue Jesus made his presence known to all, and now he has moved into the private domain of the disciples. Once the Spirit has made itself known, it must be reinforced and strengthened, supported and followed, received and accepted. Within us there are aspects that act as inner disciples, but these too are supported by other aspects. If the disciple is not supported, then he falters. So the Spirit moves to provide healing where it is needed.

♦ ♦ ♦

Studying the Gospel of Mark from an inner perspective provides us with a path to get to know ourselves in a new way. In Mark many of the details of the story are left out deliberately,[4] so that if we wish to know how the story unfolds, we must supply the details from our own lives. The action will still follow the story line in its general outline, but its particular direction will be determined by who we are and who we are to become.

There may be a constant temptation to read the story literally, to

---

[4] This was apparently frustrating to ancient readers as well as modern ones, so other gospel writers—Matthew and Luke—provided us with detailed answers to such questions as, "What happened? What did he say? What did he do?" But we are supposing that Mark's purpose was different: he did not intend to *tell* the story, but to *use* portions of the story to guide the reader. In this case then, historical details can actually be an encumbrance to personal learning.

PREPARATION

look for the "real" mother-in-law of Simon. Historically, it seems that Simon's mother-in-law plays a small part in the Gospel story. But in the "inner interpretation" we search for parts of ourselves that *function* in the way an ancient mother-in-law did—a part of ourselves that is perhaps not noticed much, but that plays a vital, continuing part in our own stories. What gave birth to what we love? What keeps our "inner household" in order? What supports us and encourages us every day? The inner power of the Gospel is not unlocked until we treat it as a tool for personal spiritual transformation. Just as the notes on a sheet of music give no sound until we play or sing them, so the Gospel does not touch us until we apply it to ourselves in the most personal way, replacing the story characters with the inner people, disciples, and Christ in our own lives.

- Look within yourself again, and consider your inner qualities as if they were "persons."
- What qualities support your hunger for God?
- If you have an "inner Simon," then who is the "inner mother-in-law?" What purposes does she serve? What functions does she perform? For example, if your "inner Simon" needs time for prayer or contemplation, your "inner mother-in-law" might be the part of you that keeps track of your schedule and your worldly needs so that quiet time is available.
- What are her strengths, weaknesses, likes, dislikes?
- What about her is important in your walk with God?
- Using your inner senses, observe your inner mother-in-law to see whether she is healthy or not.

# THE WORK BEGINS

> 1:32 That evening as the sun set they brought to him all who were diseased or possessed with demons,[5] and the whole city was gathered at the door. And he healed many who were ill with various diseases and cast out many demons, and he would not permit the demons to speak, because they knew him.

♦ ♦ ♦

From an interior perspective, the meaning of this passage is very clear. There is a healer among us, so bring everyone who is not well into his presence for healing! We are not dealing with another person, but rather the Christ is the healing presence of God within us, and the process of bringing the sick and the possessed to him is an inner action. We must learn to become aware of which aspects within us are weak or ill, which are bound by habit or addiction, which are beset by lingering influences that combine to form the "unclean" spirits of fear, abuse, anger, rejection, hatred, greed, and so on. Once we are aware of them, we must seek out the Spirit of healing within us and bring "the sick" into its presence.

Some students of the Gospel have remarked about Jesus' apparent "secrecy"—he would not permit the demons to speak, "because they knew him." This is the second instance of this behavior, and there are many to follow. Those who encounter him are forbidden to speak, or asked not to. The demons obey him; not all the people do. But remember that the goal of the story is the spiritual transformation of *us*—the persons who are reading—but not just by reading! Jesus is not interested in transforming "demons," which are no more than accumulations of negative influence that seem to acquire lives of

---

[5] The Greek is "daimon" which in this context is an evil spirit of some kind (even though in Greek a *daimon* is not necessarily evil). The writer of Mark refers to both "demons" and "unclean spirits," and it is unclear how they are different, but it is safe to say that these words are a way of indicating that people are subject to different kinds of ills.

## PREPARATION

their own, like viruses. The only thing to do with a truly destructive influence is to remove it. There is a clear difference between negative influences and the parts of ourselves that suffer from the negative influences. The story is showing the reader what to do with the parts of ourselves that are wounded by negative influences—all the crippled, lame, deaf, blind, and infirm of our inner village—bring them to the source of healing.

In reality, identifying the wounded, the negative influences, and the source of healing within us is often not a quick or simple task—nor is it an easy matter to learn *how* to bring our inner wounded to the inner healing, or how to eliminate harmful influences. Many of us do not even see the need for this work.

> o **Which parts of you need to be healed at this time?**
> o **How do you discover which parts of yourself need healing?**
> o **If you mentally scan your inner subpersonalities, you may find some whose response is, "not me, I'm fine!" If you do, I suggest that for now you leave these alone, without judgment.**
> o **I invite you look and listen within yourself—listen or look for an inner impulse or an outer behavior of fear, hurt, anger, guilt, or shame; or one of impatience, arrogance, cruelty, sadness, pride, or some other difficult quality, if there is one.**
> o **If you feel it or notice it, stay with it for a time. Just allow yourself to be aware of it without judgment. Observe it with compassion, and allow yourself to ask within, to pray, to desire that this part of your life be healed. Then let it go and mentally step back from it. We will return to this later. If you do not feel or notice anything like this, that is all right; just go on.**

***WALKING OUT THE GOSPEL: TO EXPLORE THIS FURTHER, DO EXERCISE 6 IN PART III, PAGE 405.***

## 5. HEALING, FORGIVENESS AND FAITH

PREPARATION

> ¹:³⁵ And in the morning, while it was still very dark, he rose and went out to a deserted place, and there he was praying. And Simon and those who were with him searched for him, and they found him and said to him, "Everyone seeks you." And he said to them, "Let us go to other towns, so that I may preach there also, for that is what I came for." And he went throughout all Galilee, preaching in their synagogues and casting out demons.

We see that Jesus does not linger too long in a single place. When pursued by those who would have him heal every single person who is brought to him, he responds, "Let us go to other towns." He need not be complete or thorough at this time. He arrives to *initiate* something in a particular area, to give a message, to teach, and to move on. His mission to preach and teach suggests that his ultimate mission is *not* to heal all people at this time, but to begin a process that must be carried on by his hearers, his witnesses, his disciples, and all who follow him. No one is completely passive in Jesus' presence—people come *to* him, they bring others *to* him, they *ask* him, they *reach* for him. Each plays an active part, each is called upon to contribute.

> ¹:⁴⁰ And a leper comes to him, beseeching him, and kneeling said to him, "If you choose to, you can make me clean." Moved with compassion, he reached out with his hand and touched him and said, "I do choose—be made clean." And immediately the leprosy left him, and he was made clean. And sternly warning him, he immediately sent him away, saying, "See that you say nothing to anyone, but go, show yourself to the priest, and offer for your cleansing what Moses commanded, as a witness to them." But he went out and began to tell everyone and spread the word, so that

# HEALING, FORGIVENESS AND FAITH

> he could no longer go into a town openly, but stayed outside in deserted places, and they were coming to him from everywhere.

Jesus charged the man to tell no one, but to give an offering of thanks quietly. But the man talked freely and told all to everyone. The man was *sure* that he knew what had happened and that he was qualified to publicly report the event—after all, it had happened to him! But notice we have again the signifier of an inner event—*immediately* the leprosy left him. Inner events may happen without regard to time—that is, they are not time-dependent in a linear way; an inner event may occur in an instant, or it may occur over years; remember, the word *immediately* in this text does not *describe* time, but is intended to disconnect us from time while showing us the intimate connection between the events themselves. Inner events often do not require the understanding of their beneficiaries in order to occur. In fact, inner events of great significance, like healings, often transcend the categories of ordinary thinking and are understood, if at all, only long after they occur—after their influence has permeated the life of the person who experiences them.

The healing of the leper was to have been the first step in his transformation. He was commanded to keep silence, not for the sake of hoarding a secret—because if Jesus had meant the healing to remain *secret* he would not have instructed the man to show himself to the priest. But in keeping silent the man would be able to listen better and to hear[1] what was to *follow* his healing. There was more to come! But as he went about the town crowing about what was done *for* him, he became deaf to what was done *to* him. Physical healings can be the initial events of widespread inner patterns. To some extent these patterns need conscious cooperation in order to propagate. One can learn how to cooperate with inner healing only by learning how to be quiet and listen to inner processes and promptings—thus the command to silence.

---

[1] To hear *life*, and what the Spirit had to say to him, to show him, in a new way.

PREPARATION

Afterward Jesus cannot go into a town openly because of the clamoring crowds. But he does not come to satisfy cravings. This *can* happen within us as it is described—when a wonderful transforming event happens to us, we may become so excited by it that we cannot resist the urge to talk about it and name it, to describe it, to share it, to celebrate it, to study it and preach about it. But a transforming event, such as a physical healing, is the beginning of a process, not the end. It requires an attentive, open, inquiring, receptive state of mind in order to continue. The story tells us that a "talking" kind of response may actually stifle the experience itself and prevent the transformation from continuing. We are told to keep silent.[2]

> o **What happens when you become aware of a part of yourself that needs to be healed? Does that part of you get hidden or covered up, or perhaps just set aside? Is it hard to live with this awareness?**
> o **What can you do to bring that part of yourself to the source of healing? (Do not dwell on this question. Ask it and let it go. An answer may come to you now or later)**
> o **Are you able to be quiet and watch and listen to your inner processes and changes? If not, what prevents you from doing so?**

## *WALKING OUT THE GOSPEL: TO EXPLORE THIS FURTHER, DO EXERCISE 7 IN PART III, PAGE 407.*

---

[2] I can testify from experience that receiving a healing without a truly receptive attitude can result in the healing process being interrupted for years, even decades.

# HEALING, FORGIVENESS AND FAITH

> **2:1** And when he returned to Capernaum after some days, it was heard that he was in the house. So many gathered around that there was no longer room for them, not even in front of the door, and he was speaking the word to them.

The phrase "in the house" is sometimes also translated "at home." From the inner perspective, this suggests that the Spirit makes a home within us, or that other parts of us recognize the Spirit in a specific inner location. Once the unhealed parts of us know where to turn for healing they may form an inner mob, anxious to get what they need, some crowding out others with their demands and expectations.

> o **What would *your* "inner mob" be like?—Feelings, thoughts, sensations, impulses that are not peacefully receptive but needy, craving, demanding? Do you ever see the presence of these within you?**

We considered above how to become aware of parts of ourselves that need healing and how to bring those parts to the source of healing. The following vignette begins to show us some of the obstacles to healing—one of our needs may interfere with the healing of another part of us.

> **2:3** And they come bringing to him a man who was paralyzed, carried by four others. And when they could not bring him close because of the crowd, they removed the roof above him, and after having dug through it, they lower the mat on which the paralytic lay. And seeing their faith, Jesus says to the paralyzed one, "Child, your sins have been forgiven." But some of the scribes were sitting there and questioning

> in their hearts, "Why does this one speak this way? He blasphemes! Who can forgive sins but God alone?" And immediately Jesus, perceiving in his spirit that they questioned thus within themselves, says to them, "Why do you raise these questions in your hearts? Which is easier, to say to the paralyzed one 'Your sins are forgiven,' or to say, 'Rise, take up your mat and walk?' But so that you may know that the Son of Man[3] has authority on earth to forgive sins," he says to the paralytic, "I say to you, Rise: take up your mat and go home." And he stood up, and immediately took up his mat and went out before all of them, so that all were amazed and glorified God, saying, "we never saw anything like this!"

The four men with the paralytic cannot get to Jesus, because the crowds are so eager for themselves that they will not allow a deeply needy person to enter. I think this story is describing a common experience. Once the Spirit of God has moved in a person, and the resulting peace and healing are witnessed, there are parts of us who may rush in with their own agendas. They interpret, they seek, they demand, they organize, and they create a shell around the spiritual center that can effectively isolate the Spirit and hinder it from doing its work.

These parts of us may function as spiritual insulators or gatekeepers. They block or hinder the work of God. For example, after I experienced a great healing when I was thirty I was led to attend

---

[3] Earlier we heard a voice from the heavens say, "You are my beloved son, in you I delight," (page 33) and we suggested contemplation of the meaning of the word "son." Now we hear Jesus refer to himself as "Son of Man" which would perhaps be best translated as "Son of Humanity." What is Jesus presenting to us with these words? They are not new, having been used in several Hebrew books before Jesus—although Jesus uses the terms *the* Son of Man—and I think that it again will be fruitful to contemplate the meaning of these words, especially as they may relate to Jesus *within us*. There is an essential aspect of our being human that Jesus is connecting us to, and it is important that we allow this connection to become real for us.

Divinity School out of my desire to help in the healing of others. At school I studied the Gospel, but my study became dominated by a part of me that is very intellectual and analytical, which read the Gospel According to Mark only as history, and then dismissed it as "very unlikely." But that reading prevented me from seeing the possibilities that I am presenting in this book. In my case the spiritual gatekeeper was not my reading, but the tendency to approach things only from an intellectual point of view, which effectively prevented the Spirit from speaking to me through my intuitions. Your gatekeepers may show different qualities.

The Gospel story suggests that extraordinary measures need to be taken (even measures that appear to be somewhat destructive) to overcome the obstacles created by our own spiritual need and greed. In the story, the men essentially wreck part of the house—they remove the tiles of the roof and lower the paralytic down through the ceiling. In life, we find that the work of the Spirit can be covered up and effectively limited by strong, eager parts of ourselves— ideas, emotions, habits, associations, expectations. These may respond to the work of the Spirit in our lives, but their response is often to simply use the holy work for their own ends, or, like the scribes, to limit it by comparing it to something "authoritative," like scripture or scientific "facts." The access to the real spiritual life may be denied to the parts of ourselves that most need healing, unless we find a way to get past the spiritual gatekeepers.

> o **Do you have spiritual gatekeepers?**
> o **What parts of you are excited by truth and healing? How are they important in your daily life? What beliefs, practices and qualities are connected with these parts of you?**
> o **How might these qualities act as spiritual gatekeepers by becoming restrictive, or jealous, or exacting, or proud, or particular (or some other quality)?**
> o **What can you do to prevent that from happening?**
> o **Come back to these questions whenever you feel "stuck" in your spiritual work.**

## PREPARATION

In the story the men are lowering the paralytic into the house from a hole in the roof, and Jesus sees *their* faith—the men carrying him, not just the paralytic himself—and says to the paralytic, "Child, your sins are forgiven." There are parts of us that are so crippled that they need help to even approach the healing that is needed. The healing Spirit of God may have made a home in our lives, and yet still there are parts of us that are so crippled that they must be helped even to have faith. The Spirit does *not* automatically overcome all obstacles by its mere presence in our lives. Sometimes one part of us must work to enable the healing of another part of us.

Jesus tells the man, who was brought to have his paralysis healed, that his sins are forgiven. When questioned, Jesus makes it plain that healing and forgiveness are linked closely together, for he says, "which is *easier?*"—to say one thing or to say another matters little, for *it is one process.* Again we are alerted to the inner spiritual nature of the exchange, for when the scribes question in their hearts, Jesus "immediately" perceives their attitudes in his spirit.

He is dealing with some of the spiritual gatekeepers who have crowded around him, which turn out to be the same as the inner critics we described in Section 2 on pages 37-29—the scribes and Pharisees who measure their experience against what they have been taught, who do not know how to respond to anything truly new. These gatekeepers have their own ideas and beliefs about what is allowed and what is not allowed, about who God is, and who God is not. And it is clear that one of the issues at hand is that of "authority." The scribes seem to be saying not only that God alone has the power to forgive sins, but also that God alone is *authorized* to forgive sins. The gatekeepers—the inner critics—require *permission* for forgiveness. But Jesus tells them that no permission is needed. He forgives freely and easily. The scribes and Pharisees feel that the distinction between authority and power is an important one, and they have mental rules about how to deal with each. Remember that we are not dealing with a person here, but with our own inner spiritual gatekeepers. Gatekeepers have an agenda to push, and a turf to defend. They "keep the gate"—they profit from restricting the free flow of traffic, and they construct rules to justify and enforce these restrictions. Historically, the scribes were a part of a religious legal system that was built on laws, rules and traditions, and as such they represent the inner rule-makers that we encounter.

## HEALING, FORGIVENESS AND FAITH

They make fine distinctions and accuse us when their distinctions are not observed by other parts of us. If their distinctions are ignored and forgiveness is granted freely by the Spirit, then these parts of us lose *their* power and authority, for then there is no gate to keep.

Jesus counters by asserting that he *in fact* has the authority, which arises out of the healing power that he manifests. This episode is meant to show us that holy authority and holy power are one and the same, and that both proceed out of the love that forgives. Within us, the love that forgives is what heals—breaks the paralysis that hold us back.

This is the first great teaching that Jesus is embodying: the Spirit within us is *authorized* to forgive; no other "permission" is needed, and in forgiveness the Spirit brings the power of healing.

Jesus tells the man, "Rise: take up your mat and go home;" —receive the forgiveness, receive the healing, and *take it with you.* Go back to your ordinary life *with* the healing, *with* the forgiveness. "Go home."

When we are stuck in some way, unable to go on, the story is saying that we are to mobilize whatever help is available within us and outside of us and bring the stuck part of us—our inner paralytic—to Christ, to the Spirit of God within us, and allow the hatred, the guilt, the fear, the negative feelings and thoughts, to be dissolved in forgiveness, to be released *without condition or limitation.* We will often discover that our inner (and outer) gatekeepers will object, and sometimes object very strenuously! The objections may take any number of forms: fear, logical objections, appeals to doctrine or scientific verifiability, social constraints, unwillingness to be "exposed" to public reaction, an appeal to what is "right" or "true," a need to protect someone, a demand for proof, an appeal to "justice," and so on. None of these objections is necessarily wrong or harmful in itself, but any of them may become an inner gatekeeper if it blocks healing.

> o **Recall that inner feeling or outer behavior of fear, hurt, anger, guilt or shame, etc. that you listened for earlier on page 67, and also recall the inner gatekeepers you found on page 74. Is there a relationship between them?**

PREPARATION

- What is the relationship between the wounded parts of you and the parts of you that seek God's healing and holiness? Are these parts of you aware of each other? Do they turn toward each other or away from each other? Notice your emotional reactions toward people who evoke in you thoughts of woundedness, or of holiness.
- Are your emotional reactions to woundedness the same as your reactions to wholeness, or are they opposite? What does this tell you about being healed or unhealed? About yourself? Is there a connection between your emotional reaction to the wounds of others and the healing of your own wounds?
- Does something prevent the unhealed parts of you from getting healed? If so, what? If there is an obstacle to this healing, what can you do to remove this obstacle? Will you make a commitment to do this?
- What steps can you take to get past your own spiritual gatekeepers to reach the genuine source of healing in your life?
- Do you need help identifying your inner gatekeepers and getting past them to healing?

♦ ♦ ♦

- Come back to these questions whenever you encounter inner judgment or wounding.

♦ ♦ ♦

# HEALING, FORGIVENESS AND FAITH

> **2.13** He went out again beside the sea, and all the crowd was gathering around him, and he was teaching them.

Jesus has just finished healing the paralytic, and has seen that the inner circle of people who crowded around him included not only his disciples (people eager to learn) but also spiritual gatekeepers, who are present for different purposes, and who measure both his teaching and his healing against predetermined ideas.

After the healing and after the confrontation with the scribes, he breaks the circle of insulation and goes back to open country where he cannot be surrounded by gatekeepers who will hinder his work. But he does not continue to heal people by the sea—rather, he teaches.

Word must have spread about the healing, but it seems that after the healing the spiritual priority shifts and teaching resumes—for Jesus was teaching when the men lowered the paralytic down from the roof, and the episode of healing was actually an interruption.

We do not know what the teaching was, and this is not important to the Gospel writer. It is important to know that the Spirit teaches, both before and after healing.

> o **We cannot hear the teaching unless we sit still and listen—What do you listen for?**
> o **What do you do, personally, to enable you to listen for the teaching of the Spirit?**
> o **Do you need help learning to listen inwardly?**

♦♦♦

> o **Come back to these questions whenever you have overcome a spiritual hurdle or have felt some inner healing.**

PREPARATION

> 2.14 And as he passed by he saw Levi the son of Alphaeus, sitting at the tax office, and he says to him, "Follow me," and he got up and followed him.

I believe that the elements in the Gospel of Mark are placed where they are in the Gospel, not for literary purposes, not for "historical accuracy," but for teaching purposes. Levi the tax collector is representative of a kind of opportunistic oppressor, who serves the "outer authority" (the government, in the story) in return for a share of the takings. This is part of ourselves that focuses on "outer" events, that gathers wealth and enforces an economic discipline. It is no coincidence that Jesus calls him. The Spirit within us must mobilize certain key aspects of us in order for the great transformation to take place. A tax collector uses certain inner and outer abilities—discipline, intelligence, organization, vigilance, resourcefulness, judgment, persistence—to do his job, to serve his masters. Jesus is not calling a tax collector to be a tax collector; he is calling certain qualities within us to change direction and to be mobilized in service of the spiritual life.

- Look over the qualities in Table A on page 51. Are there qualities within you that might be called your "inner tax collector?" (For example, one or more of the following: intelligent, greedy, ambitious, compulsive, superior, opportunistic, dominating; or others, like precise, hard-working or meticulous)
- How are these qualities used in your life? How can they be re-directed and combined with others and moved into the "balanced" column so that that they may serve the Spirit?

# HEALING, FORGIVENESS AND FAITH

> o  Can you identify the balanced qualities that represent this part of you? When you follow the Spirit, are some qualities not balanced but left behind altogether, or are all your qualities called?

♦ ♦ ♦

> 2.15 And it happened that as he sat at table in his house, many tax collectors and sinners were sitting with Jesus and his disciples, for there were many who followed him. And the scribes of the Pharisees, having seen that he was eating with sinners and tax collectors, said to his disciples, "Why does he eat with tax collectors and sinners?" And having heard this, Jesus says to them, "Those who are well have no need of a healer, but those who are sick; I came not to call the righteous, but sinners."

Jesus sits at table in his house, just as the Spirit feeds parts of us that come for nourishment. But as we noted earlier, some come with agendas. The scribes and the Pharisees represent the parts of us that are eager for the spiritual life—but on their own terms. They enter the house of the Spirit bringing with them established ideas of goodness, rightness, and appropriateness. They have standards of belief and behavior, against which they measure all people. For them Jesus is just another person to be measured against their ideals, and for them his response is questionable.

At this point the story is written in a way that invites us to see through the eyes of someone who compares experience by classifying others into polar opposites like responsible and irresponsible, conservative and liberal, respectable and not respectable—"us" and "them." In the story these categories are "scribes and Pharisees" (the respectable people) on the one hand, and "tax collectors and sinners" on the other hand. The classifications lead *us* to conclusions and judgments, such as that there are people who are greedy wrongdoers, *and* there are people who are educated and seekers of righteousness—or, there are people who are willing to change for the better when given the opportunity, *and* there are people who are self-righteous and arrogant and who refuse to change, from pride. The mental practice of categorizing others, dividing them into opposites (even if the categorizing seems to be true), tends to simplify things and it conceals possible connections between the categories by herding one group into the "right" camp and the other group into the "wrong" camp.

I believe we need to put aside the traditions of two thousand years in order to see what the Gospel writer wants us to see; for our tendency to classify is also a tendency to judge, and it may prevent us from seeing something important—that *our ideals* (what we judge by), whatever they may be, can get in the way of real progress, real learning, real inner connection. Tax collectors and sinners may be the parts of ourselves who are greedy and needy and constantly failing—but in the story they also know that they need help, know that change is necessary. Scribes and Pharisees are more focused on what they know to be right, to be true and good; but this focus leads them outside themselves into comparisons with others, into classification and exclusion, and in the end *away* from learning and transformation.

Our own inner scribes and Pharisees may not be self-righteous. They are just parts of us that want to be right in what we believe, and want to avoid being wrong. That part of us may believe in punishment for sinners, in preventing cruelty to animals, in the right to use birth control, or in a strong national defense, or something else, depending on who we are. An inner scribe is an ideal that will not be changed, but stands apart in some way from the troublesome aspects of our lives to keep from being compromised or betrayed. An inner Pharisee can be a part of us that is well-meaning and energetic, helpful and generous—but insulated from the unpleasantness of failures, from short-comings, from weakness. Inner scribes and Pharisees usually do not like to be challenged, and any attempt to move them toward "the dark side" of life provokes them to denial, accusation, criticism, stubbornness, resistance, fear or hostility—even perhaps some form of inner or outer violence.

We have been taught to equate "scribes and Pharisees" with narrow-minded bigots, but this caricature may obscure the truth. The sincere desire for, and belief in, our own goodness can itself become a trap that holds us back. The real spiritual life requires a flexibility that most customs and laws and many ideals do not encourage, and it requires not only a tolerance for "tax collectors and sinners," but an active loving engagement with them—with our own inner dark sides.

Jesus says, "I came not to call the righteous, but sinners." He sits and eats with all of them. Yet within us it may be the "well" and "righteous" parts of us who act as spiritual gatekeepers, who try to keep their distance from unpleasant memories, painful awareness, and unwanted habits. The inner gatekeeper may not be able to get rid of these things, but does not want to mingle with them. Jesus provides the example that the Spirit within us follows—he calls the sick who are willing to be healed, he feeds those who are willing to be nourished, he reaches for those in need, he teaches to those who can hear—all are invited to his table without precondition.

♦ ♦ ♦

- Is there a part of you that will "sit at the table" only if you are not required to change? Jesus does not require anything as the "price of admission." Do you require something, of yourself or of others?
- What parts of *you* act as inner scribes and Pharisees? What ideals motivate them? What do they require?
- How can these ideals limit you? What is your attitude toward the "opposite" of your ideal? How do you approach what is "wrong" in life?
- How might a sincerely held belief actually hinder or inhibit your own spiritual growth and healing?
- Are there parts of you that prefer not to be involved in your spiritual life?
- Does the Spirit call to all parts of you?

PREPARATION

***WALKING OUT THE GOSPEL: TO EXPLORE THIS FURTHER, DO EXERCISE 8 IN PART III, PAGE 408.***

♦ ♦ ♦

## 6. A NEW SPIRITUAL PATHWAY

PREPARATION

> 2:18 And John's disciples and the Pharisees were fasting; and they come and said to him, "Why do John's disciples and the disciples of the Pharisees fast, but your disciples[1] do not fast?" And Jesus said to them, "Can the wedding guests fast while the bridegroom is with them? As long as they have the bridegroom with them they cannot fast; but the days will come when the bridegroom is taken away from them, and then they will fast on that day. No one sews an unshrunk patch on old clothes, for the patch pulls away from it, the new from the old, and a worse tear is made. And no one puts new wine into old wineskins, otherwise the wine will burst the skins, and the wine is lost and so are the skins; but new wine is to be put into new wineskins."

In this section, Jesus is dealing with spiritual disciplines, and specifically those that involve self-denial. Jesus indicates that such disciplines are not to be followed out of tradition, but in response to specific spiritual needs, to serve a purpose. As their teacher, he feeds his disciples a spiritual food, which they are to continue to receive as long as it is directly available. He makes it clear that there will be an end to this direct feeding, and at that time his disciples will exercise a discipline in going without. In the inner interpretation we see this parable as a lesson—that spiritual exercises are to be followed for a purpose, and in response to the events of our lives. When our experience is feeding us, we are to eat, because there will certainly come a time when that nourishment will end, and then we must still go on—"fasting," living on the nourishment we received earlier, applying the lessons we have already learned when new ones are not forthcoming for a time.

---

[1] We recall again that "disciple" is a translation of the word for "learner," or "student." We sometimes attach other meanings to the English word "disciple," which may not be in the original. It is essential that we see that each teacher has learners, and the "gospel," the joyous message, is what we *learn* from Jesus. His disciples learn to *be* in a certain way, and then they learn to act from that being.

# A NEW SPIRITUAL PATHWAY

Jesus is teaching to a traditional community and indicates that new learning is not successfully absorbed by following old practices. The practice, the behavior or the ideas need to be changed in order to integrate and carry out the new learning. This change may affect not only what we do, but also when and why and how we do it. Other people may only see the outward change, which will seem perplexing or perhaps even wrong to them if they do not understand the inner change that initiates the outer change.

> 2:23 And it happened that on the Sabbath he was traveling through the grain fields, and his disciples began to make their way picking the heads of grain. And the Pharisees said to him, "Look—why are they doing what is not lawful on the Sabbath?" And he said to them, "Have you never read what David did when he and his companions were hungry and in need? How he entered the house of God when Abiathar was high priest, and ate the bread of offering, which it is not lawful for any but the priests to eat, and also he gave some to his companions?" And he said to them, "The Sabbath was made for mankind, not mankind for the Sabbath. So the Son of Man is also lord of the Sabbath."

The lesson mentioned above becomes clearer in this vignette, when the disciples are found picking grain on the Sabbath—activity that the Pharisees interpret as work, and therefore a violation of both custom and religious law. Notice the juxtaposition of this section with the previous one—both sections center on practices that have to do with eating. While the previous section had to do with spiritual discipline ("when to fast"), this one deals with outward custom and law ("when to eat"). Feeding is the story's metaphor for learning. Jesus has taught his disciples to eat when and where the food is available—and in the inner perspective this is a teaching that our learning may come at unexpected times, from unexpected sources, and that we need to "pick the grains" when and where they are available. Jesus cites the example from history to show that the most

## PREPARATION

revered king "broke the law" on a higher level, again to indicate that behavior must follow purpose, not custom. The custom and the law that we follow, he says, are designed to serve human needs. When they do not, the need must still be satisfied.

His emphasis is not on the law but on the need. Custom and law are intended to fulfill human needs, not block them. Jesus sees some custom and law as rule-bound behavior that can, on occasion, prevent us from doing what we need to do. On an inner level we have customs, habits, rules, commands, and prohibitions that govern our thoughts and behavior, which on occasion prevent us from learning. Sometimes it will be necessary to work outside established patterns in order for us to learn and grow, and changing our behavior will be challenged within us by parts of ourselves that do not want to change, who will see change as a threat.

Jesus is not advocating that we break laws at will and simply do what we want. Again, we are looking at "inner laws" and customs. He says, "The Son of Man is also lord of the Sabbath." This is a very direct way of saying that the Spirit within us has the power to discern whether customs and laws serve genuine needs or not; the Spirit also makes the decision about how to respond to an inner custom, and our responses may be different at different times.

- **Do you follow any spiritual disciplines?**
- **What purposes do they serve, and how do they serve them?**
- **Are they flexible and variable, or are they fixed and regular?**
- **If they are regular, is the regularity helpful? Why or why not?**
- **If they are not regular, is their non-regularity helpful? Why or why not?**
- **Does the Spirit lead you in your disciplines?**
- **How do your disciplines feed you? Review them regularly with these questions in mind, and make whatever adjustments are needed.**

## A NEW SPIRITUAL PATHWAY

♦ ♦ ♦

It is interesting that in the story the Pharisees do not object to the fact that Jesus heals people. They object to how and when he does the healing. The law *regulates* not only what people do, but also how and when they are allowed to do things. Jesus has asserted that the intent of the law was to promote and support life, learning and healing, and noted that the *need* for healing and learning—for life and nourishment—does not rest. Inwardly we may see that our customs and practices may be intended to preserve inner order and provide benefits such as rest, but that in fact they may get in our way when new learning dawns in our lives. When that dawn arrives we cannot rest, but we must "seize the day" and receive what is given to us.

♦ ♦ ♦

> 3:1 Again he entered the synagogue, and a man was there who had a withered hand. And they were watching him to see whether he would heal him on the Sabbath, so that they might accuse him. And he says to the man who had the withered hand, "Come forward." And he says to them, "Is it lawful on the Sabbath to do good or to do harm, to save a life or to kill?" But they were silent. And looking around at them with anger, grieved at their hardness of heart, he says to the man, "Stretch out your hand." He stretched it out, and his hand was restored. The Pharisees went out and immediately held council with the Herodians against him, so that they might destroy him.

As this passage makes clear, there are parts of us that may resist change even if the change heals or saves life. But once a healing power has begun to work in our lives, it will proceed in the face of opposition, and the opposition may intensify and attempt to stop the change, even if this means trying to stop all healing. This *can* happen

PREPARATION

to us—our attempts to learn, to be healed and to grow inwardly, spiritually, may be met with an inner backlash. Within us, we may find that our ideas of the sacred, our personal morality, our desire to be good and to do good (the inner Pharisees) may combine with our worldly knowledge and practical goals and abilities (the inner Hedodians) to stop us from growing if the growth appears to break our established patterns of thought or behavior. This action may be quite invisible to us at the time, as we believe that we are only doing what is right, or what is practical, unaware that parts of us are working to stop or squelch change that upsets our inner status quo, unaware that this change is vital for us.

The response of the Spirit to this backlash is anger and grief, because it is now apparent that for some of us there are inner parts that may be so entrenched in established patterns of behavior, thought and belief that they will work against healing, even against life. We may experience a whipsaw effect, as the powers of healing and the powers of resistance collide within us. We may experience anger and grief that we cannot account for, because the parts of us that stand opposed to the Spirit do not stand in the open, but work beneath the surface while seeming to support all holiness.

> o **Do you ever feel that you are careening between control and surrender?**
> o **Have you ever experienced a "retrenchment" after you have reached a spiritual milestone?**
> o **Can you discern when qualities within you are opposed to each other? Are there some within you that are opposed now? If there are, notice which ones.**

◆ ◆ ◆

> 3:7 And Jesus departed with his disciples to the sea, and a great multitude from Galilee followed. And from Judea,

> Jerusalem, Idumea, beyond the Jordan and near Tyre and Sidon a great multitude, hearing of all that he was doing, came to him. And he told his disciples to keep a boat ready for him because of the crowd, so that they would not crush him, for he had healed many, so that all who had diseases pressed upon him to touch him.  And whenever the unclean spirits saw him, they were falling down before him and shouting, "You are the Son of God!" And he strictly ordered them not to make him known.

As we saw earlier, some parts of us need help in approaching the source of healing. But here we see that some parts of us will not have any problem seeking the inner healing. In fact they rush to the healing, heedless of the consequences. But when our neediness drives us to seek *relief*, we may not necessarily embrace the process that is *healing*.[2] Sometimes parts of our inner selves are so eager for a good thing that they may become destructive, and this possibility is true on a spiritual level as well as in other aspects of our lives. Within us, the Spirit may withdraw a little when eagerness for healing becomes greed for relief.

- What qualities allow you to be receptive to healing? Are these always present when you seek relief from suffering? Explore the relationship of healing and relief in your own life history.
- Could getting relief distract you from going on to real healing?
- What makes it is it so difficult to keep our inner balance when we are suffering?

---

[2] For example, morphine may *relieve* the pain of a man with cancer, but it cannot by itself *heal* the tumor which causes the pain. The word *greed* comes from a root which means "to crave" and is applied when one need is followed without regard to other needs.

PREPARATION

> ○ **What qualities are most important to help you get through such times? (See Table A on page 51, or explore on your own)**

♦ ♦ ♦

> ○ **Come back to these questions whenever you feel particularly needy in some areas, or unhappy about the qualities that are being expressed in your life.**

♦ ♦ ♦

In the story Jesus continues to heal people from all countries. This is the third time in the story that Jesus is shown telling others to remain silent about him. This incident is different from the healing of the leper, for now we see Jesus called the Son of God—not by people, but by "unclean" spirits.

Word has obviously gotten out about what he does, and the response is not only from Israel and Judea but also from outside the country, from Idumea, from beyond the Jordan, from Tyre and Sidon. Similarly, when healing occurs at any "location" within us, there will be widespread interest and response across our inner landscape. So *what Jesus does* is well known, but we now have a new element emphasized—the matter of *who he is*.

We saw earlier that in the story the demons, not the people, obey Jesus' commands. Here we see that the demons, the "unclean" spirits—again unlike the people—know who he is. This presents a strange anomaly: Why is it that the spirits that Jesus casts out "know and obey," whereas people, whom Jesus has come to call and to heal, neither know nor obey?

Anomalies like this are meant to flag our attention. Events that seem to make no sense in the Gospel story are invitations to dig deeper, to allow our mental categories to expand, to allow our mental classifications to be rearranged. These flags point toward something important.

The unclean spirits crow," We know who you are!" when they say, "You are the Son of God." But they do not really know what that means. These spirits recognize a presence and a power, but what they say is a slogan that can obscure the nature of the interaction between Jesus and the people. Jesus is not interested in verbal acknowledgement, in acclamation, in outward allegiance; he desires the inner ongoing relationship between a person and God. There can be no real relationship between him and the "unclean spirits," so their acknowledgement of him is meaningless. They are in fact one of the obstacles to the relationship between people and God. He has come to remove obstacles to that relationship. Slogans and publicity, labels and notoriety are also obstacles, so he commands silence.

The demons are not interested in truth; they are "interested" in protecting their situation. Crying out "You are the Son of God!" is a great way to whip a crowd into a frenzy, and a frenzied crowd will not listen to anything, but blindly surge forward to get what it wants. If the crowd itself is screaming "Son of God!" it will not listen to what the Son of God has to say. It is a very good strategy: blind emotional belief can be used to block the work of the Spirit.

This vignette leads us to look within and ask, "When I think I know the work of God, what do I *really know*? Do I speak from personal knowledge, or does my response arise from outside influences that have shaped my thoughts and words without any experience of my own? Does my conviction come from perception, from discernment, or from indoctrination?"

Our spiritual relationship with God can be hindered by an excess of "enthusiasm" as much as by negative factors, if that enthusiasm reduces spiritual experience to labels and slogans. Again, a healing is often the beginning of spiritual experience, not the end; in order for that experience to progress, certain attitudes and actions are needed.

♦ ♦ ♦

PREPARATION

- How could you test your convictions to see whether they are held from belief supported by your experience, or whether they are simply an outside influence that you carry with you?
- Many outside influences, like the training from elders and parents, the lessons from school teachers, and the advice of friends, can be helpful and even necessary in your life. Other influences can be harmful. When we approach the Spirit for healing, it becomes more important for us to identify what moves us, for this may determine whether we actually seek healing or whether we are only craving relief while remaining unwilling to do what is needed to receive healing. As you turn to the Spirit for healing, listen within and test the spirit that guides you. Ask, "What moves me to do this? What do I bring to this process?"

# NOTES

# FOCUS

This second part of the Gospel process begins with a more direct mobilization of the inner forces that support the Gospel work with the gathering of the qualities most needed to serve the work of the Spirit. We examine these qualities in The Twelve. We also see that our understanding of the spiritual process may not be as clear as we thought, and that even though we have the name of Jesus and the story of his work, we may not really understand the identity of the One we follow, or the work he comes to do.

This next section of the Gospel will sharpen our focus. We will encounter the next levels of resistance to the work of the Spirit and be introduced to a central aspect of the Gospel: unconditional forgiveness. We will see the action of our inner family and our inner spiritual family, and be introduced to the parables of the kingdom of God. These are short stories that encapsulate the attitudes needed for walking the spiritual pathway.

The Gospel will then take us into our inner depths to heal the deepest inner wounds, and come out to show us lessons in faith. This part begins with Mark 3:13 and goes as far as Mark 6:6.

# 7. MOBILIZATION FOR SERVICE: THE TWELVE

## MOBILIZATION FOR SERVICE

> 3:13 And he goes up on the mountain, and he calls those he wanted to him, and they came to him. And he created a group of twelve to be with him, and to be sent out to proclaim the message and to have authority to cast out demons: Simon, whom he called "The Rock," ("Peter") and James the son of Zebedee, and James' brother John, whom he called "Boanerges" ("The Sons of Thunder"), and Andrew, and Philip, Bartholomew and Matthew, and Thomas, James the son of Alphaeus, Thaddeus, and Simon the Canaanite, and Judas Iscariot, who betrayed him.

There is a stage in our inner development when things begin to change. Before this point, there are events that suggest that something is "brewing," but after this point major aspects of the personality are gathered, organized, and mobilized to facilitate change. This is the time when the disciples no longer merely follow, but some of them are gathered and given tasks. In the inner perspective, this is a time when the mind, the emotions, the intuitions, and other inner aspects of the person begin to actively pursue change, healing and growth.

Again it is important to recognize that the process that the Gospel is describing is not linear. Aspects of development may occur and re-occur at different levels. As needs shift and learning is absorbed, our perspective changes and we may revisit things that seem familiar—to use the metaphor I used in Section I, our trail has many vistas from which to view the mountain, and each will offer something new as we go along our way.

What Jesus says on the mountain is not mentioned in the Gospel of Mark, because this event, from the inner perspective, is highly individual and personal. The Spirit within us will communicate to each of us in a unique way, and gather together the inner helpers to promote the great transformation in us. The helpers are not sent out to preach to other people—they are *inner* helpers sent to the lost and troubled aspects of our own multifaceted beings, to harmonize them

FOCUS

and transform the many into one, to bring wholeness to our fragmented and fractured personalities and to our persons.

The gathering on the mountain, in this story, is indicative of a gathering that happens only when we are ready and when the Spirit moves within us. The work of the Gospel now takes on a focus which is represented by the gathering of the Twelve, and I believe that the new focus is highlighted in their names. In the culture in which the Gospel was written, peoples' names were not merely labels for a person. The names had meaning that had significance to the family into which the person was born and in the culture at large. The Twelve are the family into which the Gospel was born, and the names of the Twelve carry meaning for anyone to whom the Gospel is given—to us, its readers.

The root meanings of the names of the Twelve suggest qualities mobilized by the Spirit within us: "Simon," whose name comes out of the root meaning "hearing with understanding," becomes "Peter" which means the "rock,"[1] indicating that hearing with understanding is the rock-foundation of the work.[2] "James" (the same as "Jacob") is an "overcomer" or "one who seizes opportunity." "John" is the bringing of God's favor. Together, James and John are the "sons of thunder," suggesting that they will deal with commotion, upheaval, anger and wrath, bringing God's favor and overcoming obstacles. Spiritual transformation is often not a quiet, peaceful process, but one in which there is great storm and stress. "Andrew" (a Greek name) brings "humanity" to the work. "Philip" (another Greek name) means a lover of horses, and this aspect brings in the "animal" part of our natures—our bodies—to be part of the work. Together, these aspects suggest the employment of a full range of human qualities, including physical senses and other human and so-called "animal" qualities. "Bartholomew" is a son of the furrows—a farmer— and brings in the hard work, the patience, and the trust of a farmer to the endeavor. "Matthew" brings the gifts of God. "Thomas" is a twin, suggesting both separation and identity, and brings a joining, a coupling together, for completeness. "Thaddeus" brings "large-

---
[1] So perhaps "Peter" is the Greek equivalent of the English nickname "Rocky."
[2] And perhaps it may also suggest that *not* hearing is a boulder that can block our way.

## MOBILIZATION FOR SERVICE

heartedness," courage and generosity, and "Judas" brings praise and worship, without which the work is self-serving and dead-ended.

We see that the list of disciples includes two Simons and two James, that Matthew and John bring kindred qualities. These disciples represent qualities that are being emphasized: hearing with understanding; a willingness to grapple with what is holy and to seize opportunity, overcoming obstacles; and the gifts and favor of God. In the work of God, effort is always twinned, doubled and redoubled, repeated, and the presence of the name Thomas ("twin") among the disciples emphasizes this aspect of the work. We prepare, and we prepare again. We try and try again. These qualities are intended to be two-directional—listening both inside and outside ourselves; seizing opportunities and overcoming obstacles both within and without; receiving gifts within us and from the world.

We notice that Mark's Gospel *introduces* Judas Iscariot as the betrayer. Why is this? No betrayal has taken place at this point in the story, Jesus is only calling his chosen ones up to the mountain. If the Gospel were a history, it seems likely that the writer would withhold this information until the point in the story when the betrayal occurs. We are seeing the disciples as representing qualities that are mobilized in the service of spiritual growth and transformation. A message is conveyed in Judas' being identified as the betrayer as soon as he is introduced—that a quality that is drawn upon for the work of the Spirit is also a quality that can be used to sabotage that work. We have examined how qualities can move from deficiency to balance to excess in Table A on page 51. The same qualities may move us in one direction when they are balanced, and in another direction when they are extreme, or polarized. In the Gospel of Mark, those qualities that in the end work against the Spirit are praise, celebration and worship, symbolized in the name "Judas."

Judas is identified in the story as the betrayer as soon as he is named, and it is vital to any person on the spiritual path to realize that some—perhaps any—of the qualities we use to follow God are also the very qualities that can be used to end our journey, or to sidetrack it.

We looked at a large list of inner qualities in Table A on page 51, and at this stage we are narrowing our focus to a dozen particular qualities. The "disciple qualities" of the Twelve can play a special role in our spiritual life. Like the qualities in the larger list in Table

## FOCUS

A, each of these twelve disciple qualities is a balanced quality, poised between extremes, and when tried or tested these qualities may be tipped or pressured into the extreme of excess or deficiency. The balanced qualities work on behalf of the Spirit, but the extremes may not, and their fruits may not be what is really needed. It is of the utmost importance for us to realize that the dual potential of these qualities does *not* diminish with time; rather, it increases as we progress. People further along the path are liable to be tested or tempted *more*, not less, than beginners. The temptations may be very subtle or they may not even be visible to us, yet they can be powerful nonetheless, and may not become evident until they have been at the work for some time. Throughout the Gospel we will see examples of the disciples speaking or acting out of balance.

Some commentators have wondered at the way Mark's Gospel portrays the Twelve, for as we will see in the sections to come, they will repeatedly miss the point, go the wrong way, succumb to fear and misunderstand what is happening around them. Why are these human exemplars portrayed this way? I believe that by identifying the disciples with human qualities represented by their names we answer this question, and the distinction between the balanced and unbalanced qualities is essential to our understanding the role of discipleship in our lives. The disciples are shown missing the way often because it is exceedingly easy for us to miss the way in our lives. Comparing the disciples' names with their behavior is a model for us to compare the ideal with the real in our lives, and to learn some of the lessons that the Gospel has for us. As we will see, the disciples veer between affirmation and denial, fear and faith, arrogance and timidity. Tracking the disciple qualities in our lives and working with them will enable us to learn what Jesus' disciples learned, and will enable us to receive what they received.

Mark's Gospel says that Jesus appointed the Twelve to proclaim the message and to have authority to cast out demons. From the inner perspective this is all one process—being with Christ, being sent to teach, and healing. Within ourselves these things may happen "immediately," since it does not take time or distance for an inspired part of ourselves to take an interest in a weak or injured part of ourselves. But it does take awareness, will, training, compassion, and a guiding inspiration—and work, and for many of us this means that the overall process will evolve over time.

## MOBILIZATION FOR SERVICE

Here is an example how the healing process might proceed: A part of me (a "disciple" part) that wants wholeness and a spiritual relationship with my Source may become very impatient with another part of me that just wants to enjoy good food and music. And both of these parts of me may have no patience with another part of me—an inner child, maybe, who may be angry, self-centered and demanding. And that part of me may have absolutely no interest in another part of me that is sensitive, lonely, artistic, and shyly self-conscious. There is yet another part of me that is fearful, having been injured by both abuse and neglect. The Spirit of God within draws all to itself, but will work through some parts of us to reach and heal other parts. The Spirit may send a compassionate parent part of us to be with the injured child; it may send a joyful part of us to be with the "sad one," and a quiet, thoughtful part to be with the wild, thoughtless part, and a shy part to be with the arrogant part.

In the example above, we may notice that our disciple quality of "patience" may turn into "impatience" if another part of us that we may label as "lazy" does not respond after a while. If we try to remain completely self-reliant, our disciple qualities may cease to do the work of the Spirit in patience and resort to "spiritual butt-kicking" to get what we want; so in this way a spiritual intention may yield a very un-spiritual fruit. Help may be (and usually is) needed if this happens to us, for other qualities—such as perception and discernment—may be needed to keep us balanced and following the guidance of the Spirit; that help may come from within us or from outside ourselves, or both.

There is, in effect, a complex community within each of us, and the Gospel suggests ways that the Christ, the Spirit of God within us, gathers inner resources to reconcile and harmonize the disparate parts of us, bringing all parts eventually together so that the person can become "single minded" and inspired to live manifesting the spiritual qualities of peace, love, compassion and joy. The qualities and subpersonalities that are used by the Spirit may change over time, but the quest for balance, healing and wholeness remains constant.

♦ ♦ ♦

FOCUS

> - What qualities are called to serve the Spirit in *your* life?
> - What subpersonalities are prominent or noticeable in your spiritual work?
> - What parts of *you* most need healing?
> - Can you see whether one part of you is trying to influence another part? How?
> - Come back to these questions regularly.

***WALKING OUT THE GOSPEL: TO EXPLORE THIS FURTHER, DO EXERCISE 9 IN PART III, PAGE 410.***

♦♦♦

### Qualities Associated with the Twelve

In the Gospel the Twelve are people whom Jesus gathered into a group that would become immersed in their close association with Jesus and absorb his teaching and ministry in a unique way. It seems appropriate in our inner interpretation to focus on the qualities that these men may represent for us, as the original meanings of their names suggest qualities that have particular significance in the spiritual walk, and this is perhaps why certain of the disciples (Simon, James and John) are singled out and repeatedly chosen by Jesus to accompany him in the Gospel of Mark. The following table, based upon the root meaning of the disciples' names, shows the core disciple quality of each of the Twelve in the center column, and also gives some suggestions as to how that quality can be pulled off-balance into an excess or a deficiency, in which the disciple quality is diverted from truly spiritual purposes and can work against the purpose of the Gospel.

## Table B: Qualities Associated with the Twelve

| Deficiency | Balanced Qualities | Excess |
|---|---|---|
| **Simon** | | |
| Unheeding, intolerant | Alert, hearing, listening, understanding | Pandering, gullible, too willing to believe what is heard |
| **James** | | |
| Defeatist, timid, negative-minded | Overcoming obstacles with will and energy | Usurping, dominating others |
| **John** | | |
| Spiritually fearful | Bringing or being open to God's favor | Egotistical, self-righteous, having an ego that masquerades as spirit |
| **Andrew** | | |
| Devaluing what is "merely human" | Loving all of what it is to be human | Substituting what is human for what is divine |
| **Philip** | | |
| Devaluing what is physical, earthly | Appreciating what is animal, physical, earthly | Substituting what is physical for what is spiritual |

FOCUS

### Bartholomew

| Unwilling to work, mistrustful of self | Willing to work, patient, trusting self and God | Too trusting in self and accomplishment to the exclusion of spirit |

### Matthew

| Closed to spiritual guidance | Open to the gifts of God | Having a "mind in the heavens and being no earthly good" |

### Thomas

| Isolated, alone, excessively independent, habitually doubting | Joining, supportive, empathetic | Dependent upon others, having no boundaries, too group-minded |

### Thaddeus

| Hard-hearted, withholding | Large-hearted, generous, courageous | Foolhardy, profligate |

### Judas

| Skeptical, cautious, critical, negative-minded | Praising, celebrating, worshipping | Excessively zealous, "spiritually" aggressive |

> - Which qualities or combination of these qualities do you see in yourself?
> - How do these qualities work together in your life to form your "disciple subpersonality?"
> - Where along the spectrum of extreme or balance are they?
> - What pressures in life move your qualities toward one extreme or another?
> - What helps you to move into balance in each area?

♦ ♦ ♦

> 3:19b And he comes home, and the crowd comes again, so that they cannot even eat bread, and when his companions heard of this, they went to take hold of him, for they were saying he was overwhelmed.[3]

In the story Jesus returns to his home after the time on the mountain. We notice that there is a fairly regular alternation of going out to do the work, and of returning home to rest. This is illustrative of the normal rhythm of spiritual work. We are not to continually "charge ahead"—which is impossible for most of us anyway. Just as Jesus reaches for the least of people, the Spirit within us reaches for the slowest and weakest parts of us, bringing them together with the quickest and strongest parts of us, for this is the only way we are made whole. But for us the process often feels like "two steps forward and one step back," and the work of transformation requires rest periods because it is difficult. When we make progress, it is necessary to pause, so that the learning can be assimilated and put into practice, and the weak parts made stronger.

But we see again that as soon as Jesus is "at home" he is mobbed by crowds of people. The crowds are becoming frenzied in their

---
[3] Greek: literally "beside himself."

greed to get what they want or need. In the story there is a suggestion that some people think that the crowds are "driving him crazy."

We have seen two episodes in which Jesus is mobbed by crowds, and in between these episodes is the gathering of the Twelve. The Spirit must mobilize inner helpers, because there is much urgent work to do that needs to be organized through the qualities of the personality. Our inner development does not consist solely of the direct contact of our wounded ones with the Spirit. The process involves our inner subpersonalities learning from the Spirit through disciple qualities such as hearing with understanding, overcoming obstacles, trust, patience, hard work, praise, worship, joining, courage, generosity and the full range of our humanity and our bodily senses. Until these qualities begin to participate in the work, the healing process can be chaotic, and may at times seem to be going nowhere.[4]

> o **Might physical illness or symptoms, such as acne, headaches, arthritis, cancer or fibromyalgia (or some other symptom) be ways that "the frenzied crowd" is manifested in your life?**
> o **Could "the mob" be manifested in repeated patterns of negative experience in your outer life, such as being accident-prone, or repeatedly getting into arguments or conflicts, getting regularly fired from jobs or being ill-treated by strangers?**
> o **What other phenomena in your life may be a manifestation of urgent inner needs pressing for healing?**

---

[4] Training exercises in some kind of spiritual psychology may be helpful to you to learn to discern your inner qualities and subpersonalities, and to learn how to open to love and interpret them in service to the Spirit. For myself, I found that experiential training in psychosynthesis provided many perspectives and techniques that helped me to become more whole on a human level, which enabled me to become open to the Spirit and respond to its call in a more balanced way, with my inner disciples and my whole Self.

The Gospel here presents another level in which balance is necessary. Work must be balanced with rest; learning must be balanced with reflection and assimilation.

♦ ♦ ♦

# 8. IDENTITY AND SPIRIT: "WHO IS THIS, *REALLY?*"

## IDENTITY AND SPIRIT

> 3:22 And the scribes who came down from Jerusalem said, "He has Beelzebul, and by the ruler of demons he casts out demons." And he called them, and spoke to them in parables, saying, "How can the adversary[1] cast out the adversary? If a kingdom is divided against itself, that kingdom cannot stand. And if a house is divided against itself, that house cannot stand. And if the adversary has risen up against himself and is divided, he cannot stand, but his end has come. No one can enter a strong man's house and plunder his property unless he first binds the strong man; then indeed the house can be plundered. Truly I say to you, all will be forgiven the sons of mankind for their sins and whatever hurtful talk[2] they utter; but whoever speaks evil of the Holy Spirit is not forgiven quickly, but is guilty of a sin that endures." [3] — for they had said, "He has an unclean spirit."

We find sometimes, within ourselves, when a new force appears within us and stimulates major changes, that we feel beset on all sides—the voice of the hurt parts of us, struggling to be healed; the voices of the suppressed parts of us, demanding to be heard; and the voices of an inner skeptic, which questions whether this new force in our lives is "for real," or whether we are just making it all up, putting on a show, or soothing ourselves with wishful thinking. All

---

[1] Greek: *the satan*

[2] Greek: *blasphemies*

[3] Literally in the Greek, *has no forgiveness in this age but is in danger of a sin that lasts for an age.* I believe that translations that render this passage in modern English as "guilty of an eternal sin" are mistaken. Jesus spoke of "ages," and *all* ages pass. The original Latin *aeternalis,* derived from *aeviternus* meaning "of great age," was equivalent to the Greek. But the word "eternal" has evolved, probably from the influence of Greek or Roman theology or philosophy, so that it means something like "endless" or "forever" or "timeless" in modern English. The concept of endless sin is incompatible with Jesus' fundamental teaching of forgiveness.

FOCUS

of these voices focus in one way or another on this new force within us.

This leads to a very important question about this new force: Who is this, *really?*

In the Gospel story, the worldly scribes have seen every spiritual act and sideshow there is to see, and they are looking for fakery. And with good reason. The only "magic" they have ever witnessed is fraud: spiritual sleight of hand and trickery. They believe that if they cannot uncover the trickery, then there is still something wrong— they are more afraid if they *cannot* discover "the catch," for to them real power is really frightening.

Our culture, like the ancient culture of the gospel story, abounds with hucksters. Many of us know of supposedly "spiritual" people whose "spirituality" is a show to cover over base behavior. Some such people start out with a sincere desire to be teachers, preachers and healers, only to fall prey to base behavior later. When we meet a spiritual teacher or are confronted with an unknown power within us, we ask a legitimate question when we ask, "Who is this, *really?*"

Self-deception is all too easy—even when base behavior or evil intent are not involved. A spiritually eager part of us, a strong subpersonality, may take over our inner reins, leading and driving us toward new heights and new learning, instilling discipline, changing our behavior to reflect lofty spiritual ideals. But a spiritually ambitious subpersonality is not the Holy Spirit—is not the voice of God within us, no matter how eager it is and no matter how commanding and authoritative its voice. How do we tell the difference? How do we discover "who is this, really?"

In the Gospel story the scribes suggest that Jesus is only pretending to be godly, but that his motive and power derive from an evil source. They think, either he is a fake, or—far more frightening to them—that his power *is* real and he is up to no good.

Jesus provides one of the clues to answer our question. It can be helpful here to consider not only what he says, but what he does *not* say. He does not defend or demonstrate the consistency of his actions, yet his demeanor, his behavior, his words, and his results are all consistent— they lead people toward God in every way. He reminds people that there is always an inconsistency, somewhere, in the

## IDENTITY AND SPIRIT

behavior of a fake, an imposter, or of one with evil intent. Evil relies upon a certain amount of inconsistency, for if "the adversary" works against *everything*— even itself— then it becomes self-destructive and, as Jesus says, "comes to an end." Inner and outer inconsistency is something we do well to watch for. For example, an ambitious "spiritual" subpersonality within us may show itself by using base means to achieve an ideal— inciting guilt, spiritual "butt-kicking," rigidity, spiritual greed, arrogance and using fear as a motive are some of the signs that we are dealing with an unhealed aspect of our own personality, not the Holy Spirit.

Jesus' parables are meant to stimulate thought, not to provide "answers." A profound parable can yield multiple valid interpretations from different perspectives, and its value lies precisely in the fact that no one interpretation is the "correct" one, because *every* valid interpretation arises out of the particular individual qualities that are brought to bear in considering the parable. A parable, then, is designed to draw you out. If you do not apply some effort to it and connect it to your own life, experience and circumstances, its value will be lost to you, and the "meaning," although apparently true and perhaps even universal, will be merely academic and lifeless.[4]

Looking at this issue from the other side, we can heed what Jesus does show us. Jesus shows in the parable that nothing is accomplished when one works against oneself. The scribes indulge in an absurdity to try to discredit him, even ascribing holy work to Satan. But Jesus moves to different ground and does not engage with his adversaries' accusation.[5] Notice that he does not continue the first metaphor and say that he is plundering Satan's house. He moves away from the scribes' accusation, and he moves away from their mindset, which is a defensive attitude focused on evil. He speaks of a "strong man" instead. Who is this? What is his "property?"

Jesus says that you cannot plunder a strong man's house unless you first bind the strong man. Tie him up! He uses strong, graphic

---

[4] This is also true of this book, which makes no claim of "correctness," but is meant to offer one perspective which may bear fruit if it is used, but is likely to be less useful if it is not applied personally by the reader.

[5] See Section 2 pages 36-43 for the discussion about the adversary. Notice that Jesus does not engage his accusers beyond a summary refutation. He moves on to engage these people on his own terms.

language. But he is also suggesting that when the Spirit begins to work within us, it encounters a "strong man" standing opposed to its work, which is to clean our inner house of harmful influences, of evil, of fear, of disease, of sin—any condition, thought, feeling, habit that separates us from our holy source. The work of the Spirit, then, is to "plunder" the property of the "strong man," who may be any part of ourselves that undermines or opposes healthful and spiritual pursuits, that keeps us divided and that stands in the way of wholeness and healing. The "property" is the power of life within us, which is to be transformed and redirected. The "strong man" regards spiritual transformation as an attack—"plundering his house," for he is satisfied to control things as they are.

I wrote earlier that we are made whole only as the Spirit reaches for the slowest and weakest parts of us, bringing them together with the quickest and strongest parts. What if the quickest and strongest parts of us do not *want* to mingle with the slow and the weak? The strong may not be secure in their strength, nor the quick in their speed. They may not want wholeness. We may find it to be so in ourselves. Parts of us may be afraid of being weakened, slowed down, or "compromised," or "plundered." We may easily see the agent of any constructive change to be "the adversary" or "the enemy" as we strive to keep ourselves "strong" or "pure" or "correct" in our own minds. Each of us has something within us that resists healing at one time or another.

♦ ♦ ♦

- Is there a "strong man" in *your* life, standing between you and your spiritual maturity?
- Is it the same quality or subpersonality always, or does it change?
- How does "he" defend his "house?"
- What is the meaning of "binding the strong man" in your life?
- How do *you* overcome your own inner resistance to change? What helps you to do this?

## IDENTITY AND SPIRIT

> ○ **Come back to these questions whenever you feel an inner conflict as you try to learn and grow.**

♦ ♦ ♦

Many times we instinctively regard any force that tries to change us as threatening. Even when we *know* that the force is well-intentioned, still the question remains, "Who is this, *really?*" How do we know that the change is for our good? Isn't it natural to protect ourselves from harmful change? Perhaps resisting harmful change is how we develop an inner "strong man." If we do, it is easy for us to suspect that *anyone* who tries to change us is really out to "plunder our house." We may resist even the Spirit of God. So how do we know the difference?

Jesus, in the story, tells us that we must make an important distinction. It is easy to be misled, and everyone will be forgiven their mistakes. There is, however, one thing we must avoid: in the story this is "speaking evil (often translated "blaspheming") of the Holy Spirit." Is Jesus merely telling us not to curse? No. He is giving us vital practical advice about the question we raised earlier: how do we know "who is this, really?" For the Holy Spirit is the source of all forgiveness and blessing, and the person who rejects the source of forgiveness cannot at the same time seek forgiveness. This would be like expecting water to flow after we have dammed up the stream. It simply will not happen—not because it is "impossible," but because forgiveness and blessing require our cooperation and acceptance. They are neither imposed upon us, nor bestowed upon us unaware; they require a positive response from us on some level.

The key to understanding "who is this, really" is whether the voice within us forgives *all*. Jesus tells us that *all* sins will be forgiven *all* people as long as the person will accept forgiveness. When we hear a voice that denies forgiveness, we may be sure that it is not the voice of God or of God's Holy Spirit. Jesus suggests not that God will do whatever we want, but that when we change our behavior, when we repent and turn away from our mistakes and misbehavior, then forgiveness is *always* God's response. Many times we may desire forgiveness and at the same time we refuse to change our attitudes or our behavior. This refusal is actually the denial of forgiveness. Jesus simply tells us that so long as we deny forgiveness, it will not come to us—not in this age, nor in the age to come.

Does this mean that there *is* no forgiveness for us if we refuse to cooperate? Not at all—it is there waiting for us, but there is both a giving and receiving involved, because forgiveness is an act of relationship. If we do not receive it, then the relationship is incomplete, and it remains incomplete *until* our part is accomplished.

Does this mean that God's forgiveness is conditional? Does it depend on our "consent?" If forgiveness does not come to us because we deny it, does this mean "forever?" I believe that here is where accurate literal translation is crucial. Jesus does *not* say that deniers have no forgiveness *ever*, but *for an age.* Again he is showing that the Spirit mirrors us. Since Jesus' time people have interpreted these words according to their own fears. For a fearful person a time of unforgiveness often *feels* like an age, and an age may *feel* like forever. This is a psychological fact that many therapists and psychologists will affirm, but it is *not* a depiction of God's response to us. The work of Jesus is to heal and forgive, and the work of God is love, and those people who believe that this work can be stopped or thwarted get their answer at the end of the Gospel story. See the discussion at the end of Section 47 on Page 361.

◆ ◆ ◆

> o  **Who is the one within you that wants to "bind the strong man?"**
> o  **Is the one within you that desires wholeness willing to forgive all people, all offenses, all injuries, all "blasphemies?"**
> o  **Do you need to forgive God for what has happened to you?**
> o  **What changes in your attitude or behavior are needed for you to be forgiving of all and everything?**

- What are needed for you to accept forgiveness from any and all people, from God, for all offenses, all injuries, all blasphemies that you have ever committed?
- What will you do to make this happen?
- Over time, notice what effect that forgiveness of *all* has on your life—your values, your politics, your behavior, your friendships, even your health.

♦ ♦ ♦

- Come back to these questions whenever you notice that you are condemning yourself or someone else for something that you or the other person has done, or not done.

## 9. THE FAMILY OF HABIT
## AND
## THE FAMILY OF SPIRIT

> **3:31** And his mother and his brothers come, and standing outside they sent to him and called him. And a crowd was sitting around him, and they said to him, "Your mother and your brothers and sisters are outside asking for you." And he answered them, saying, "Who are my mother and my brothers?" And looking around at those who sat about him, he says, "Look— my mother and my brothers. Whoever does the will of God is my brother and sister and mother."

From the inner perspective, we see in this story the claims of old ways, old teachings and training trying to assert themselves against the new force that moves us toward transformation. A whole familiar family of voices may beckon us at one time or another: "I've always done things *this* way;" "I was taught that *this* is right;" "This is what I am used to;" "We expect you to respect our ways;" and many others. Jesus is demonstrating that the Spirit within us is committed to transformation and that the old thoughts, habits, beliefs, and attitudes that we have lived with and supported all our lives —any that do not work for wholeness, healing and forgiveness —are not sufficient if they are not part of God's will for our lives. He shows that in spiritual work we acquire a new inner family of support: new attitudes, thoughts, feelings and behavior become our inner "family" and their support is vital.[1]

> o **What thoughts, habits, beliefs and attitudes are your "inner family of origin"—the ones you grew up with?[2]**

---

[1] Again we recall that in this "inner interpretation" the Gospel does not urge anyone to reject real family members, but rather to gather to oneself the attitudes that support our response to the Spirit.

[2] Some of these may be more recognizable as the thoughts, habits, beliefs and attitudes that were held by your parents and other family members. These are your inner family, too — even if you didn't like them or rejected them. Attitudes and habits that we dislike may nevertheless be very active in our lives.

FOCUS

> - Do these support the path you are now on, or do some of them hinder it?
> - What thoughts, habits and attitudes are your inner spiritual family, and how do they support you?

♦ ♦ ♦

> - Come back to these questions whenever you feel an old habit, attitude, thought, feeling or behavior surfacing in your life, one that does not support you on your spiritual path.

♦ ♦ ♦

In this parable the Gospel of Mark has introduced us to another key point. The objective of the transformation is to do "the will of God." "Will" here means "choice" or "purpose," and this leads directly into the next section of the story, which presents parables meant to give clues of what it is like for one's life to be governed by a higher purpose—what the Gospel calls "the kingdom of God."

## 10. PARABLES: THE KINGDOM OF GOD

FOCUS

> 4:1 And again he began to teach beside the sea. And such a large crowd gathered around him that he got into a boat, and sat in it on the sea, and the whole crowd was beside the sea on land. And he taught them many things in parables, and in his teaching he said to them, "Listen. A sower went out to sow. And it happened in the sowing that some seed fell by the roadside, and the birds came and ate it up. And some seed fell on rocky ground where there was little soil, and it sprang up quickly because it had no depth of soil, and when the sun rose it was scorched, and since it had no root it withered away. And other seed fell into thorns, and the thorns grew up and choked it, and it yielded no grain. And other seed fell into good soil and brought forth grain, growing up and increasing and yielding thirty, sixty, and a hundredfold." And he said, "Whoever has ears to hear, let them hear."

Certain things are needed for one's life to come into harmony, and Jesus tells parables designed to engage us in this process. In the parable of the sower he tells the people that a certain attitude is needed for us to understand, to "get" the meaning of events in our lives. The "word" that is sown is understanding, and the Gospel shows that there are many levels of understanding, each one containing a barrier that must be overcome before meanings can flow into awareness. First Jesus tells a parable to the crowd, in which images from everyday life contain the meaning that he is conveying; and he invites the people to look for meanings in these images, saying "whoever has ears to hear, let them hear."

> 4:10 And when they were alone, those who were around him along with the Twelve asked him about the parables. And he said to them, "To you has been given the secret of the kingdom of God, but for those outside, everything comes

> in parables, because they 'may indeed look but not perceive, and they may indeed listen, but not understand, then they might not turn back and be forgiven.'" And he says to them, "Don't you 'get' this parable? Then how will you understand all the [other] parables? The sower sows the word. There are some along the path where the seed is sown. When they hear, the adversary immediately comes and takes away the word that is sown in them. And these are the ones being sown in rocky ground, who when they hear the word immediately receive it with joy, and they have no root in themselves, and endure only for a while; then when the trouble or persecution arises on account of the word, immediately they stumble and fall away. And others are the ones sown among thorns; they are the ones who hear the word, but the worries of this age, the seduction of wealth and the desire for other things come in and choke the word, and it becomes fruitless. And these are the ones sown in good soil, who hear the word and receive it and bear fruit, thirty and sixty and a hundredfold."

The parable of the sower is the first parable of the Kingdom of God. If we do not understand this parable and walk it out in our lives, we will not understand the other teachings of Jesus that follow this one. He explains it for us— if we do not *grasp* the teaching and hold it to ourselves, it will be taken away. If we grasp it without *depth* and *balance* and *grounding*, then the teaching will not survive the inevitable testing that will occur in our lives, and it will come to nothing. If we measure the teaching against the values and standards of the world, then it will merely take its place among those values and standards—which will outshine it, out-shout it, out*perform* it, and it will yield nothing. But when the teaching is grasped and held to oneself, balanced and deeply grounded in its own soil, then the results are astounding.

He tells the disciples that they have been given the secret, or mystery, of the kingdom of God. But this, too, is a parable designed for the person who reads the Gospel, for what distinguishes the disciples from other people? Only that they have chosen to follow

## FOCUS

Christ in all things. We have said that a disciple represents qualities in our lives, and the first of these qualities is "listening with understanding" represented by the name *Simon*. When significant effort and focus in our lives are dedicated to *listening* for the spiritual significance of events, then the meaning of events is opened up for us, just as the parables are explained to the disciples by Jesus.

But for the other parts of our lives, that may listen briefly to words of inspiration as the crowds listened to Jesus, the events of our lives are like the words of the sower— some are heard but not understood, others are absorbed lightly but lost, others are understood at some level but abandoned, and some are understood, absorbed, *and followed.* Without commitment and dedication, our chances of understanding the meaning of our lives and the events we experience are a lot lower. Even with understanding, without action there is no harvest—no result.

> 4:21 And he said to them, "Is a lamp brought in to be put under a basket or under a bed, and not on a lampstand? For nothing is concealed except to be revealed, nothing hidden except to be brought to light. Let those with ears to hear, hear!"

♦ ♦ ♦

> 4:24 And he said to them, "*Pay attention* to what you hear. The measure you give will be the measure you get, and it will be brought to you; for to whomever has will more be given, and from him who has not, even what he has will be taken away."

♦ ♦ ♦

## PARABLES: THE KINGDOM OF GOD

> 4:26 And he said, "The kingdom of God is as if a man should scatter seed on the ground, and he should sleep and rise, night and day, and the seed sprouts and grows, he knows not how. By itself the earth bears fruit, first the blade, then the stalk, then the full grain of wheat in the stalk. But when the grain is ripe, immediately he goes in with the sickle, because the harvest is come."

♦ ♦ ♦

> 4:30 And he said, "How might we liken the kingdom of God, or what parable will we use for it? Like a mustard seed, which when sown in the ground is the smallest of all the seeds on earth, yet when it is sown it grows up and becomes the greatest of all plants, and puts forth large branches, so that the birds of heaven make nests in its shade."

♦ ♦ ♦

> 4:33 With many such parables he was speaking the word to them, according to their ability to learn. He did not speak to them except in parables, but when they were alone, he explained all to his disciples.

Jesus says, plant in our lives the smallest seed of dedication for spiritual truth and commitment to the higher purpose, and it will grow—seemingly without effort by us, with a power that is beyond our own—until it is the greatest thing in our lives, providing shelter and returning our efforts many times over. But he also says that we have a part in this process, for we must gather the harvest that this planting produces— we are meant to *use* the results that the Spirit produces in our lives.

Jesus tells us explicitly that there is a secret (or *mystery*) to this process, but that what is secret is not meant to be kept concealed, but to be revealed. However, it may not simply be *given*, or shown or explained. Revelation is *experienced*, not merely thought. Jesus explained the parable to his disciples, yet at this point in the story they do not really "get" it, because they have *only* heard with their ears. This is where the process begins again and again on each successive level of learning. Jesus says, "*Pay attention* to what you hear!" What you take in, what you focus on, *matters*.

He explains that "to whomever has will more be given, and from him who has not, even what he has will be taken away." This is a principle of all life that is particularly crucial on the spiritual path. We can see how it operates in everyday life in many ways. People who have experience at something do it better than people without experience; people who *practice* at something get better at it, while people who neglect something often lose it. From the inner perspective, attitude is everything, and "you get what you focus on." Spiritual practice is an inner focus that concentrates power into experience. If that power focuses an attitude of attainment, of openness, of progress, of "having the things of God," then these are projected into experience and our lives change accordingly. If we repeatedly focus on attitudes of failure, of fear, deprivation or incompetence, then these too are projected into experience and our lives show it.

The "things of God" are not *things* like cars and houses and money. Jesus is talking about "things" that become integral parts of ourselves— that become "rooted" in us. In the earlier parable he spoke of the one who has no "root in themselves," and here is a key to what he is talking about. When he speaks of "whomever has" he means what they "have *in* themselves," for what we have within ourselves gathers other similar qualities to it with an inner momentum—inner qualities are "cumulative" in a way. If, for example, we have a little "courage" in one instance, we have the basis for more courage in the future. Also we will find that this quality gathers supportive qualities to it and they become rooted within us, so that

## PARABLES: THE KINGDOM OF GOD

the courageous person may become bolder, more generous, more aware, more willing to take risks, and so on.

This "cumulative" aspect of inner qualities also applies to undesirable qualities, so that, for example, anger or fear tend to build on themselves within us. Because our inner qualities are never static it is important that we come back to this— Jesus says "Pay attention to what you hear." Listen *inside* your mind with your inner ear, as well as outside with your physical ears.

♦ ♦ ♦

Who are those that "have," and who are those that "have not?" Another way of looking at this question can be expressed this way: Within us the parts that "have" are those that express love, trust, confidence, joy, compassion, generosity, tolerance, assurance, comfort, hope and abundance. Those that "have not" are those that express hatred, fear, suspicion, arrogance, possessiveness, prejudice, pessimism, agitation, misery and scarcity — the absence of the qualities of "having" listed above. Both these stances tend to be cumulative within us. For example, a person whose feeling of "I have love" is rooted deeply within them will find evidence for that feeling and it will be confirmed in life, and one whose feeling of "I have no love" is deeply rooted will see that feeling confirmed— the quality is cumulative, and the "have-not" person will experience more inner "not-having," *regardless* of what happens in his or her life.

For example, a young man who once aspired to be a writer had a very "have-not" attitude buried deeply within him. He had a deep sense of being unworthy, inferior, and "not good enough" (that was, nevertheless invisible to most people who met him). But he was also a brilliant person and a hard worker. He wrote a play and submitted it to an older man who was an experienced writer and editor. After reading the play the older man listed five aspects of the writing that were good and strong, and he mentioned one aspect in which the play was weak and needed work. He told the young man that his writing was good and encouraged him to revise his work and submit it again. But the young man's "have-not" attitude was deeper and stronger than his "have" attitude, and he literally did not hear the praise that was given, only the criticism. He went home discouraged and never wrote another play. His "have-not" attitude accumulated support from the older man's criticism and overwhelmed his ability and his talent (and the praise he had received), and he "lost what he had."

The "kingdom of God" is a place of choice— the choice to hear and respond to voices within and without. In the Kingdom no voice is stifled; all are heard, and *heard out*. We may then choose a way to respond that projects love, joy, trust, compassion and generosity like a man who plants a seed. He can wake and sleep without worry, for the seed will grow and bear fruit, and even the smallest choice to "have" the things of God will bear fruit.

We are confronted many times every day with the opportunity to respond to our experience with an attitude of "I have," "I am," "I can," or "I have not," "I am not," "I cannot." Each attitude plants a seed and will tend to increase the more it is used.

We get what we focus on, which may be very different from what we *say* we desire. For example, suppose something difficult happens at home or at work. We may notice a thought like, "I can't stand it when that happens," or "I hate that!" or "This kind of thing always happens to me." We may notice a feeling of hurt or bitterness, resentment, anger, or fear. Or we may *not* acknowledge such feelings, as we bravely affirm "Everything is fine!" or "everything will be all right." Jesus tells us directly to *notice* and to pay attention, for while the voice of our mouths says "yes" the voice of our hearts or the feelings in our bellies may be repeating "NO! It is NOT all right!" over and over. Or the opposite may happen and we say "no" with our mouths but our inner voices may cry out "Yes!"

There is an inner giving as well as an outer giving. When the inner voice speaks words of discouragement, of lack, of futility; when the mind thinks out of despair, or condemnation, or revenge; when the inner perception sees futility, lack, failure—these are forms of inner giving as well as outer behavior— then the self is visited with such words, judgments, and perceptions, which do not *feel* like gifts!

The self may just accept such words, judgments and perceptions, or it may choose to respond to the negative voices with a compassionate, healing attitude. When the inner self chooses encouragement, hope, praise, forgiveness, and love, and plants these in the soil of life even while acknowledging the presence of all that is seen and

## PARABLES: THE KINGDOM OF GOD

heard, then these positive, life-affirming qualities begin to grow in our lives; they become our habits and attitudes, and they become a shelter for all things in our lives. The qualities that we bring to our every day living have everything to do with the attitudes we respond with. If the most deeply rooted qualities we see in ourselves are the "not having" attitudes, we may need help from others — because these qualities may hinder our own ability to choose to change those attitudes.

> o  Which of the inner voices that you hear are rooted in you, and which seem to come and go?
> o  Do you listen to all of your inner voices, or are some muffled or ignored?
> o  Is it sometimes better not to listen to some voices within? Why or why not?

♦ ♦ ♦

> o  Over time, take an inventory of your observations about your life, your work, your family and friends, your abilities, thoughts and attitudes.
> o  Where do you observe yourself "having," and where "not having?" If you would like to explore this issue, go the qualities in Table A, page 51, and Table B on page 104, and compare the qualities with the areas in your life where you feel you "have" and that you "don't have." Is there a relationship?
> o  Which qualities of "having" do you wish to strengthen in your life? Which do you wish to leave behind?
> o  Which qualities of "not having" are obstacles to your spiritual life?
> o  Which qualities do you need help with?

FOCUS

♦ ♦ ♦

This entire section of the Gospel presents important guidance for the spiritual seeker, in several concise lessons that are available to those who earnestly seek for meaning. The first lesson is that we must become aware that while guidance is available for all, not everyone will receive it fully and walk it out to fruition at any given time. Those who prepare themselves psychologically and spiritually, who then accept the guidance and apply it, will be ready to carry it through to completion.

A second lesson is that the process will proceed according to the attitude of the participant— the attitude of "having" will itself accelerate learning, growth and accomplishment, whereas the attitude of "not having" will not only sabotage progress, and it may erode previous accomplishment. Learning how to live in faith, applying attitudes of "I am, I do, I have, I see" in the *present* tense (not "I will" or "I should" in the future, not "I did" in the past, but *I do— now*), with an assuredness and persistence that goes far beyond mere confidence in facts, because it derives from our connection with and reliance upon God—this is the key. Faith works together with an act of will rather than an affirmation of belief. Anyone can have the experience of "having" or of "not having" something. The faith that chooses to act upon what we "have" gathers power.

Finally, he shows us in a parable that spiritual progress involves more than individual work and effort. We approach the issue with a powerful faith, in a way that manifests our inner guidance from the Holy Spirit; we act; and then we release the process to unfold. These steps are all necessary aspects of the spiritual process: reliance on God, inspiration, action, and release. The result, Jesus says, is a bountiful harvest. And part of our work is to gather this harvest and use it.

This section of the story finished with a repetition of the observation that Jesus taught all people in parables, but to his disciples he explained everything. The writer of the Gospel is emphasizing that the people who *actively* follow Christ, who *actively* seek the truth, get the guidance they seek. Those who listen passively, or who merely follow an intellectual interest, get hints—that may unfold if they follow them, or maybe evaporate if they do not. The lesson is applicable not only between people, but within ourselves as well, and applies to the Gospel itself as well as to the stories within the Gospel. There are parts of us that have little interest in spiritual growth, while other aspects of us thirst for it and work hard to learn. For many of us on the path, life may be an alternation from the eager subpersonality to the indifferent, to the hostile one. For us to grow, it is necessary that our inner disciples learn these lessons, for they can easily be pushed aside or co-opted by other aspects of ourselves. We may then get a feeling one day that "I learned this years ago— but then I forgot it."

Our inner spiritual walk is more like trying to change an entire community than changing a single mind. The inner process in many ways mirrors what we observe in society, so the living poetry of the Gospel is very apt in showing what happens within us. "Evangelism," then, begins with healing within ourselves, for we cannot help others while within ourselves there remain aspects of us that are violent, diseased, hurt, arrogant, "self-righteous" or seeking power over others.

We influence people by who we are more than by what we say. The unhealed "evangelist," then, is likely to convert people to his or her own way of *being*—unhealed—despite holy words and good intentions.

We seek to be healed and transformed. We cannot then be content to change one idea, or one attitude, or one behavior. Many who seek the Kingdom seize an idea, a feeling, or a behavior, but do not reach in and reach out for all the ideas, all the feelings, all the behaviors that bring us into the Kingdom. We do not need to "have it all," however— Jesus says, just plant the seeds, scatter them, everywhere, and watch them grow!

♦♦♦

## WALKING OUT THE GOSPEL: TO EXPLORE THIS FURTHER, DO EXERCISE 10 IN PART III, PAGE 412.

♦♦♦

## 11. INTO THE DEPTHS

# INTO THE DEPTHS

> 4:35 And on that day, when evening had come, he says to them, "Let us go across to the other side." And having sent the crowd away, they took him just as he was in the boat, and other boats were with him. A great windstorm arose, and the waves were beating into the boat so that now the boat was filling. And he was in the stern, asleep on the cushion, and they wake him and say to him, "Master, do you not care that we are perishing?" And he woke up and rebuked the wind, and he said to the sea, "Peace, be still." And the wind ceased, and there was a great calm. And he said to them, "Why are you fearful? Do you not trust yet?" And they were filled with great awe, and said to one another, "Who then is this, that even the wind and the sea obey him?"

This is a fascinating segment of the story, a truly "inner" episode. They go on a journey across the sea by night. In the outside world one does not usually begin a sailing trip in the evening, but the inner nights are often times when important journeys are undertaken, and this one is very significant. Jesus tells them, "Let us go across to the other side," and they took him in the boat "just as he was," and other boats are with them. He goes to sleep while a great storm arises.

Jesus is the Spirit leading us away from the crowd and clamoring of everyday life, into a different, more interior realm — and seemingly a more fearful one. This only occurs with the full cooperation of many aspects of our personality, but does not involve anything unusual from the spiritual perspective—he goes "just as he is." But instead of directing them, he goes to sleep. This is precisely how it feels for us when we embark into new, unknown, spiritual territory— it may feel as if we are sailing in the dark and our leader is asleep while the storm comes up. The storm is what we may experience when we allow ourselves to be led "to the other side"— things within us get churned up and overturned, awakened, and they may occur with a force that can be very frightening. The ordinary aspects of our personality fear for their survival, but they often do

FOCUS

nothing until the boat is nearly ready to sink. Then, in a panic, they turn to the Spirit—who has been with them all the while. The Spirit only seems to sleep from the perspective of the parts of our personality, which have hitherto seemed to live "on their own." For these parts of us, the Spirit seems to awaken, but the truth is that it is we who awaken to the Spirit when we finally call upon it.

It is hard to imagine someone calming a storm with a word. Those of us who have experienced something like this within ourselves can attest to how it feels— a violent, deadly storm transformed—immediately—into a peaceful calm that stays with us for the rest of the journey. Following our Spirit inwardly and in every other way *does* take us into the dark night of our souls, and it *does* provoke storms in that night. These storms are provoked precisely so that on a new level we will learn to open ourselves to spiritual power.

When we go on such an inward journey we find ourselves in uncharted territory and a deep pervading calm overtakes the entire inner landscape when we call upon the Spirit from this depth. The surface parts of ourselves are astounded, for they did not believe it possible that such overwhelming inner turmoil could yield to such a profound peace—and yet it does.

And again, our inner disciples and other aspects of our personality, who thought they knew where they were going and what they were following, find that the inner reality outstrips their expectations. Again they ask, "Who is this, *really*?" This question is repeated in the Gospel because it is important— and it is also important for us to ask this question as we look within.

---

5:1 And they came to the other side of the sea, to the country of the Gerasenes. And when he had gotten out of the boat, immediately he was met by a man out of the tombs, who had an unclean spirit, who lived among the tombs, and no one could bind him anymore, even with a chain, for he had often been bound with shackles and chains, but the chains he wrenched apart and the shackles he broke in pieces, and no one had the strength to subdue him. Night and day among the tombs and on the hills he was howling and cutting himself with stones. Having seen Jesus from a

> distance, he ran and bowed down before him, and with a great shout he cried, "What have you to do with me, Jesus, son of the most high God? I adjure you by God, do not torture me!" — for he was saying to him, "Come out of the man, unclean spirit!" And he asked him, "What is your name?" He replied "My name is legion, because we are many." And he begged him eagerly not to send them out of the region. Now there was a great herd of pigs grazing there on the hillside, and they begged him, "Send us into the pigs, let us enter them!" And he allowed them, and they came out and entered the pigs, and the herd of two thousand rushed down the steep bank and were drowned in the sea. And the swineherds fled, and told it in the city and the country, and people came to see what had happened. And they came toward Jesus and saw the demoniac sitting there, clothed and in his right mind, the one who had had the legion, and they were afraid. And those who had seen it told what had happened to the demoniac and the pigs. And they began to beg him to leave the area. As he was getting into the boat, the man who had had the demons begged him that he might be with him. But he did not allow him, and said to him, "Go home to your own people, and tell them how much the Lord has done to you, and the compassion he showed you." And he went away, and began to proclaim in the Decapolis the great thing Jesus had done to him, and all were amazed.

◆ ◆ ◆

This scene has taken place (in daylight) "on the other side." The boat does not land at a town, but near "the tombs," and they are met by a wild man, who appears to be deranged and completely uncontrollable. The symbolism of this episode is very powerful and suggestive. Many of us have inner aspects and subpersonalities that we hate, that rage and flail away uncontrollably, that are so unpleasant to us that we effectively banish them from our conscious waking lives into a sort of inner nether world, where they seem to be dead—and we wish they *were* dead. But they are not dead, only living "among the tombs"—and on that level, they not only live, but are very powerful and resist all attempts to stifle or control them, and their power may be abusive, wild or self-destructive.

The Gospel is showing us that when we open up to a full life in the Spirit, we will journey into the "night" to reach the banished parts of ourselves, the parts that have been left for dead, the parts that may contain unacceptable urges and represent great power.

In the story the spirits in the man recognize Jesus as the son of the most high God, and ask that he not be tortured. As we discussed earlier, a "demon" or "unclean spirit" in the story is an influence that is not our own, that has entered our lives and seems to have taken on a life of its own within us. Anyone who has ever been addicted to drugs, medications, alcohol or tobacco, for example, and who has tried to fight their addiction or dependence, will know exactly how this feels, and will appreciate the difficulty of "casting out" the unwanted influences. Some of us know the experience of being subject to a legion of these influences simultaneously— for example, multiple addictions and compulsions, personality disorders; or the lingering influence of abuse by parents or peers; early life trauma and physical disabilities. Negative influences may come from a variety of sources and there are many different ways that such influences may be present in our lives, whether they are visible or not.

Whether these influences are on the surface or deep within our inner recesses, when we choose to follow the Spirit we will inevitably be led to confront them at some point. When we are ready, the Spirit will work to cast out what does not belong to us and in us, for spiritual healing is a process of coming to our true selves. From the perspective of the negative influence, inner healing is viewed as torture. When healing of a negative influence is attempted on a solely mental or emotional level, the resulting conflict may be experienced as torturous. A peaceful resolution to inner conflict must involve all levels of the person and be led by the Spirit. The process may be tempestuous and extreme and it may take a long time— weeks, months, or even years. Yet for some people it may not be experienced

## INTO THE DEPTHS

in a dramatic way, for sometimes we may seem to just wake up one day (after days, or maybe years), and the outside influences simply seem to be gone. When the healing occurs we are in our "right minds," sitting peacefully. The actual process is as different as people are different— the parable is showing us only the outline of a process.

The swine and swineherds are symbols that may not "work" for all of us, as many of us have no tradition against or aversion to pork or to pigs. But in the story, pigs (as food especially) represent forbidden or unhealthy "pleasures" and practices, and swineherds represent those who cultivate unhealthy practices. In our culture, probably the nearest simile might be drugs and prostitution, drug pushers and pimps, as the story uses graphic images to make a point. For many of us, the inner bondage will not be so apparent, or its effects so extreme, but the example is there for us to use and to explore. When Jesus allows the "unclean spirits" to "enter the pigs," he is figuratively sending an unhealthy influence to be with its own kind. When an unhealthy influence in us is "sent to its source," the source ceases to be an influence on us, just as the pigs in the story run into the sea. This, of course, is alarming to any person or any part of us that profits from our enslavement to the unhealthy influences. Such persons or parts of us become sources of resistance to healing. It is vital that we understand that there is an "economy" of inner "dis-ease," addiction and enslavement— certain purposes are served, "profits" are gained, something is supported and nourished.

o **Do you have a habit, a thought pattern, or an attitude that is self-destructive or counterproductive? One that stays with you despite your efforts to control or eliminate it?**

o **If you do, reflect on this unhealed part of yourself, one that seems resistant to change. What does the "unhealed part" do *for* you? What hidden purpose does it serve? What feeds it? What supports it? What is its real object? What need does it try to satisfy?**

FOCUS

> ○ **Is there an essential element that you need to know about before you can begin to be healed?**[1]

When Jesus arrives we cannot tell the difference between the man himself and the legion of spirits that dominate his life, yet we can tell something— for it is the *man* who approaches Jesus, even as the spirits within him cry out against Jesus. Within ourselves, too, we may find that we must go through the negative influences on the outside to reach the person on the inside, and be careful to keep our focus on the person— taking care not to confuse the person with what *influences* the person.

When healing has occurred, the part of us that is healed knows, on some level, what has happened to us and wants to continue the process, just as the healed man in the story wants to follow Jesus. Notice that this time Jesus does not command him to be silent. The entire episode is representative of a deep healing within us, and the healed part of us is aware of the true work of the Spirit, and is not tempted to spread misunderstanding. The healed part only wants to follow the Spirit from which it has received healing, and it is this part of us that can *truly* tell us about God—about "what the Lord has done to us." What *this* part has to say, now that it is healed, is not

---

[1] For example, I smoked cigarettes for over twenty years, and tried unsuccessfully to quit several times. As the years went on the inner conflict became severe and began to manifest in physical symptoms. I could see that smoking was having a variety of negative effects in my life, the shortness of breath being only the most obvious one. Only after I understood that I had been afraid of my emotions, and that smoking effectively suppressed my emotions, was I ready to really quit. First I had to be willing to face and deal with my emotions—an unhealed part of me that the smoking was covering up, kept invisible with a "smokescreen." It was essential for me to see that my smoking served a purpose, and to see what was at the root of the purpose (fear, in my case), and then to choose to serve a different purpose, before I could really open myself to healing. Only then could I begin to see that underneath the craving was the need to be loved. Before that time, any effort to quit was torture to me, and peoples' innocent attempts to help me (like flushing my cigarettes down the toilet) provoked violent reactions from me. But after the Spirit gave me the gift of awareness, I was (with some help) able to quit in a short time with no pain, no anguish, no violent reactions, and no desire to go back to the habit.

tradition, not expectation, not ideas, not dogma, not excitement, not glory and emotion. When we are healed on a deep level we share peace and a profound *knowing*, a truth that has been *experienced*, and the Spirit of God encourages us to share this in whatever way is appropriate *for us*. This is the heart of the joyous message, the good news.

◆ ◆ ◆

- **What is the difference between your self and *what influences your self?***
- **Here is a brief exercise to help you look at this:**
  - **Take a moment to be quiet, allowing your thoughts to settle. Put all daily concerns aside for a few moments and breathe deeply a few times, relaxing your mind and body. Pause for a moment.**
  - **Notice your thoughts, your feelings. Be aware of your overall feeling tone — happy, sad, tired, vigorous, content, nervous, etc.**
  - **Now notice *that you are noticing.* Allow yourself to *be* that witness that notices. Notice the difference between your *self* that is witnessing, and the thoughts and feelings your self *has*, that are being witnessed.**

## 12. THE WORK OF FAITH: LIFE AND HEALING

# THE WORK OF FAITH: LIFE AND HEALING

5:21 And when Jesus had crossed again in the boat to the other side, a great crowd gathered about him, and he was beside the sea. Then one of the leaders of the synagogue named Jairus comes, and seeing him, he falls at his feet and was begging him earnestly, "My little daughter is at the point of death. Come and lay your hands on her, so that she may be healed and live." And he went with him, and a large crowd followed him and pressed in on him. And there was a woman who had had a flow of blood for twelve years. She had suffered much under many healers, and had spent all that she had and got no better, but rather grew worse. She had heard about Jesus, and came up behind him in the crowd and touched his garment; for she said, "If I can even touch his clothes, I will be healed." And immediately the source of the blood dried up, and she knew in her body that she was healed of the disease. And immediately Jesus was aware within himself that power had gone forth from him, and turning around in the crowd he said, "Who touched my clothes?" And his disciples said to him, "You see the crowd pressing in on you, and you ask 'who touched me?'" And he looked around to see who had done it. But the woman, knowing what had happened to her, came in fear and trembling, fell down before him, and told him the whole truth. But he said to her, "Daughter, your faith has made you well. Go in peace, and be healed of your disease." While he was still speaking, some [people] come from the house of the leader of the synagogue, saying, "Your daughter died; why trouble the teacher any further?" But Jesus ignored what they reported and said to the leader of the synagogue, "Do not fear; only trust and believe." And he allowed no one to follow him except Peter and James and John, the brother of James. And when he comes to the house of the leader of the synagogue, he sees a commotion, people weeping and

> wailing loudly. When he had entered, he said to them, "Why do you make a commotion and weep? The child is not dead, but sleeping." And they laughed at him. But he put them all outside, and takes the child's father and mother and those who were with him, and goes in to where the child was. And taking the child's hand he says to her, "Talitha cumi," which means "Little girl, I say to you, arise." And immediately the girl got up and walked about— she was twelve years old. And they were beside themselves with great ecstasy. And he strictly charged them that no one should know this, and told them to give her something to eat.

Jesus has again crossed to "the other side," returning in our inner interpretation to a more accessible level of our awareness, for in the episode of the man in the tombs the story has taken us to the depths of our self-awareness and beyond. The leader of the synagogue represents the part of us that controls our attitudes toward what is sacred, which governs our worship and religious practice: "Jairus" means "enlightener" and his daughter is dying. Here is an episode representing our experience of disillusionment with religion, the death of spiritual joy. The inner part knows that the revival of the faith within us is not accomplished by practice, by works, or by anything else unless we are in genuine contact with the Spirit.[1] In the person of Jesus in the story, the Spirit is willing.

Now the story pauses for a moment, as a woman with a "flow of blood for twelve years" comes to touch his robe, convinced that she will be made well by the touch. She touches his robe and then *feels* in her body—immediately—that her hemorrhage has ceased and she is healed of her disease. Jesus likewise *feels* that power has gone out of him without his conscious intent. He is being pressed upon by numbers of people and his disciples ask, "You are being mobbed by people, and you ask, 'which *one* of you touched me?'"

---

[1] I am not suggesting that practice and works are useless; but only that without the Spirit, faith is not quickened.

## THE WORK OF FAITH: LIFE AND HEALING

Here is a mob of people who want something, and all are touching Jesus if they can, but only one is actually prepared to receive what he has to give—is so ready that her slightest contact allows her to receive her healing. It is her receptiveness[2] that allows the healing power to enter her, and this healing does not require a conscious intention or act by Jesus.[3] He represents the Spirit within us, whose power is available to all but is not released by desire, nor by clamor, effort or eagerness, but by the absolute faith that healing is hers.

This is the example that Jesus then brings to our conscious awareness—and to Jairus, our inner "spiritual governor:" Do not fear, only believe, only trust, only accept your daughter's life as a *fact*. The work of the Spirit is here being demonstrated on many levels, as only a story can do. The "child" —spiritual joy—is revived by the Spirit, but what is needed is the absolute faith of the *elder*. The faith of one part of us allows the revival of other parts of us, and that faith is not about *getting* what we want but about *giving* life with love, and about *receiving* the power that makes faith possible.

It is likely that we will not understand what has really occurred when this happens, and the revival of spiritual joy is only the beginning of a larger process. Again Jesus commands silence,[4] but he tells them to give the girl "something to eat." In the Gospel feeding always refers to spiritual nourishment, but this is also a recognition that spiritual love includes loving the body.

When we say "our inner child" it seems from the words that there is only one; but our impulses, needs and feelings change over time. First we are infants, then toddlers, little children, adolescents, teenagers. Each of these lives within us, and there is a parent in spirit in each of us also, who loves and cherishes each child within us, and wants healing, life and wholeness for each child.

---

[2] And her courage, for in that ancient culture a menstruating woman was considered "unclean" and was forbidden by law and custom to touch any man.

[3] It also does not require that Jesus have any idea of what the woman needs to be healed: the Spirit knows, and the power goes to where it is needed.

[4] The command to silence is symbolism that is meant *for the reader*, since in the story the girl's death is already public knowledge.

FOCUS

> - Identify one of your inner children, and allow yourself to become aware of the needs and feelings of that child part of you. If you have an inner child that is hurt or wounded, focus on this one.
> - Now, identify an inner parent and see what attitude the inner parent has toward the child. Your inner parent may be supportive and nurturing, or it may be critical and impatient.
> - If your inner parent is critical, negative or impatient, bring this part of you to the Spirit and ask for healing. Allow the Spirit to lead you. This may be something you need to do over time.
> - When your inner parent is in a positive, nurturing attitude, allow the parent to embrace the child, allow the child to receive this embrace, and allow the Spirit of God to be there between them in the embrace.
> - Scan your inner being— is there a part of you that seems to be "dead," that needs to be revived? If there is, what will you do to bring the life of the Spirit to that part of you?
> - How do you feed your inner children?
> - What nourishment sustains a childlike faith?
> - What kind of care and love of your physical body is an expression and extension of spiritual love?

***WALKING OUT THE GOSPEL: TO EXPLORE THIS FURTHER, DO EXERCISE 11 IN PART III, PAGE 415.***

♦ ♦ ♦

We notice in the story that the woman had been hemorrhaging for twelve years, and at the end the child was twelve years old— the

# THE WORK OF FAITH: LIFE AND HEALING

two "twelve's" are a flag for our attention.[5] In the ancient near east a childless woman was considered a "failure" as a person, unfulfilled and probably unwanted by a husband or family— virtually an outcast, and this woman would also be considered "unclean" because of her condition. Opposite her we see a man who is successful— a father and the leader of a synagogue, which was the hub of religious and social activity in a town. Their positions are of long standing— twelve years. They approach Jesus from opposite positions, and yet the response is the same— life flowing forth from the Spirit, facilitated by faith and trust.

The woman cannot conceive a child while she has the flow of blood; the leader of the synagogue has had a living child for twelve years, and she dies—apparently. Here is a graphic representation of how the work of the Spirit allows inner birth to occur, and it reverses inner death. These two vignettes are interwoven deliberately, to show us that without the Spirit the inner life does not begin, and without it the inner life is not sustained. With the Spirit our inner life is given birth, and it is renewed. This process can be at work in us on several levels simultaneously. Notice that the "outcast" is healed *first*, and her faith needs no teaching— she believes and is healed. Her example is set before us as we return to the "successful" man, who needs help and instruction.

♦♦♦

> o **Is there a part of you that is unable to bring forth something new in your life, unable in some way to conceive, to give birth, begin a new project?**
> o **Is there some part of you that is inwardly bleeding in some way?**

---

[5] I will not speculate on the meaning of the number itself, but 12 does appear to have special meaning to biblical writers. There are 12 tribes of Israel, 12 inner disciples of Jesus, 12 signs of the zodiac, etc. See the following website for more information: http://www.biblestudy.org/bibleref/meaning-of-numbers-in-bible/12.html. You may find analogies so that the number twelve speaks to your own life in a specific way.

FOCUS

> o **How can you bring this part of you to the life that flows from the Spirit?**
> o **What will you do to make that connection?**

From our vantage point, the key to this process is what Jesus calls "faith:" it brings forth life, it brings healing, it overcomes death.

♦ ♦ ♦

What is faith? Jesus uses the word in the same breath as "do not fear," but faith is more than confidence, more than assurance, more than desire, more than conviction. What else? Jesus has not impressed a teaching on anyone, he only said, Believe that she lives, this is the truth—despite the evidence of your senses. Believe that the Spirit works, despite the lack of proof. Come *with me*, and believe. Faith is belief *with connection*, belief with acceptance, with love, with involvement and trust. He will show us more later.

## 13. HISTORY, KNOWLEDGE AND FAITH

FOCUS

> 6:1 And he left there and came to his own country, and his disciples follow him.[1] And on the Sabbath he began to teach in the synagogue, and many who heard him were astonished, saying, "Where did this man get all this?" and "What is this wisdom that has been given to him?" and "What power comes through his hands! Is not this the carpenter, the son of Mary and brother of James and Joses and Judas and Simon? And are not his sisters here with us?" And they took offense at him. And Jesus said to them, "A prophet is not dishonored, except in his own country, and among his own kin, and in his own house." And he could do no powerful work there, except that he laid his hands on a few sick people and healed them. And he marveled because of their unbelief.

Here in his home town, people are for the most part offended by him, by his presumption. The Spirit of God flows in our lives only after we have decided to change, to reform, to repent. The parts of us that learned life in the bosom of our families are often the most resistant to change, and the last to learn. Jesus says elsewhere that "the first will be last," knowing that on one level our inner children, our oldest habits, our earliest perceptions, are among the last to respond to the healing work of the Spirit. It is precisely the familiarity that is the difficulty— people say, "we *know* who you are," which in a slightly different sense is the same as what the unclean spirits said to Jesus when he healed people. The demons "knew" him to be the son of God—but they did not really know him. His neighbors "knew" him to be the boy who grew up in their midst and was an

---

[1] Notice that this sentence begins with Jesus in the past tense, but ends with the disciples in the present tense. To us this seems odd, but many such mixings of tense occur in Mark. Many translations simply change the words so that all the sentences are consistent— in the past. But I feel that the author knew what he was writing, and that the tense shifts are deliberate. Look to see how past and present interweave in the Gospel and in your life.

## THE WORK OF FAITH LIFE AND HEALING

ordinary person like everyone else—but they did not really know him.

Similar obstacles may be present in our lives. When we think we "know" the Spirit of God (maybe we believe we are already "saved," for example), we may limit it and hinder it from doing its work within us. When we think we "know" reality, we may limit ourselves and prevent ourselves from responding to healing.

There are different kinds of knowing, and the Gospel shows us that some kinds of knowing are in fact obstructions. We may find that our religious knowledge bars our ability to understand science, or that our scientific knowledge may make it impossible for us to understand how faith works. Things learned in early life may stand in the way of new learning, and things that we *believe* may make it impossible for us to understand evidence that is right in front of us. The evidence we perceive with our senses may blind us to realities that cannot be sensed or measured.

This section closes as Jesus "marveled because of their unbelief." What the Gospel calls "unbelief" is in fact another species of "belief"— the negative kind. In the previous vignettes the Gospel showed how belief can be a springboard to healing and revival, whereas in this section the "unbelief" or negative belief is an obstacle to healing.

In the previous section we saw people who believe when there is no proof, and here we have seen people who disbelieve despite the evidence of their senses. Again we ask, What is faith? What is missing when we do not have it? Not only "belief," or conviction, or assuredness, but also a willingness to engage the unknown, a willingness to allow the miraculous to emerge from the familiar; a willingness to be led, to be taught, to be transformed. Faith also requires us to look at our experience without preconceptions, to be open to *what is*.

> o **How might knowledge (your knowing, or what you know, or the knowledge of others) help you in your spiritual work, and when might it become a hindrance?**
> o **What happens when your faith follows after your knowledge?**

FOCUS

> o **What happens when your faith tries to go on without knowledge?**

Many "skeptical inquirers" as well as "true believers" in our times see faith and knowledge as polar opposites. Jesus is asking us to be involved, connected and trusting; aware, loving and accepting— this attitude allows us to embrace faith and knowledge together in a synthesis that produces results and effects that are not possible to one who remains detached, distant or uninvolved.

For example, what is now commonly called "the placebo effect" in medicine is often a manifestation of faith in action. But the scientist who attempts to make an "unbiased" test of its "objective reality" by removing the personal involvement, knowledge, commitment or faith of the participants from the test do not realize that this is like trying to unplug the cord and then prove or disprove the presence of electricity. Of course they consistently "disprove" its presence, and announce that the placebo effect is a mystery or a fraud or "something else." If they assume that belief and faith—even of the commonest sort, such as faith that a pill will work—is behind the effect, their experiments might yield different results. Because faith cannot be "quantified" does not mean it is not real. Faith *is* a real phenomenon, but it is inextricably connected to the person having the faith: there is no such thing as "objective" or "impersonal" faith. It is also a phenomenon that is unique to a particular person and circumstance that is, strictly speaking, not "repeatable" even though the process is analogous from one situation to another.

♦ ♦ ♦

> o **Can you identify times when your faith and your knowledge seem opposed to each other?**
> o **What is the relationship between "knowing" and "believing?" to you? What parts of you get**

engaged in knowing, what parts in believing? Your mind, emotions, intuition, body?
- Some things in life seem to be just plain "facts," like the sky is blue and the chair I sit on is solid. Are these "facts" knowledge or belief, or both? Does this make any difference to you? Do you need "certainty" or "permanence" in order to know or to believe something?
- Sir Isaac Newton's theories of physics in the 17th century were supported by proofs and demonstrations, and people believed in the laws of physics that he explained. But in the 20th century Einstein's theories of physics were also supported by proofs and demonstrations, yet the theories do not agree. Is acceptance of such theories "knowledge" or "belief" or both — or neither?
- How do changes in "knowledge" change your faith? Think of some examples in your life.
- How can a clinging to old "knowledge" get in your way? Think of some examples in your life.
- How does your life change when faith and knowledge go hand in hand, each supporting and relying upon the other?
- What kind of personal involvement is needed for your faith and your knowledge to be mutually supportive instead of polar opposites? Can you find examples in your life where this can occur?

# NOTES

# PRACTICE

This part of the book leads us more into the active work of the Gospel. It begins with the active participation of our inner qualities in the Gospel process and immediately encounters major resistance. An inner child may play a major part in our lives as we experience attempts to sabotage our inner growth. Conscience may be stifled; an inner death may occur. We learn about spiritual resources and develop the ability to recognize inner events, and learn that recognition does not guarantee that we have a correct interpretation of the meaning of what we have seen. We begin to understand the difference between a defensive spiritual posture and the faith that allows spiritual resources to be tapped and spiritual power to flow. We see how the Spirit may multiply our resources.

The false dichotomy between "practical matters" and "spiritual matters" is made clear and we see how a spiritually defensive attitude develops as a result of fear of exposure to what is "unclean," false, alien, "wrong," or improper. The Gospel leads us to cross boundaries of many kinds— boundaries of awareness, thought, custom, practice and care. We learn the power of seeking validation from our own experience in faith and in action rather than from precept and law. The Gospel leads us to confront our fear of the "other" and to see habits of mind that become a "victim mentality" which the Gospel invites us to overcome with faith.

This section of the Gospel provides the groundwork for an understanding that will change everything in our lives. This part begins with Mark 6:6 and goes as far as Mark 8:26.

## 14. ACTION AND REACTION

PRACTICE

> 6:6b And he was going about among the villages, teaching. And he calls the Twelve and began to send them off two by two, and gave them power over the unclean spirits. He charged them to take nothing for their journey except a staff[1] — no bread, no bag, no money in their belts; but to wear sandals and not to put on two tunics.

When our inner disciples are first "sent out" within ourselves, they are to "take nothing with them:" no arguments, no ideas, no means of persuasion, but only the power that has come from the Spirit.

> 6:10 And he said to them, "Whenever you enter a house, stay there until you leave the place, and if any place will not welcome you, and they do not listen to you, as you leave shake off the dust beneath your feet as a witness to them."

Witness of what? —that the disciples do not allow rejection to cling to them. Shaking off the dust is a way of saying, "I forgive. I release. I go on." The core of Jesus' teaching is to be applied whether the disciples are received or not. Within us it may be thus— there are parts of us that are just not interested in "the spiritual life." The story is suggesting that even within ourselves, we are to go where the work will be received and where it will be effective. "Spiritual butt-kicking" is our term for attempts to coerce unwilling parts of ourselves, or others, whether they seem like sincere efforts or not. Jesus is instructing us not to be coercive— not even to be slightly "pushy." Do the work where it is *welcome,* he says. Jesus is telling us that the best teachers and persuaders and attractors are love and good example. Talk is only as good as the talker. If one part of us

---
[1] A walking stick

begins to experience the benefit of love and healing, other parts of us may want the benefit, too—but if not, let it be and move on.

> 6:12 And they went out and preached that people should repent. They were casting out many demons, and anointing with oil many who were sick and healing them.

At a certain point in our spiritual seeking, the Spirit will mobilize the resources it has gathered within us and "send" these influences into our larger life. The healed parts of us, the parts of us that are dedicated to our spiritual life, are "sent out" to influence our thoughts, our habits, our outward behavior, and every other aspect of our lives. This is not the same as being sent to "convert" other people. The Spirit sends its inner messengers, the disciples (learners) within us, to the parts of ourselves that interact with the world, to change the rest of ourselves— change our minds, our perceptions, our understanding and our behavior.

The inner transformation happens in stages, and the particulars of change are unique to each person. The inner disciples are sent to the parts of us that may have little or no obvious connection to "spiritual things:" our "worker" selves, our sexual selves, our shopping subpersonality, our gardening subpersonality, our bird watching subpersonality, our political activist part, our sports fan, and so on.

Jesus, as representative of the Spirit within us, does not instruct the disciples to break down doors, or to argue, or convert, or try to overcome resistance. He tells them, if you are not welcomed, go to where you are wanted. If you are welcomed, stay. The message of the inner disciples is very, very simple: "change." Repent. Turn away from practices that do not work, that cause pain and harm. Take a step, and you will be *met*. The inner disciples now begin to assist in the process of healing. On all levels of inner transformation, a willingness to change and *to be changed* is the first step— without this, nothing happens.

Our attempts to change and to grow are to be focused within us on where these attempts *will work*. We are not to pick our most

## PRACTICE

intractable problem and charge in like a bull in a china shop. Rather, the inner disciples need to make *allies* within us by working with parts of us that are amenable to the work, that welcome it.

Remember who the "inner disciples" are: they are the particular qualities that begin our inner transformation—hearing with understanding, caring, a willingness to wrestle with difficulty, an ability to endure conflict and face the issues, reverence, respect, courage and worship, steadfastness, patience, hard work, generosity and a willingness to take risks. For you, other qualities may be part of the group. Jesus sends the disciples out by twos, for even within ourselves we need support and balance. Boldness must be tempered by prudence; hearing must be balanced by vision; steadfastness must be balanced with humor; reverence must be accompanied by the willingness to take risks, and so on.

> o **Which qualities within you can be used to temper and complement other qualities to keep them balanced? You may want to use Table A on page 51 and Table B on page 104 as a starting guide.**

The qualities we develop in exercises, in study, in prayer and meditation, in spiritual discipline, are sent into our daily lives with a message of healing and forgiveness, of faith, hope, love, joy, and peace. They preach only when invited, and do not attempt to go where they are not wanted. If I invite these qualities to come into my job, my leisure time, my love life, my relationships, my attitudes toward my family, then I will see a difference. It is harder to invite these qualities into my conflicts, my failures, my doubts, my fears, my resentments, my self-abuse or my anger; yet it is in these areas that the need for healing is the greatest, and this is the focus of much spiritual work.

For example, if I am in the heat of anger about something, it is really hard for "mercy" to get any "air time" in my mind. "Mercy" will need some help, from "patience" maybe, to get heard. If I am angry enough, my inner disciples may have to wait for the angry part of me to cool off a little. Continuing the example, the message of "mercy" will begin with asking me to be merciful with myself, for

## ACTION AND REACTION

rarely is there any anger toward others that does not also involve inner anger as well—and often an anger toward some part of myself. This is where the "twinning" (Thomas) of qualities is important in our lives, for our qualities and emotions — and the focus of our spiritual work — need to be bi-directional. For example, hatred directed outward often mirrors unconscious hatred directed inward; and it is the same for other attitudes and emotions. When the Spirit sends inner disciples to help us heal, we need to invite them in "two's" to meet us coming and going, inner-directed and outer-directed, light and dark.

We are the disciples, and we are also the ones to be healed. There is a Third Party who joins our parts together when we are ready, who heals the wounds and the disease, and makes us one.

When we, or parts of us, are not ready for this work, our inner disciples have been instructed by the Spirit not to urge, coerce or even try to persuade; but rather to shake off the dust beneath their feet as they leave, to witness to us that they have no negative response to our refusal— they experience no need or distress. God *does* work in our lives, and a time will come when we are ready for them. At that time they will come to us. Until then, they work elsewhere.

- Which inner disciples are at work in your life now?
- What work are they doing?
- Which inner disciples (qualities) do you want to invite to work within you?
- Have you ever felt yourself rejecting the work of an inner disciple? If you have, notice how you felt when you said, "no." If it was a true inner disciple sent by the Spirit, you felt no guilt, only an acceptance that the work was not right for you at that time.
- What makes the time "right?" or the work "right" for you?
- Which inner parts of you are ready for the work now?
- Which inner parts of you most need spiritual work now?

PRACTICE

> o  Come back to these questions whenever your life changes direction in some way, or when you want it to change direction

♦♦♦

6:14 King Herod heard of him, for his name had become known. Some were saying, "John the Baptist has been raised from the dead, which is why the powers work in him." But others were saying , "It is Elijah!" and others were saying , "It is a prophet, like one of the prophets of old." But when Herod heard of him, he said, "John, whom I beheaded, is raised." For Herod himself had sent men to arrest John and put him in prison on account of Herodias, his brother Philip's wife, because Herod had married her. For John said to Herod, "It is not lawful for you to have your brother's wife." And Herodias held a grudge against him, and wanted to have him killed, but she could not. For Herod feared John, knowing that he was a righteous and holy man, and he protected him. When he heard him he was greatly perplexed, yet he liked to listen to him. But an opportunity came when Herod on his birthday gave a banquet for his lords and commanders and leaders of Galilee. Herodias' own daughter came in and danced, and she pleased Herod and his guests, and the king said to the girl, "Ask me for whatever you want, and I will give it to you." And he swore a great oath to her, "Whatever you ask of me, I will give to you, even half of my kingdom." She went out and said to her mother, "What shall I ask for?" She replied, "The head of John the Baptist." Immediately

> she rushed back to the king and asked, saying, "I want you to give me the head of John the Baptist on a platter." The king was greatly grieved, but because of his oaths and the guests, he did not want to refuse her. And immediately the king sent a soldier of the guard with orders to bring John's head. He went and beheaded him in the prison, and brought his head on a platter, and gave it to the girl; and the girl gave it to her mother. When his disciples heard of it, they came and took his body and laid it in a tomb.

◆ ◆ ◆

This section of the Gospel has brought us to yet another level. Many people have remarked that spiritual growth resembles peeling the layers of an onion. Events are never repeated, however we often must do similar work at successively deeper levels. At every level of growth we may encounter some sort of negative energy: resistance, temptation, sabotage. The story of the execution of John the Baptist shows how our desire to change can run into opposition. Herod represents a ruling "worldly" subpersonality that has characteristics that do not welcome spiritual work—arrogance, egotism, love of power over others, loose or relaxed morality. He also represents a person with what psychologists call "boundary problems." The Herod subpersonality within us may seem hospitable to the work, but when its preferences are challenged it will find a way to silence the voice of conscience. At every level it is useful to ask ourselves:

> - **Do you have qualities within yourself that could be called an "inner Herod?" (A part that rules one aspect of your life)**
> - **If you do, look within to see whether this part of you pays lip service to your conscience, but keeps it locked up so that nothing actually happens.**

PRACTICE

> - **What parts of you protect themselves against the challenges of inner growth? What do they protect—pleasures, privileges, self-esteem, reputation, self-image?**
> - **Do you ever side-step growth because of, or out of concern for, someone else?**

♦ ♦ ♦

Here is a significant point: Herod did not like John's challenging him, but still he listened to him, both wanting to grow and resisting growth. The inner conflict is beautifully illustrated in the story, as Herodias (a different, "feminine" aspect of the inner Herod— notice the same name with a changed gender) would have killed John, but Herod protects him, until Herodias finds the right stratagem to undermine Herod's will. The conscience is sacrificed to pleasure and pride, but the trigger is an apparent act of generosity (but one that tries to minimize or trivialize this exercise of raw, brutal power. John — the conscience — is served on a platter like a dessert). But even this point contains a flag for our attention. Historically, princesses did not customarily dance for guests, for this was a function ordinarily performed by professionals; and rulers do not usually grant virtually unlimited power to children. What else is happening in this vignette?

Maybe we have an "inner child" that is wounded, weak and needy. But a wounded inner child may express itself in ways that are vicious, selfish, provocative, and ultimately dangerous to us when we give unchecked power to these expressions. This may happen when other adult or spiritual parts of us are weak or confused and are manipulated by our child-needs (for love, approval, etc.), and as a result our mature judgment may be undermined and even our normal preferences may be overruled by pride, craving or some other inner influence.

The manipulations of a needy inner child can be seductive, yet the story suggests that, in addition to the manipulation of needs, it takes a kind of unnatural narcissism and inner lust to accumulate and

## ACTION AND REACTION

unleash the power to stifle our conscience; the boundaries between our inner functions may be crossed, even violated. We may find our will to reform, to grow, is eroded by seemingly benevolent, even noble impulses that are actually in the service of needs or cravings or demands that are not healthy—in the language of the story, "not lawful." And one such craving may lead us to another.

This Herod part of us, manipulated into a position of inner conflict, will give in when the going gets rough or the seductive power of needs is strong, and the voice of conscience may be stilled, at least for a while.

We notice that the death of John is placed in the story right in the middle of the account of the travels of the disciples. Why? Because it is precisely when our inner disciples are sent to work that the resistance to the Gospel process will intensify. Spiritual growth is *work*, and at times that work is experienced as conflict, and it may seem that the voice of conscience is extinguished. But even as Herod wonders whether Jesus is actually John raised from the dead, so within us, once the path of growth is taken, no avenue of growth is ended unless another is begun; no door is closed without another opening. And what is opened is much greater than what was closed.

> o **Do you have an inner "dancing princess," whose demands or allure may blind you to the existence of hidden desires, needs, cravings or rage?**
> o **How might the needs of your "inner children" cause you to lose or abandon your spiritual balance?**
> o **Have you ever shut your conscience down?**
> o **If so, why? What happened as a result?**

♦ ♦ ♦

> o **Come back to these questions whenever you find yourself regretting something you have done.**

## 15. SPIRITUAL RESOURCES

> ⁶:³⁰ And the disciples returned and gathered together around Jesus, and told him all that they had done and taught.[1] And he said to them, "Come away by yourselves to a deserted place and rest awhile." For many were coming and going, and they had no opportunity even to eat. And they went off in the boat to a deserted place by themselves. But many saw them going and recognized them, and they ran on foot from all the towns and got there ahead of them. As he went ashore, he saw a great crowd; and he had compassion on them because they were like sheep without a shepherd, and he began to teach them many things. When it grew late, his disciples came to him and said, "This place is deserted, and it is already very late. Send them away, so that they may go into the surrounding country and villages and buy themselves something to eat." But he said to them, "You give them something to eat." They say to him, "Are we to go buy two hundred denarii worth of bread and give it to them to eat?" But he says to them, "How many loaves have you? Go and see." And when they had found out, they say, "Five, and two fish." Then he told them all to sit down in groups on the green grass. So they sat down group by group, by hundreds and by fifties. And taking the five loaves and the two fish, he looked up to heaven, he blessed and broke the loaves, and gave them to his disciples to set before the people, and he divided the two fish among them all. And all ate and were filled. And they gathered twelve baskets full of leftover bread and fish. There were five thousand men who ate.

The opening door mentioned above is confirmed in the story as the disciples return from their travels to tell Jesus of what they have

---

[1] Note that now the disciples are not only healing, they are also teaching. What do they teach at this point?

done. He responds by telling them to rest, away and by themselves. Spiritual work is punctuated by periods of rest and re-integration. But again, in the story, the crowds press in upon them to such an extent that they cannot rest, or even eat. To get the rest and reflection that is needed they must get in a boat and leave—they must separate themselves and withdraw for a time from the work. This is what is needed within us: occasionally it is necessary to rest, to withdraw, to allow the results of our work to integrate with the rest of our lives.

In the story, however, the needy crowds do not leave them in peace. They run ahead to their "place of peace" and are waiting for them as they approach the shore. And so it is within us, that when one needy, wounded part of us senses that healing is possible, it may give us no peace until it gets what it needs. It may not be patient, or reasonable, or even considerate. It may "run ahead" of the healing process, which is perhaps why we may experience a "two steps forward—one step back" kind of progress as we go toward healing. It is not the disciples who respond, but Jesus himself—but this time he does not heal; rather, he teaches, he invites them to become involved and learn rather than to merely take what they want and leave. And the people respond— they stay and learn.

This part of the story reflects how parts of us may respond when we are in great need— on the one hand, we may just "want what we want" with no particular desire for anything greater. For some of us, some of the time, that will be the end of things. But, if we are willing, our hour of great need can be an opportunity to break through our neediness and learn. So we might welcome the times of inner need, and watch for when our need becomes so great that we will go to unusual lengths to get what we need. Awareness at such a time may be very difficult, as our need may nearly drown it or like the princess, seduce our will. But nevertheless, awareness is still possible, although we may likely need help to maintain it. If we watch and listen inwardly at such times, we may arrive at unique points of learning.

This vignette expands upon the lesson in the story of the woman with the issue of blood, for that section of the story suggested that desire and need combine to make us receptive to the work of the Spirit.

And then something unusual occurs in the story. The disciples suggest to Jesus that it's late, they are a long way from anywhere,

## SPIRITUAL RESOURCES

why doesn't he tell people to leave so that they can go get some food? He says, "You give them something to eat." And they answer, "with what?" And he says, in effect, "with the bread and fish that you yourselves were going to eat." They know this is very little, not enough to feed a crowd; but in the inner life the one can become the many.

The Spirit has given the disciples a brief rest, and now their learning is to be continued. On the inner level we are dealing with a community—some parts of us that are eager to grow, and some that are not; some parts that are relatively healthy and strong, and some parts that are hurt or afraid. We also have the Presence that is a fountainhead of peace and healing and joy. The inner disciples have few resources, but they do have some, that will not go very far by themselves. But when we bring those resources to the Spirit, they are multiplied. The lesson is in what to do with what we have— by themselves, our resources quickly run out; brought to the Spirit, they go as far as they are needed—and more.

This lesson is for each of us. When our intention is to feed the hungry, to heal the sick, to clothe the naked, to help the needy, we will come to the end of ourselves quickly. When we try to help ourselves we find ourselves distracted, frustrated, exhausted. The dedication to and invocation of the Higher Power in our lives does not magically make us stronger than we are, more patient than we are, more wise than we are. But it does open a connection to One who is ourselves and yet much more than ourselves, and power and wisdom begin to flow in ways that are beyond ordinary understanding.

We do not run out and spend all we have on bread and fish; we do not go and "get" more—rather, we take inventory of our resources, we bring the small amount we have to God, and then watch and help as people are fed. We take part in the process, but we do not "do it" ourselves. Needs are met, with a lot left over.

A miracle is one way that a story presents something that is not susceptible to the "normal" categories of human thought. Jesus, the miracle worker, represents in the story what is both essentially human and what is divine within us, combining categories that we normally keep separate, to demonstrate an experience that ordinary linear

PRACTICE

reasoning or logic cannot account for.[2] The purpose of this section of the story is not to induce us to "believe in miracles," but rather to invite us to act with faith, with utter conviction, with care, with generosity, with dedication, *with the Spirit*, feeding others and the "others" within ourselves, and being fed by the Spirit. The story is showing us that when we act in this way our resources will be multiplied and our best intentions will more than be fulfilled. Remember that Jesus told the disciples, "*You* give them something to eat," and in fact it is the disciples who pass out the food, not Jesus. Using the amplified resources made available by the Spirit, they can give the people something to eat. And so it is with us— the resources of our inner qualities are increased by the Spirit.

How can this happen? We do not literally bring a loaf and a fish to Jesus. Our inner resources might be things like an ability to do something, a memory of something, a knowledge of something, a connection, an awareness, a desire, a relationship, an idea, an intuition, a feeling. Getting our resources oriented to the Spirit allows the power of the All in All to flow through them.[3]

> - **What are some examples in your life of resources being multiplied?**
> - **What are your "inner bread and fish?" What resources are available within yourself that the Spirit of God may use to nourish the needy, both within you and outside of you?**
> - **When you see a need, where do you go first to get help? To your thoughts, to prayer, to a book, to a friend, to God?**
> - **How can you bring the resources you have to the Spirit?**

---

[2] Classic logical categories of contradiction and identity are both poured into a creative soup here, for the bread and fish are what they are, and yet they are more. In the inner life such creativity is always possible and Jesus is demonstrating how it flows.

[3] This book is itself an example of resources being multiplied.

## SPIRITUAL RESOURCES

- What does this— bringing your resources to the Spirit— mean to *you*? What is your own way of doing this?
- Does it take time for your inner resources to be multiplied? What is your part in the process?
- Does bringing your bread and fish to the Spirit change how you do things?

♦ ♦ ♦

- Come back to these questions whenever it seems that you have "too much to do," or when it seems that what you desire is impossible.

♦ ♦ ♦

# 16. CROSSING BOUNDARIES: REALITY AND THE MIND

> **6:45** And immediately he had his disciples get into the boat and go on ahead to the other side to Bethsaida, while he dismissed the crowd. After saying farewell to them, he went up on the mountain to pray. And when evening came, the boat was out in the middle of the sea and he was alone on the land. And he saw that they struggled to row, for the wind was against them. Before dawn he comes toward them, walking on the sea, and would have passed by them. But when they saw him walking on the sea, they thought it was a ghost and they cried out, for they all saw him and were terrified.

Why would he have passed by them? The disciples are being trained in spiritual discernment. He is close enough for them to see him— if they are able. It is the darkest hour of the night. If they do not see him, he will pass by. But what happens? They do see him, but misinterpret what they see— "a ghost!" So this vignette represents a stage in their learning in which they are to understand that their own mental baggage will color and maybe distort their perceptions: even a direct perception of spiritual truth may be misinterpreted. This tells *us* also that as we progress in the spirit, we will discern more, perceive more— but at this stage we may not be able to understand what we see. We may get things so mixed up as to confuse the living for the dead. As they learn more, their ability to interpret will become more accurate, and so it is with us.

> o  **Have you ever experienced a strange perception or feeling, an incredible "coincidence," or an uncanny occurrence that made you wonder? How did you "explain" what happened? Could the reality of the situation have been something greater than you supposed?**

PRACTICE

> 6:50b But immediately he spoke to them, saying, "Take heart, it is I;[1] do not be afraid." And he got into the boat with them and the wind ceased. And they were utterly astounded, for they had not understood about the loaves, but their hearts were hardened.

We have encountered an episode of particular spiritual significance, as "immediately" Jesus sends his disciples to "the other side" by boat while he himself withdraws to the mountain to pray. Why? The Spirit has just finished a mighty work that we, as readers, easily recognize as something unusual, even miraculous. But did the *disciples* recognize the full significance of what has just occurred? Probably not at the time, perhaps because they were perhaps too busy handing out bread and fish to thousands of people to stop and watch to see what exactly was happening. The story tells us that we too may fail to recognize the significance of some events in our lives unless we are alerted to their meaning.

Again, we are dealing with inner characteristics, and there are times when things go better than we expect them to. And so to drive home the point one notch closer to understanding, he separates from them and sends them away.

> o **What does "the other side" mean to you? Does it mean different things at different times?**
> o **Why are the disciples sent there?**
> o **Why might you be sent there? How might this happen, practically, in your own life?**

♦ ♦ ♦

---
[1] Or, literally, "*I am.*" This is a kind of formula, a phrase that is used elsewhere only in verses 13:10 and 14:22. The phrase "I am" recalls the passage in Exodus 3:14 when God gives this name: "I am that I am."

The Spirit continually sends us out "on our own," for its teaching is meant to build up our spiritual strength and abilities. On rough water at the darkest hour of night, they are having a very hard time getting on, and the wind is against them. Jesus crosses effortlessly, walking on water as if it were land, not hindered by the storm that opposes *them*, but not him.

The disciple parts of us are accustomed to walk on dry land, accustomed to living with the clear contours of "outer" life, the life that perceives with the senses. They get into the boat onto water, but the waters of the inner life are not their native element, and they are at the mercy of forces beyond their control. Jesus represents the Spirit who moves freely through all the levels of our lives, inner and outer, day and night. The disciples do not understand this, and when they see him they mistake him for an apparition and are afraid. A ghost is an "entity" whose very existence seems to be in violation of our mental categories, in which ground and water, life and death, waking and sleeping, are segregated and understood to be opposites. In feeding the five thousand, Jesus has crossed the boundaries of our waking logical categories, and here he does so again, calming the storm as he gets into the boat with his disciples—who are afraid, amazed, and do not understand. They also do not notice that they are *seeing* clearly in the darkest hour of the night! But as we noted above, there is a difference between seeing and right understanding.

We saw earlier how people came to Jesus to be healed, how they were willing to tell what had happened without really understanding what had happened to them or who they were dealing with. Here we see that the inner parts of us, those most eager to follow the spiritual path, may repeatedly witness miracles of spiritual work, and still be lost in fear and amazement, failing to understand. Parts of us may feel the presence of the Spirit, but they are sometimes not encouraged by it, but instead are frightened because the boundaries between our mental categories have been crossed.

Seemingly miraculous events have not been documented by repeatable, verifiable experiments performed by scientists in our times, yet the "anecdotal evidence" for such events is nearly ubiquitous and has been reported on all continents, in all cultures and in all historical eras. Some people would like attribute these

PRACTICE

occurrences to the ubiquity of wishful thinking, but many such occurrences have been reported by very scrupulously honest, conscientious people. Because a scientist cannot measure an effect does not mean that there *is* no effect. Quantum physics has shown that there are distinct limits to what can be measured. A scientist cannot measure "love" or "hate" or "respect" or "fear," yet the seemingly miraculous transformation of hate into love has occurred in numerous people. Phenomena whose characteristics apparently defy currently accepted theories of science abound and have been reported in books, journals and scientific papers, but the prevailing attitudes of established thinkers has consistently been to dismiss "inconvenient" evidence — that does not conform to current theories. Pioneers of thought and understanding, both religious and scientific, have always found their breakthroughs in "marginal" or "exceptional" phenomena— in events that defy current understanding. Such pioneers are often ridiculed or attacked by the mental and spiritual gatekeepers of their times. It was true of Jesus as it was true of Copernicus and Galileo, and it is true also of the "new biology" and the "new physics" that are creating bridges between scientific and spiritual thought. What contemporary thought labels as "impossible" is usually something not yet understood. Jesus was not in the business of "hawking" miracles. Rather he was demonstrating the results of a way of life.[2]

Activity on a non-physical level (what some people call "supernatural power") was commonly accepted by people and "driving out demons" was within the spiritual vocabulary of the times when this story was written. This was an activity well within the accepted framework of the "warfare between good and evil" (although I believe that the neighborhood exorcist's activities were not the same as what Jesus does in the Gospel story). Much as people loved and appreciated the healings, they did not "marvel" about them because, for them, no boundaries of mental categories were crossed. It is we, the readers, who are shown that the actions of Jesus are miraculous. When we embark on the spiritual path, following the Holy Spirit,

---

[2] To explore the areas of religious "phenomena" more, I suggest William James' *The Varieties of Religious Experience:* New York, New American Library, 1956 as a starting place. James looks at spiritual phenomena from the outside, whereas the Gospel looks at them from the inside.

amazing things begin to occur in our outer and inner lives. In our inner lives we may find that what seems to be miraculous can happen all the time, and the Gospel is a training ground for us to learn to turn inner miracles into facts of life.

I interpret the sea to represent our inner mind. Jesus and the disciples at various times cross from one "side" to the other. The particular characteristics of the "sides" of our minds will vary from person to person, but certain challenges will confront many of us—inner storms, conflicts, the violence of wounded subpersonalities, the resistance of spiritual gatekeepers, the presumption of the commanding ego.[3]

The Spirit within us taps into the life and power of our spiritual Source, which lies at the root of our being. It is that power that is able to calm inner storms, because once that power is "recognized" and received by the other parts of ourselves, it simply renders conflict insignificant. The power of the Spirit takes the conflict out of our lives in the same way that light "removes" darkness— it does not negate or suppress real issues, but rather *adds* the element of "light," of indescribable love and peace to *both or all* sides of an issue, making resolution possible, indeed almost inevitable. The Spirit does not take sides in inner or outer warfare, but in love — and with love— it overcomes the *impulses* to warfare.

So the boat in which the disciples sail may represent our attention, which crosses from one side of the mind's experience to another. When the Spirit of the Higher Self (not "my" self, but Jesus represents a greater Self who is both within us and transcends us— a transpersonal Self) is received into this boat, the element of conflict is simply gone. Peace and clarity make choices and positive action possible. However, at this stage of growth we are still unlikely to understand what is truly happening, and we will be amazed when we

---

[3] I am not using a psychological technical term here. I use the word "ego" loosely as a term to describe that part of ourselves which is, at any given time, calls itself "me" and is in overall control of our outward functioning and our surface awareness—sort of like the person in the driver's seat of a car. There may be several "people" in the car, but at any time only one is the driver. But the "ego," like some drivers, may not pay attention to where other "inner travelers" need or want to go, and sometimes one of the other travelers "grabs the wheel," and we are amazed at how a person may seem to change when this happens.

## PRACTICE

have such moments of peace and clarity, not knowing where they come from and not being able to experience them consistently or at will. But when we do experience them, healing will occur at one level or another.

♦ ♦ ♦

> - Allow your awareness to move from your thoughts to the physical sensations in your body, your arm for example. What is the difference in your awareness when you move it like this?
> - Try moving your awareness to a person, then to a memory, then to an emotion, then to a thought, then to an intuition. Now allow yourself to hold all of these things together in your awareness, not focusing on any one thing, but being aware of all.
> - Then allow your attention to withdraw a little from all those "things," and picture it sort of sitting off by itself for a moment, away from everything, being "attentive" but not "doing" anything, anywhere. What does this feel like?
> - What different levels of awareness can you discern in your own life? For example, mental awareness, or emotional awareness, or physical awareness, or others that are appropriate for you. What do you call these levels?
> - Examine how your attention travels not only from one object to another, but also from one level to another.

# 17. THINGS OF THE HEART

> ⁶:⁵³ And having crossed over, they came to land at Gennesaret and moored the boat. And when they got out of the boat, people immediately recognized him and rushed about the whole region, and began to bring the sick on mats to wherever they heard he was. And wherever he was going, into villages or cities, into fields or in the markets, they brought the sick and begged him that they might touch even the fringe of his clothes, and all who touched him were healed.

The story here tells us that something important has changed: now, unlike the episode with the woman with the flow of blood, "all who touched him were healed." Not *some*, not only the believers, not only those who followed him—*no one* was excluded. All were healed. This is an important thing to remember, for our tendency to judge what is right from wrong, worthy from unworthy, and good from bad might suggest to some of us that the "wrong," the "unworthy," or the "bad" ones are not eligible for healing. The story says explicitly that *all* people who touched him, even in the slightest way, were healed. Our interpretation sees that all parts of all people will be healed by the Spirit, who abides in each of us.

> ⁷:¹ And the Pharisees and some of the scribes who had come from Jerusalem gathered around him. They noticed that some of his disciples ate bread with unclean— that is, unwashed— hands. For the Pharisees and all the Judeans[1]

---

[1] I translate the word as "Judeans," not "Jews," for the way the Gospel has been written suggests that the writer and many people in the story distinguished Judeans (residents of Judea) from Galileans, but it is not evident to me that he classes them all together as "Jews." For middle eastern people, ethnicity was local. Jesus, in this view, was *not* a Judean but a Galilean. Romans like Pilate, however, did view their conquered peoples in terms of overall class and ethnicity based upon their own political divisions, so we use the word "Jews" later in translating his words to suggest that he lumped all the "Jewish" people in a single group.

## THINGS OF THE HEART

do not eat unless they wash their hands,[64] keeping the traditions of the elders; and they do not eat anything from the market unless they wash it; and there are many other traditions that they observe, the washing of cups and pots and copper vessels. And the Pharisees and the scribes ask him, "Why do your disciples not walk by the tradition of the elders, but eat with unclean hands?" He said to them, "Isaiah prophesied rightly about you hypocrites, as it is written, 'This people honors me with their lips, but their hearts are far from me; in vain do they worship me, teaching the commands of men as learning.' Having abandoned the command of God, you keep the tradition of men." And he said to them, "How nicely you set aside the commandment of God so that your tradition may be kept. For Moses said, 'Honor your father and your mother,' and 'Whoever speaks evil of father or mother —let him die.' But you say that if anyone tells father or mother, 'Whatever support you might have received from me is Korban, (that is, an offering [to the temple])' then you allow him to do nothing for the father or the mother—invalidating the word of God through your tradition that you have handed on. And you do many things like this." Then he called the crowd again, and said to them, "Hear me, all of you, and understand: there is nothing outside of a person that can defile them by entering; but what comes out of a person, these are what defile a person. Those with ears to hear, let them hear." And when he had left the crowd and entered the house, his disciples asked him about the parable. And he says to them, "Are you also uncomprehending? Do you not see that whatever goes into a person cannot defile them, because it does not enter the heart but the stomach,

---

[2] Literally, wash their hands with the fist— rubbing one hand with the fist of the other hand

> and goes out into the sewer?" (Thus he declared all foods clean.) He said, "What comes out of a person is what defiles. From within, from the human heart, come evil intentions, sexual immorality, theft, murder, adultery, greed, wickedness, deceit, debauchery, envy,[3] slander,[4] pride, foolishness. All these evil things come out from within a person, and they defile a person."

We are again in different "territory," for Jesus and his disciples are here confronted at their meal (spiritual nourishment) by the spiritual gatekeepers, the scribes and Pharisees. It is a fair assumption that some of Jesus' disciples were not Judeans or possibly even Israelites (recall that Philip and Andrew are Greek names). At any rate, some of his followers do not follow current Judean traditions of hand-washing, purification of implements, and so on. The spiritual gatekeepers challenge Jesus because he does not require uniformity of practice by his followers, because he does not attend to the outward rituals and preparations of the disciples. Jesus is teaching *us* directly when he says, "Hear me, all of you, and understand: there is nothing outside of a person that can defile by entering; but what comes out of a person, these are what defile a person." He is presenting a fundamental distinction that is basic to spiritual life. Sacredness, holiness, goodness, purity are not connected to what we are exposed to, which comes into us from outside; for if they were, our basic spiritual attitude would be defensive and our response to exposure would be fear. But Jesus constantly tells us, "Fear not." Sacredness, goodness, holiness are connected to our inner source, to what comes out of us, and therefore our attitude is assertive and affirmative, and our response to exposure is love.

♦ ♦ ♦

---

[3] Literally "evil eye"
[4] Literally "blasphemy"

## THINGS OF THE HEART

The spiritual gatekeepers are concerned with their own purity, which they define, at least in part, as a successful defense against exposure to what is alien, wrong, illegal, "unclean," immoral, unauthorized, or indecent. Their ritual purifications are their defense against this exposure. It is significant that Jesus chooses as an example the traditions and laws revolving around the treatment of parents. Our parents gave us our first food, both spiritual and physical. Our natural response to them is gratitude — thus the biblical commandment; yet Jesus shows that the Korban tradition was used to nullify both natural response and commandment, creating a dichotomy where there was none— creating a response of ingratitude in the name of God, which is the hypocrisy he speaks of.

- **Notice how you react to the events and circumstances that influence you from outside yourself.**
- **Reflect on something negative or unfavorable or upsetting that has happened to you today, or this week; see how you have reacted— defensively, angrily, mechanically, resignedly, deliberately, lovingly?**
- **In what ways can you respond to what happens in your life without allowing outside influences to *control* your response?**
- **In yourself, observe the difference between when you *react* to something automatically, and when you *respond* to something deliberately out of choice. Which types of events or people cause you to either respond or react? When do reacting and responding produce the same results for you? When do they produce different results?**
- **When your automatic reactions produce the same behavior as your deliberate choice responses, what does this tell you about yourself? When the reactions are different from your choice responses, what does this tell you?**

PRACTICE

He shows that some widely accepted spiritual traditions may work to create a false opposition between spiritual needs and worldly needs. He makes it clear that attending to spiritual requirements is not a reason to neglect worldly requirements.

♦ ♦ ♦

> o  Can you think of a situation in which, for you, the practical or worldly requirements of the situation have seemed to be opposed to spiritual requirements?
> o  How does Jesus' teaching speak to you in this situation?

♦ ♦ ♦

Here is an important lesson for all of us who walk the spiritual path: no genuine commandment of God sets up false oppositions between genuine spiritual needs and genuine worldly needs. Only a "tradition of men" will create such dichotomies and demand that we choose between them. Such choices truncate our experience, limit our vision, and separate us from what is vital to our lives.

Jesus is making it clear that what is vital in our lives has everything to do with the choices we make, and *where* we make our choices— whatever physically goes into us cannot defile us,[5] for whatever goes into the body just comes out again. The best example of this is food, which provides nourishment and passes on. Food, he says, does not enter the heart. What, then, *does* enter the heart? For this is where the issues of holiness, goodness and sacredness are resolved. *Out* of the heart, he says, come the evil things that defile us. And out of the heart also come things that show that we are healed.

---

[5] The Greek word that is translated as "defile" means "to make unclean." We discussed this in Section 4, pages 57-67.

## THINGS OF THE HEART

What we "take to heart" matters, for what we take in at this level is also what comes out of us as ideas, feelings, behavior, relationships. We cannot always choose what we are exposed to, but we can choose how we *respond* to what we are exposed to. Jesus' teaching about food is no different from his teaching about other people, or about parts of ourselves. There are no foods, no people, no parts of ourselves that are "unclean," or to be shunned, or are inferior, or evil *in themselves*.[6] It is important that we approach ourselves, things and other people with life-supporting, life-sustaining attitudes, for these are the essence of holiness, goodness, sacredness: restraint, self-control, generosity, honesty, respect, support, encouragement, modesty, wisdom, compassion, love.

Even if we must avoid something or someone, we may do so with respect, compassion and blessing. Our attitudes toward "inner" exposure are as important as toward "outer" exposure. We may discover a part of ourselves that is filled with malice, hatred, bitterness, envy, greed, or some other quality that Jesus lists as "defiling." It is important that we approach these inner subpersonalities with the same life-supporting, forgiving attitudes that we use to respond to other people, for these are the attitudes that heal. Jesus makes it clear that here is where the challenge is—to "cleanse" (heal) the inner person is the first work to be done; not with fear, but with faith; not with artificial discriminations, but with inclusive responsiveness.

We may notice that the defensive attitude that we adopt to protect ourselves from what we see as wrong, harmful or "defiling" is itself a two-sided thing. The inner wall that we erect to keep out

---

[6] This is not a suggestion that anything and everything is "all right." There are things that we must not eat because they are harmful to us. The behavior of parts of ourselves, as well as that of other people, can be harmful. We may avoid something that is harmful to us without believing it to be evil *in itself*. For example, I now must avoid drinking coffee (which I used to love); it now does unpleasant things to my metabolism. I also have to avoid music played above a certain volume level, because a band's loudspeakers caused damage to my ears many years ago. Each of us will discover that some things are good for us, some things are not; some are good now but not always; some are harmful to me but not to others. This is different from things being good or evil *in themselves*.

## PRACTICE

harm may also keep out love and healing.[7] The Pharisees demonstrate this repeatedly, rejecting Jesus on "defensive" grounds.

---

- Who are some people you avoid?
- What are some ideas or practices you keep out of your life?
- What is something that makes you angry or disgusted?
- What do you do to keep yourself true, or faithful, or on the right path?
- How do you usually treat people who are not true, not faithful, or "wrong?"
- How do you react to yourself when you do wrong, do something foolish or "stupid," or when you discover that you have done something against your own beliefs or principles?
- What are some attitudes, beliefs and behaviors that can enable you to live with compassion for others and for yourself?
- What are things you can take to heart—ideas, proverbs, stories, practices—that can help you to live compassionately?

- Come back to this section and to these questions whenever you struggle with error, opposition, difference of opinion or harmful behavior in yourself or in others.

---

[7] In *The Biology of Belief* (New York: Hay House, 2008) Bruce H. Lipton, Ph.D. shows us an intriguing analogy to this in the activity of living cells. He shows us that a cell cannot grow (move, eat, etc.) and defend itself at the same time. The cell must close up to defend itself, but then it cannot eat or dispose of waste material. It must open itself to grow, and then it must become vulnerable.

## 18. LOVING "THE OTHER," THE ALIEN

PRACTICE

> 7:24 And he stood up, and went from there to the region of Tyre. He entered a house and wanted no one to know, but he could not escape notice. And immediately a woman, whose daughter had an unclean spirit, heard of him and came and fell down at his feet. Now the woman was a Greek,[1] a Syrophoenicean by birth. She begged him to cast the demon out of her daughter. He said to her, "Let the children be fed first, for it is not good to take the children's bread and throw it to the little dogs." But she answered and said to him, "Master, even the little dogs under the table eat the small crumbs of babies." And he said to her, "Through this word the demon has left your daughter; go home." And she went home and found the child lying in bed, and the demon gone.

This vignette illuminates for us part of what Jesus (and what the writer of the Gospel) means by "the word." The gentile woman has spoken "the word" through which the demon has left her daughter. She has spoken in the power of her faith *to* Jesus, begging *insistently* that her daughter be healed. Jesus responds, telling her that indeed "through this word" power has flowed and her daughter is well. "The Word," then, can come from or through anyone—even an "unbelieving foreigner"—for the love of God can come through or to any person, and is available to all.

In this episode of the story Jesus literally leaves the country in order to rest from his work. He goes to Tyre to be alone, to walk for a time and not be recognized, for wherever he is seen he is besieged with people. But even here he is recognized, and a Syrophoenicean woman begs him to heal her daughter. His response may seem arrogant, exclusive, or even cruel at first reading. However, an inner interpretation of his words yields some light. Sometimes a spiritual teacher may "insult" a student to test the student's desire for learning and healing. If the student's hurt feelings are stronger than his

---

[1] "Greek" was a term often used to indicate anyone who was non-Hebrew.

## LOVING "THE OTHER"

or her desire to learn, then perhaps the learning will stop for a time. But if the need for growth and healing is great, the student will not allow her or his hurt feelings to stand in the way, and the purpose will be met. Some barriers to freedom must be removed, and some must be broken through.

This section is a continuation of the lesson presented in the previous section. Some people who live "defensively" not only avoid certain foods, but also believe that some people are to be shunned because of race, religion, political affiliation, nationality, or some other pretext. Sometimes people who are victims of such ill treatment begin after time to accept it as "normal," and even expect it. Jesus offers her the words of condescension that she may have come to expect, to see whether she will break through the barrier of lowered expectations.

From the standpoint of the story, the woman is a foreigner and probably an "unbeliever." But she does believe that Jesus can heal her daughter and presses on to receive what she needs. There are parts of ourselves that may be so "alienated" from our dominant personality that they are never seen or felt in our ordinary lives, and they may be like a person living in a foreign country; for example, a meek childhood subpersonality that has been set completely aside in the mind of a hard-driving businessman. The Spirit will take us to unusual states of consciousness in order to allow such voices to be heard and we may find ourselves intensely disliking what may emerge at such times, responding with disdain, scorn, hatred, anger at this voice within us; saying, in effect, "healing and growth are for the spiritual parts of me! I don't want anything to do with this other stuff. Get away from me!" The story is encouraging us — encouraging the disliked, alien, foreign, unlikable parts of us — to press on, to come forward and claim the healing. In the process the story is implicitly telling us to open ourselves to these experiences, because healing is for all.

- **In a quiet moment, ask yourself, "what part of myself do I like least?**
- **Ask, "What part of myself or my life do I prefer not to acknowledge? What part do I not accept?"**

PRACTICE

- What happens if you allow that part of you to have a voice (but not control) in your life?
- What does it need? What kind of healing does it require for you to be whole?

♦ ♦ ♦

- Come back to this section and these questions whenever you feel inferior in some way, or like an "outsider," or if you notice an impulse of non-acceptance or condemnation within you.
- Come back to this section if you notice an impulse or inner voice that protests or does not accept your own usual attitudes or thoughts.

## 19. HEALING IS A BEGINNING

## PRACTICE

> ⁷:³¹ Then he left the region of Tyre, and went through Sidon to the Sea of Galilee in the middle of the region of the Decapolis. And they bring to him a man who was deaf and could hardly speak, and they begged him to lay his hand on him. He took him off by himself, away from the crowd, and put his fingers into his ears, and he spat and touched his tongue. And looking up to heaven, he murmured a prayer, and says to him, "Ephphatha!"—that is, "Be opened!"—and immediately his ears were opened, his tongue was released, and he spoke plainly. And he commanded them to tell no one; but the more he commanded them, the more zealously they were proclaiming it. And they were astonished beyond measure, saying, "Everything he does is wonderful! He even makes the deaf hear and the mute speak!"

This vignette brings Jesus into contact with a person who is closed up—he cannot hear or speak normally. Jesus' response to the man is a demonstration that the Spirit responds to us in a flexible way that meets us where we are, for Jesus takes the man aside where he can communicate with him one to one. How does one communicate with a deaf mute? — with touch, gestures, signs and pantomime. Jesus is, again, interested in communicating, and the work of the Spirit within us will adapt to break through our closedness and deafness in a way that we can understand.

Again Jesus charges the healed one to tell no one, but the more he commands them the more zealously they proclaim—speaking with the healed tongue—but not really knowing what they are talking about. Their ears are opened, but they do not listen to what he has said. The voice is healed, yet it is used to disobey the healer. The excitement is so great that understanding and obedience are pushed aside. This kind of scenario is repeated in the Gospel for a reason— for within us, we believe that we *know* something when we have experienced a healing or some other significant progress in our lives. The Gospel story is repeatedly urging restraint and self-control, and showing us that it is not unusual or unlikely that many of us will fail in this way repeatedly. Our amazement and excitement may get the better of us, more than once.

This vignette illustrates what we noted earlier: that a "healing" is only the beginning of a process, not the end— for if healed ears do not listen and healed voices speak in disobedience to the healer, we can see that the real healing has only begun. The healed person has much to learn and to practice before the healing is complete.

> - **Is there an impulse in you that sometimes "doesn't want to hear" something?**
> - **What is the difference between "not wanting to hear" and listening but not responding or agreeing?**

♦ ♦ ♦

> - **What is to be learned or practiced <u>after</u> a healing?**

♦ ♦ ♦

## 20. SPIRITUAL RESOURCES, PART 2

## SPIRITUAL RESOURCES

> 8:1 In those days, when again a great crowd had gathered, and they had nothing to eat, having called his disciples he says to them, "I have compassion for the crowd, because they have been with me now for three days and have nothing to eat. If I send them away hungry to their homes, they will collapse on the way—and some of them have come a long way." And his disciples answered him, "How can one feed these people bread here in the desert?" And he asked them, "How many loaves do you have?" They said, "Seven." And he commanded the crowd to sit on the ground, and he took the seven loaves and after giving thanks, he broke them and gave them to the disciples to distribute; and they passed them out to the people. And they also had a few small fish, and after blessing them he told them to distribute these also. And they ate and were filled; and they took up the broken pieces, seven baskets full. There were about four thousand people, and he sent them away.

We are approaching the climax of the story. This section begins in the place we have been walking, and rises to a new level for a revelation that changes everything. At the beginning of this section we again see Jesus feeding a multitude of people from what seem to be few earthly resources. But notice the differences: they are in the desert, and the people have been with him for days. Not only the disciples, but many others also are spending extended periods of time with Jesus. In the inner interpretation this scene is describing a person whose life is changing, who has left behind certain worldly preoccupations for a time in order to follow the Spirit, and the story suggests that the Spirit provides nourishment in the desert—which represents our inner landscape after we have left the comfortable environment of our established ideas, habits, associations and desires. We find in the story that spiritual nourishment is followed by physical nourishment, even though few physical resources seem to be available. We see again that physical health and well-being are a *spiritual* concern, as Jesus follows his teaching with attention to

PRACTICE

physical needs. Again we find the alternation of focus, with the story showing the necessity of balance between our spiritual and physical needs.

As before, the power of the Spirit breaks through the boundaries of our mental categories and magnifies our resources in a way that can only seem miraculous by the logic of physical, outer existence.

> ○ **In what way does your spiritual practice include physical practice?**
> ○ **How do your spiritual beliefs include attention to physical health and well being?**
> ○ **Are these two areas balanced in your life? If not, what might you do to bring them into balance?**

◆ ◆ ◆

> 8:10b And immediately he got into the boat with his disciples, and went to the district of Dalmanutha. And the Pharisees came and began to argue with him, seeking from him a sign from heaven, to test him. And sighing deeply in his Spirit he says, "Why does this generation seek a sign? Truly I say to you, no sign shall be given to this generation."

Although the last vignette occurred in the desert, they were spiritually "by the sea," for they have *immediately* gotten into the boat and crossed over. In the "inner landscape" each region is not far from the others. This interruption is interestingly placed right after the miraculous feeding of the four thousand, as Jesus is accosted by Pharisees seeking from him a "sign from heaven." He answers that no such sign will be given. His disciples and others must hear

## SPIRITUAL RESOURCES

this, and we see that Jesus does *not* regard the feeding of the multitude as such a sign, but as the practical results of faith. No "sign" will be given— Jesus *acts*; he does not give "signs."

What are the Pharisees seeking when they ask for "a sign?" They do not trust in their own experience, much less the experience of others. They need validation from beyond their own experience, something "out there" like a "sign from heaven," but as Jesus tells them, no such validation will be given to them. The only validation they will get must come from their experience—but when that happens (because the presence of Jesus is its own validation) the Pharisees do not recognize it for what it is.[1]

> o **What kind of "proof" or validation do you need in order to believe something? Some people of faith look for confirmation in everyday events, while some scientifically-minded people require a more rigorous kind of evidence. How much validation can you accept from your own experience, and how much confirmation from the experience or agreement of others do you need?**

♦ ♦ ♦

> 8:13 And he left them, and getting into the boat again, he went across to the other side. And they forgot to bring

---

[1] This response seems to be not unlike that of some modern skeptics whose idea of scientific validity requires a particular theoretical presentation and experimental repeatability in order for a concept or procedure to qualify for acceptance, and who will cheerfully debunk anything less as "pseudo-science" even if credible evidence exists that the concept or procedure has produced undeniable results in a practical context. Such skeptics' demand for theory is similar to the Pharisees' demands for "signs"— they are both more interested in "rightness" than in results.

PRACTICE

> bread, and except for one loaf they had none with them in the boat. And he cautioned them, saying, "Watch! Beware of the yeast of the Pharisees, and the yeast of Herod!" And they questioned one another, saying, "It's because we have no bread." And knowing this, he says to them, "Why do you say you have no bread? Do you not yet perceive or understand? Are your hearts hardened? Do you have eyes but do not see, or ears but do not hear? And do you not remember? When I broke the five loaves for the five thousand, how many baskets full of broken pieces did you gather?" They say to him, "Twelve." "And the seven for the four thousand, how many baskets full of broken pieces did you gather?" And they said to him, "Seven." And he said to them, "Do you still not understand?"

In the path of change, we cannot always retain what we have learned, nor do we always realize the significance of what we have done or not done (and somewhere within us, we may not *want* to understand). So it is here— the four thousand have been fed and there were seven baskets of leftovers, yet the disciples leave it all behind in their eagerness to follow, and find themselves in the boat with only one loaf. Jesus tells them to beware of the yeast of the spiritual gatekeepers (Pharisees), or of those who live for worldly things (Herodians), in effect telling them that people who teach fear or greed, even in the name of God, will cause them problems.

Why does he say this *now*? And this is just what the disciples ask themselves. They realize that they have forgotten to take the bread and fish with them, they have only one loaf between them, and they think that Jesus is rebuking them for forgetting. But he *now* rebukes them, not for forgetting the bread, but for forgetting something much more important. In their response to Jesus they have fallen into a mindset of fear and scarcity— the very teachings (bread) of the Pharisees and the Herodians, made to "rise" by a spiritual "yeast" that seems to make it increase. The yeast (the hidden catalyst) of the Pharisees and the Herodians is fear.

## SPIRITUAL RESOURCES

Pharisees teach holiness and "rightness" as an avoidance of sin, impurity or wrongdoing, while the Herodians teach prosperity as an avoidance of disease and poverty. These negative "shadow" sides are essential to the teachings of each group. Jesus realizes that when we do not fully understand the work of the Spirit, we forget; and when we forget, we "tilt" almost imperceptibly through fear into considerations of scarcity and self-defense.

He says to them, Remember! Twice we have been without resources, and twice we have obtained enough to feed thousands with baskets of leftovers! Twice you were going to go outside to get what you needed, and I took what you already had and exceeded your needs. *This* is what you need to remember: this walk is not about doing *well* (the way of the Herodians) or about doing *right* (the way of the Pharisees), but about faith, and reliance upon power that is available to you through me.

Jesus is leading the disciples into a fuller awareness of reality. For them, bread is something to buy, to get, to obtain, to keep. If they forget it, it is lost to them, left behind. Jesus is turning their attention to the direction and source of power— not from things, but from the Spirit; not from outside, but from inside. It is *with* them, in the boat!

---

- When you find yourself in physical want or need, where do you go for help? Do you rely on the Spirit in your quest, or only on your material resources?
- What is the relationship between spiritual power and physical resources in your own life?
- Do you maintain an awareness of this relationship, or do you need to be reminded?
- How is spiritual power translated into physical reality for you?
- What is the difference between being fed from the power of the spirit and being focused on "getting things" using spiritual power?

♦ ♦ ♦

PRACTICE

Implicitly, we again begin to feel the rise of the question, "Who *is* this?" but before Jesus makes the question explicit, we have a short vignette inserted to illustrate what has just occurred.

> 8:22 And they come to Bethsaida. And they bring a blind man to him and beg him to touch him. He took the blind man by the hand and led him out of the village, and when he had spit into his eyes and laid his hands on him, he asked him, "Do you see anything?" And he looked up and said, "I see people, but they look like trees walking around." Then he laid his hands on his eyes again, and his eyes focused and he was restored, and he saw everything clearly. And he sent him home, saying, "Do not even enter the village."

Jesus not only touches the man, he takes him by the hand and leads him completely away, out of the village. Jesus works on him (saliva was considered to have curative properties), but the man sees only dimly. After the second laying on of hands, he sees everything clearly. Healing and restoration is a cooperative process; not all healings are "one-touch" affairs. The disciples of Jesus do not seek physical healing, but to *see* all things clearly—yet after repeated demonstrations of the power of the Spirit and the power of faith, they see only dimly. When Jesus warned them of spiritual error, they look to their material resources, answering "we have no bread." There is a confusion of levels— there is a relationship between what is spiritual and what is material, but the disciples do not yet understand how it works. The blind man in this vignette is standing in for the disciples in the reader's eyes, seeing only dimly at first touch, but finally being restored.

When he is restored, Jesus sends him home but tells him not to go to the village from whence he has come, where he is sure to be drawn into speculation and excitement that follows upon such a healing. He may see with his eyes, but like the disciples he still does not understand.

SPIRITUAL RESOURCES

♦ ♦ ♦

> o What can you do to maintain your focus on your heart, on the power that comes out of you from the Spirit?
> o What is something you can do to acknowledge that power, and to align your own will with it? I invite you to choose to do something specific for this acknowledgement, today or this week.

♦ ♦ ♦

> o Come back to this section and to these questions whenever you feel lacking in resources, unsuccessful in your endeavors, or off-track in your spiritual walk.

♦ ♦ ♦

*WALKING OUT THE GOSPEL: TO EXPLORE THIS FURTHER, DO EXERCISE 12 IN PART III, PAGE 417.*

# NOTES

# REALIZATION

We have arrived at a watershed in the Gospel. Things begin to move in a different direction from here on. From the inner perspective we have seen that some preparation of mind, body and attitude has been needed, and then we have needed to turn our focus toward qualities that serve the Spirit, which are gathered in support of the work of transformation. In the course of this gathering we may have had to confront inner or outer dis-ease, sabotage, resistance, and skepticism. We began to understand that faith is at the center of the work, and that faith works miracles within us that can be translated into fact. Yet we are still prone to interpret the changes from a material point of view, forgetting the power of the Spirit in an automatic reaction of fear over doing well or doing right. We have begun to practice reliance on the Spirit, and we have also been aware that some inner need or greed can still work to quash conscience and stop the transformation. We have begun to change our focus to what is validated by our experience, yet we are still prone to see "dimly" and need help to stay on the path.

There has been a work going on in us, and while we have focused on our own actions, beliefs and attitudes, we have been taught by a power greater than ourselves. Now it is time to confront directly the question, "Who is this, *really?*" for we need a greater understanding of the life-context in which our transformation is to take place. We will realize Who is behind the changes in our lives. Yet we will find that with this new understanding come new tests and temptations, new ways in which understanding must be honed, clarified, focused, put into faith and action.

We will take the next steps in the education of our faith and use of power. This part begins with Mark 8:27 and goes as far as Mark 10:52.

## 21. WHO IS THIS, *REALLY?*

## REALIZATION

> 8:27 Jesus and his disciples went on to the villages of Caesarea Philippi, and on the way he questioned his disciples, saying, "Who do people say that I am?" They answered him, saying, "John the Baptist; and others say Elijah, and others one of the prophets."

Jesus, in asking his question, is aware that people often do not see or investigate the reality of their own experience, but constantly refer it to something *else:* something that they may not *know*, but that they know *of.* This is just another way of asking for "signs," of looking for "proof" or validation outside of experience. People say he is Elijah or one of the prophets, names associated with teachings and stories that are reassuring and familiar—and safely distant. People say that he is someone else, because this seems to explain things, and does not require real attention, real awareness, real presence. Similarly, when we begin to experience transforming occurrences in our lives, we may easily attribute them to one cause or another, to something that explains events satisfactorily — a theory, a doctrine, a hypothesis, a dogma, an *answer* of some kind.

> 8:29 He asks them, "But you—who do you say that I am?" and Peter answers him, "You are the Christ." And he sternly ordered them to tell no one about him. And he began to teach them that the Son of Man must suffer greatly, and be rejected by the elders, the chief priests and the scribes, and be killed, and after three days rise again. And he said this bluntly.

Here Jesus takes the question we have asked earlier and he makes it explicit: Who is this, *really?* The disciples report that people believe him to be John the Baptist, Elijah, or one of the prophets—the revived conscience, or a new manifestation of a powerful voice of the past. Jesus asks and Peter (no longer "Simon," the listener, but

"Peter" the rock, the stone, the foundation built on inner hearing) answers, "You are the Christ," the consecrated one.

It is clear that the disciples had some ideas of who "the Christ" was, or was supposed to be, for there is no discussion of Peter's statement— it is taken as something understood and accepted. But Jesus is making it plain that people really have no idea what "the Christ" really means and who He is. The Christ has been walking among the people for some time now, and they have been quite unaware of the fact— their beliefs leads them to expect certain things, and they (like Herod's advisors) attach their experience to something wonderful in the past. Notice that all the names that people bring up are those of the dead and departed great ones: John, Elijah, one of the prophets. Peter has made the connection between his experience and a spiritual reality, and his answer provides everyone with a context in which to see what Jesus has been doing.

What is the significance of this, from the inner perspective? Jesus' question asks us, What— or who— moves our lives toward healing, toward peace, toward wholeness? What, or who, within us, will love every part of us and accept us with unconditional forgiveness and heal us? Is this a part of ourselves, or is it *more*? Is it a variation on what we have known in the past, or is it new? The Gospel will speak to each person on the level at which she or he can hear. It is a spiritual tool designed for the use of a spiritual seeker to assist that person on the path, and it must be fitted to the user.

> o **Ask yourself Jesus' question: What — or Who — is behind the changes in your life right now? Is there something greater than yourself that calls you, draws you to change?**
> o **What is the source for you of love, acceptance and healing?**

As we follow the path we become increasingly aware that some changes occur within us that are not of our own doing—we are led in a certain way, events synchronize in a certain way, we are challenged and tested, we are encouraged or healed, we receive

## REALIZATION

thoughts or inspirations, direction, leading, or inner rebukes, corrections, prohibitions or revelations, that will be unique to each person. Each of us will have our own ideas of what has happened to us, and we will make sense of things in ways that work for our lives.

The Gospel stresses repeatedly that our responses are likely to cause problems. Jesus heals people and then commands them to be silent, because the presumption of knowledge—even when that presumption is based upon incontrovertible personal experience—can be an obstruction to true understanding, to the work of the Spirit, and to the unfolding and fulfillment of the person and of the work of God. Here he orders his own disciples to remain silent, suggesting that they too have more learning ahead of them, which they may hinder if they proceed to talk or act in ignorance. Jesus' command that the disciples be silent about him is a command to us for inner silence, for in stillness we may begin to hear and understand.

Jesus' question, "Who do people say that I am?" is an invitation to us to see the inner connections between the significant events of our lives, and once the connections are realized in awareness, we are invited to become open to where the connections lead us. The question is asked only after much has already occurred, after much learning and much healing have changed our lives in a perceptible way; and only after the inner disciples have been sent out to heal and to teach.

The question does not come from us, but rather from within. When we are sufficiently prepared to deal with this question, it will be asked of us: what is the source of all that has been happening in my life? What does it all mean? Before that moment, we are to remain silent, work with what we are given, learn the lessons that experience offers us, and grow as best we can. The question is not asked to put a label on the events of our lives, "This is Christ!" because clearly nobody— not even Jesus' closest disciples— really knows what that name means. But attempting to answer this question forces us to put our lives into a framework, a context. When change is stimulated by The Christ we will probably give the matter more attention and take it more seriously than if we are doing something only for our own satisfaction. This realization gives us power.

Yet even after we know the "answer" to this question, Jesus tells us to remain silent, for we have only begun to know. We must learn to distinguish what in our lives comes from God, and what does not.

## WHO IS THIS, REALLY?

Some very good and important things may actually be in the second category, so it may be easy to confuse the two.

♦ ♦ ♦

- o **We are not ready to ask about the identity of the Christ until we have already begun to actively manifest the qualities that come from the Christ: healing, reconciliation, and love.**
- o **When you feel ready within yourself, consider this: What does it mean to you to look upon the changes taking place in your life and ask about what causes these changes, "Who is this?"**
- o **Ask yourself, "Who am I?" and give the first answer that comes to your mind.**
- o **Explore your awareness of yourself with this question: A second time, ask "Who am I?" and respond again with the first words that come into your mouth— allow the answer to just come, without censoring.**
- o **Ask again, and answer; continue to ask and answer until you feel content to say no more. Reflect on what your answers tell you about yourself. Write down your reflections if you find that helpful.**
- o **What is the connection between asking "Who is this?" about what moves the events of your life, and asking "Who am I?"**
- o **Reflect on the things that move your life, that heal and transform you, and ask again, "Who is this?" Again, simply allow an answer to emerge.**

---

- o **Come back to these questions whenever you feel a significant change in your life, or when you have learned an important spiritual lesson.**

# REALIZATION

Jesus is presented as a model for us to emulate, to a limited degree, but much more importantly he is presented in the Gospel as one with whom we are to be in relationship. We are not meant to *be* the Christ, but we are meant to be in a living relationship *with* the Christ— a relationship that goes two ways.

Who is the Christ? One way of answering that question, for the moment, is this: The Christ is the personification of the living umbilical cord that unites each of us with our Creator. We only relate in the fullness of our being on a *personal* level, person to person. Our relationships to things, events, ideas are always with only a part of ourselves, whereas we can relate to another person in a way that involves us completely, for personhood is the essence of what we are. God the Creator, All That Is, The One, "I am that I am," relates to each of us through a personal aspect, whom we call The Christ.

When Peter answers Jesus' question by saying, "You are the Christ," he says "you are manifesting our connection with God in the flesh."[1] Within us, when the deep question is asked, we then realize—we do not speculate, we do not theorize, we do not guess, but we *know*—that the power that has led us, healed us, moved us, taught us, is the power of the Ultimate, of the ALL, of God, in the particular form that is God's connection to ourselves, personally and uniquely. The Gospel is describing an event that *happens* at some time in our lives— in the past, now, or in the future. We make the connection, we realize that healing change in our lives happens within a larger context, and that it has a direction and a purpose, and that it is sustained by a Power greater than ourselves.

> ○ **Has such a realization occurred in your life?**

---

[1] This is my personal interpretation. I have no desire to upset or tamper with other peoples' beliefs about Jesus and The Christ, and I will not attempt to answer the question, "what is the relationship between Jesus and The Christ" or other Christological or theological matters beyond what I have written above. I am providing an interpretation of the Gospel which intends to say something to you, the reader, and I am allowing the inspiration I am given to choose my words here. If you find that another sentence expresses the reality of Jesus and the Spirit in your life better, I invite you to connect your own faith to the inner interpretation and allow it to work in you.

> - If it has, what was the practical result of this realization, if any?
> - If such a realization has not occurred to you, this is all right too—just go on.

Once we have realized this connection, the Spirit's instruction is clear: tell no one. The connection is our own, and *knowledge* of the connection is still a presumption concerning what is, in truth, a gift that we may *realize* yet not understand. Telling others implies an understanding which at this stage we do not have.

At this point in the Gospel story, at the very moment when the story reveals plainly for the first time that Jesus is the Christ—that is, from our perspective, that the power that moves in our lives, and that moves us, is a direct connection with God— Jesus himself announces that he must die an ugly death at the hands of enemies, and rise again after three days. The sequence of the telling of the story is significant: fully half of the Gospel has been devoted to describing a process in which the disciples become gradually aware that the man they are following is more than they think he is, until finally the full realization of who he is dawns. And the *first* response of Jesus to this realization is to tell them that he will leave them, indeed leave the world completely—but to return in three days. Why now? Because we cannot *begin* to understand his death and resurrection until we realize who he is. They are essential aspects of his mission—not in an outward, worldly way, not in a political way, but in a way that will complete the disciples' understanding of who he is and what he is teaching— and in a way that will change us. This will unfold as the Gospel story continues, because understanding Jesus' mission is in fact the task of understanding how the Spirit of God works in our lives.

At this point it is important to hear what the story is telling us: once we realize that this inner person, this voice within us, is in fact our connection to God, then we must also realize that the flesh-and-blood incarnation or physical *image* of this connection must leave us.

REALIZATION

> 8:32bAnd Peter took him aside and began to rebuke him. But turning around and facing his disciples, he rebuked Peter, saying, "Get away from me, adversary! For you focus not on the things of God, but of men." And he called the crowd to him with his disciples, and he said to them, "If anyone would come after me, let him disown himself and take up his cross and *follow me*. For whoever seeks to save his life will lose it, but whoever loses his life because of me and the joyous message, will save it. For what benefit is it to a person to gain the whole world and lose his life? For what can a person give in exchange for his life? For whoever is ashamed of me and my words in this sinful and adulterous generation, of them the Son of Man will also be ashamed when he comes in the glory of his father with the holy angels." And he said to them, "Truly I say to you, there are some standing here who may not taste death before they see that the kingdom of God has come in power."

Peter speaks for all of us when he says, in effect, "I *just* realized who you are, and you say you are leaving? No way!" And of course he finds it inconceivable that the Christ, the Son of God, can be murdered. Also within ourselves, once we understand that the Spirit of God is responsible for the changes in our lives, we do not want to let go of this, we cannot give it up![2]

Jesus tells us in no uncertain terms that the path to God involves the ultimate surrender. We cannot *keep* the selves we know, the faith we know, the God we know, or the life we know, for these are all too limited for God's Spirit to flow through. The life Jesus invites us to lose is the life *we know*—the one we make sense of, the one we *control*. He says, whoever would save his life will lose it, and whoever loses his or her life for my sake and for the joyous message

---

[2] Jesus rebukes Peter, saying "Get away from me, Adversary!" But he does not say, "Get away from me, Peter!" He continues to teach Peter and the other disciples. See the discussion on p.63 about non-engagement with the adversary.

## WHO IS THIS, REALLY?

I embody, will save it. Jesus says that in gaining the world we would lose our life. And what can a person give in exchange for his life? This saying makes sense in our inner interpretation, for here we are not talking about physical death to save our souls, but the death of the physical, limited *image* of God within us. Jesus himself is *not* The Father, the ALL, the One, and there are limits to what he can do. The Holy Spirit of God is intended to come into our lives with glory and with power, but only after the worldly incarnation and image, the limited manifestation—Jesus—is gone.

He says clearly that some of the people who are with him, who give up their lives in the way he means, will experience the "kingdom of God" *with power* in this lifetime—*before* they die. We are not considering the "afterlife." The Gospel is communicating the most difficult concept in ordinary human experience: that when we give up our "egotistical" control of our lives in favor of the direction of the Deep Self, Christ within us, our real life begins. The transition requires a total commitment that is as radical as death versus life, for no partial measures or commitments are possible. This is not a commitment that can be made in a moment, for it requires preparation, focus, practice and more. Even among his own disciples he says that *some* will see the kingdom of God come with power in this lifetime.

What does "the coming of the kingdom of God" mean for us? From the inner perspective it means that one's life is guided in a deeply peaceful, harmonious way under the direction and leading of the Spirit, so completely connected to our spiritual source, without obstruction or inner conflict or destructive impulse, that the full power of our spiritual source flows in us and through us. This is the power that forgives, heals, restores, loves, gives life. It will manifest differently in different people, but it is unmistakable when it is present, no matter what it is called. For some of us it has been present at times, and it has been marvelous to experience, its results are wonderful. Jesus is telling us that it is possible to live this way, not merely to have a taste of it, and that some of us *will* live this way, in *this* lifetime.

◆ ◆ ◆

REALIZATION

> - What attitudes build your relationship with God?
> - How do you strengthen these attitudes?
> - What practical actions confirm these attitudes?
> - What does it mean to you to "take up your cross and follow" Jesus?

◆ ◆ ◆

The way to this life is through a death. With the inner interpretation of this "death" we look for what needs to "die out" in our lives before we can open ourselves to being transformed. The Gospel is making it plain that Jesus himself — within us — must die before this transformation can occur. Making death a prerequisite for life seems ludicrous on one level of our awareness, but the apparently absurd is, again, a flag for our attention—the Gospel is inviting us to explore how this may make sense for us, how it may actually *work*.

We know that in order to follow one path at a fork in a road, it is necessary to abandon another path, and this may be a key to allow us to understand what Jesus is telling us. We cannot follow two divergent paths at once, as Robert Frost wrote, and "be one traveler." We must leave one— that path must die for us, and we must die to that path. Jesus is telling Peter and the others, "if you want to follow me, you must accept whatever difficulties come along the way." He feels it is essential that they — and we — know up front that the path we will follow will lead us to the death of the very one we are following. We start by following a *person*, and the person must die— after which, what do we follow? What do we do? In our own lives, what happens when we follow an ideal, and then the ideal is destroyed? What if we follow a desire, and the desire evaporates? What if we follow a philosophy or a creed, and our faith in it dies? Where do we go? What becomes of us? Jesus is telling us that we *will* experience this kind of loss at the deepest level if we choose to follow him, and he is also telling us that we will come through this loss into a greater life — our life will be *saved*. Can this be explained in advance? Can you see the mountain *before* you have seen it? No. There is a path to follow. The purpose of the Gospel is to bring us along in this process, guiding us toward experiences that will bear

## WHO IS THIS, REALLY?

fruit and lead to the completion of the process— the coming of the kingdom of God in power.

The relationship between us and the Spirit is not an "if-then" conditional connection, but it *is* reciprocal. Jesus says, "whoever is ashamed of me, of them the Son of Man also will be ashamed." He is saying that the relationship is two-sided. When we approach Jesus with fear and shame, the Spirit will mirror us with fear and shame, for the Spirit meets us where we are. Why would Jesus bring this up? Why does it matter? He is not threatening or judging people when he says this, he is explaining why our experience with the Spirit will be as varied as we are, because the Spirit *responds* to us. If we find ourselves met with fear and shame in life, this does not mean that the Spirit has abandoned us. It is an invitation to change. When we meet the Spirit with love and faithfulness, we are met with love and faithfulness, and there is power in this meeting.

How do we experience this? Some of us may have a direct experience of the Spirit, some of us may not, but this is not the point. Jesus often teaches the same lesson on many levels. In the previous vignette in the boat he was teaching the disciples that the difference between fear and faith plays out in practical life, and here he amplifies that teaching to show us that our attitudes toward the Spirit cannot follow two divergent paths any more than our bodies can. He is teaching us that life *responds* to us, and if we react (as Peter began to) with refusal of the invitation of the Spirit, the power of the Spirit is shut off for us and in us. It is *exceedingly* difficult to respond with faith when events hit us with tragedy, pain, loss or death, and Jesus tells us that the loss will hit us right at the core. Yet he beckons, "Follow me." There is more.[3]

> o **Can you see an aspect of your life that needs to die, or die out? If so, look to see whether this is a "fork in the road" situation, where you need to take another path.**

---

[3] The reciprocal relationship is developed more in the parable of the rich man. See Section 28, especially pages 254-255.

REALIZATION

- What does the death of Jesus mean to you? In what practical way does this meaning have effect for you?
- Do you experience any reluctance or negative feeling when you contemplate death? Where does this come from?
- How, in your own life, could a death of some kind become a springboard for new life?
- Is a (real or potential) connection with Jesus something you are happy about, proud of, ashamed of, uncomfortable with?
- Is your attitude and approach to spiritual things the same as your attitude and approach to "ordinary life," or do you have to respond differently? Why, or why not? Think of some examples from your recent life to reflect on.
- Come back to this section and these questions whenever you feel that you are responding to the events in your life with a negative attitude.

## 22. LISTENING FOR MEANING

# REALIZATION

> ⁹:² And after six days Jesus takes Peter and James and John with him, and leads them up to a high mountain by themselves, alone. And he was transformed before them, and his clothes became dazzling white, such as no fuller on earth could bleach them. And Elijah with Moses appeared to them, and they were talking with Jesus. Peter responded, and says to Jesus, "Master, it is good that we are here. Let us make three tents: one for you, one for Moses, and one for Elijah." He did not know what to say, for they were terrified. Then a cloud enveloped them, and a voice came from the cloud, "This is my beloved son. Hear him!" And suddenly when they looked around they no longer saw anyone but Jesus alone with them. And as they were coming down the mountain, he charged them to tell no one what they had seen until after the Son of Man had risen from the dead. So they kept the matter to themselves, questioning what the rising from the dead meant. And they asked him, "Why do the scribes say that Elijah must come first?" And he said to them, "Elijah does come first to restore all things. And how is it written that the Son of Man must suffer greatly and be despised? But I tell you that Elijah has come, and they did whatever they pleased to him, just as it is written of him."

The scene of transfiguration on the mountain makes some connections in the spiritual tradition out of which the Gospel has emerged. Moses is the figure of law, and Elijah of the prophets, and together they represent the core of the spiritual tradition before Jesus, the "law and the prophets," which have guided spiritual life among these people up to this time. In the vision they communicate with Jesus, telling us that there is a living connection between spiritual rules, prophetic inspiration, and the new spirituality embodied in Jesus. When the vision ends, the images of Moses and Elijah are gone, and what remains is the living reality of the Spirit, embodied

# LISTENING FOR MEANING

in Jesus. The voice from the cloud tells *us* the essential message: the Spirit within us is from God, and our task—our responsibility—is to *listen.* Remember, Peter is the "first" disciple, whose name Simon means "hearing with understanding." When we go forward in the spiritual path we find our primary work is in listening, and learning to respond to the Holy Spirit within us— not once, or once in a while, but all the time.

The most difficult time to listen is when we are afraid, excited or impressed, like the three disciples on the mountain, quaking with fear and not knowing what to do. One of the things we may do when we are confused is to try to separate things out, to try to hold on to things and make sense of them, and the disciples act this out, offering to make tents for spirits. This confusion dissipates as we are led to listen to the voice of the Spirit. When we feel the presence of the divine we may also feel charged up or confused. The voice from the cloud emphasizes this, as the three disciples are in the midst of a "peak experience:" it says, *"Listen!"* Don't just be impressed or awed. With this the experience of the disciples dissolves into clarity— Jesus alone.

Again Jesus charges them to tell no one—the repeated caution to people who do not fully understand what they have experienced, not to speak in ignorance and cut off their opportunity to learn. They are enjoined to keep silence until the Son of Man has risen from the dead. Earlier, the Gospel has indicated that Jesus has told the disciples "bluntly" what is to come, but here they keep the matter to themselves, questioning what the rising from the dead *means.*

The point of the story is not to tell a miraculous event over which one marvels and wonders; the point is to *convey meaning,* which we are to understand if we can and put into practice. At some point, and possibly at more than one point in our spiritual journey, there will be death and resurrection. Only a few of our inner disciples will be able to see it coming, and they are, like Peter, likely to resist and deny it, or to be struck into confusion, or to try to "capture" it or to contain it in inappropriate ways, such as wanting to build tents for spirits. The death and resurrection experience will exceed our expectations, it will defy our mental categories, it will upend our understanding. We are to *wait* for the meaning of the experience to become clear.

## REALIZATION

The disciples have a linear, "up-the-hill" vision of spiritual progress, in which the voice of conscience begins the call, and one goes forward into glory. Jesus tells them and us that the journey into spiritual life involves the stifling of conscience ("they did whatever they pleased to him") and the contempt of the worldly aspects for what is spiritual ("the Son of Man must suffer greatly and be despised") — the journey into spiritual life goes downward before it goes upward. These statements are made as they are coming *down* from the mountain (the "peak experience") as the landscape of the Gospel reflects what the story is communicating to us. Jesus tells us that our "up and down" experience on the spiritual path will involve not just a little letdown, but major onslaughts.

♦ ♦ ♦

> o **Are there connections between your own spiritual teachings and traditions and the interpretation of the Gospel According to Mark that is presented here?**
> o **What do you listen for in a spiritual teaching? How do you listen for the voice of the Spirit?**
> o **What does "rising from the dead" mean to you now?**

♦ ♦ ♦

> o **Come back to this section whenever you sense a possible conflict between what you have been taught and your own inner inspiration.**

## 23. FAITH

## REALIZATION

> 9:14 And when they came to the disciples, they saw a great crowd gathered around them, and some scribes arguing with them. And immediately all the crowd, when they saw him, were greatly amazed and ran to greet him. And he asked them, "What are you arguing about with them?" And someone from the crowd answered him, "Teacher, I brought my son to you, for he has a spirit that makes him unable to speak, and whenever it overcomes him it convulses him, and he foams and grinds his teeth and becomes rigid. And I asked your disciples to cast it out, but they could not." And he answered them, saying "O faithless generation, how long will I be with you? How long will I hold you up? Bring him to me." And they brought him to him, and when the spirit saw him, immediately it convulsed him, and he fell on the ground and rolled around, foaming at the mouth. And he asked the father, "How long has this been happening to him?" And he said, "From childhood. And it has often cast him into the fire and into the water, to destroy him. But if you can do anything, have pity on us and help us!" And Jesus said to him, "*If* you can! All powers come to the one who has faith." Immediately the father cried out, "I have faith! Help my lack of faith!" But Jesus, seeing that a crowd was quickly gathering, rebuked the unclean spirit, saying, "You deaf and speechless spirit, I command you—come out of him, and never enter him again!" And after crying out and convulsing him terribly, it came out, and he became like a corpse, so that most of them said that he died. But Jesus took him by the hand and lifted him up, and he stood up. When he had entered the house, his disciples asked him privately, "Why could we not cast it out?" And he said to them, "No one can cast this kind out except in prayer."

Coming down from the mountain, they find the disciples in the middle of a dispute. Jesus' response is often translated conversationally in a way that makes him appear to be impatient: "O faithless generation, how much longer must I be among you? How much longer must I put up with you? Bring him to me." I do not hear impatience but sadness, for he is looking over an entire generation which tries to live without faith, and at this point even his own students still need propping up. The entire episode has to do with the issue of faith, and its central place in spiritual life and healing. Listening, we hear Jesus say, in effect, "You have been arguing over the facts. The facts do not provide a channel for inner power. You are without faith, and yet you desire *me* to heal. How long must I wait for you to bring your *faith* to this relationship? In your faith, *bring* your issue to me—do not sit by and argue and hope for something to happen!"

The father says, "If you can do anything, have pity on us and help us." His words are those of someone who is pleading for the work of faith while remaining in doubt, remaining uncommitted to the healing. Jesus responds by stressing the power of the commitment—*all* things are possible to one who believes. And the man's response is a lesson for those of us who must learn faith: I believe; I want to have faith; I am willing; Help my unbelief, my lack of faith! Faith is something learned, that needs help in the face of "facts." The healing is an interaction between the faith of the man and the power of the Spirit. When the man takes the step in the level of faith that is possible for him, the Spirit responds— the "facts" change.

Again we ask, "what is faith?" It is more than "belief that something is true;" it is more than confidence, more than desire. Faith is a response to the will of God, and Jesus will show us more later in the story.

The disciples ask why they were unable to cast out the infirmity, and he answers that only prayer drives out this kind. And by prayer, he means full engagement of the healer with God, with the spiritual source of the healing, a full commitment *for* and *to* the ones to be healed, along with the full will and engagement of the ones to be healed, or their supporters. There must be full faith on both sides, and Jesus is teaching his disciples not only to have faith themselves, but also to draw out (encourage) faith from others.

We see the central place of healing in the spiritual journey. From the inner perspective, every stage of spiritual growth is marked by an encounter with dis-ease, with dispute, with opposition, with failure. The aftermath of spiritual "high points,"—being on the

## REALIZATION

"mountain top"—may be a descent into dispute, doubt, and dis-ease. It is vital that we be aware of this, even though we may not understand it until later.

The vignette of the father and his epileptic son suggests that removing the spirits of anger, rage, self-hatred and self-destruction may be something we are afraid or reluctant to do, for we may not see how we can live any other way. We may discover that we rely upon such influences in many ways that are not apparent at first. Maintaining an angry attitude toward life may be a way to stay stable without confronting the fear that lies beneath the anger, which may be too overwhelming to face. Self-hatred may have been inculcated into us from childhood by abusive parents, and we may find it easier to hate ourselves than give up our one object of love— even if it is a false one. What are often called our "vices" are variations on "defense mechanisms," which we adopt unconsciously so that we can survive traumatic existence. Removing such defenses from our lives should not be attempted lightly or without help and support, for as the story shows us this process itself can be traumatic—everyone thought that the boy had died as a result. Some inner influences — and the defenses we have developed to deal with them — may seem so much a part of our lives that we may feel that we have been born with them, and that we will die without them. Nonetheless, the Gospel indicates that we will live after they are gone, for our defenses are designed to compensate for the absence of the faith that is an essential aspect of healthy life.

Again, as in Section 4 (see page 57), the spirit convulses the boy— terribly— and cries out as he goes out of him, leaving the boy seemingly dead. Some inner healing does not go smoothly and easily, for the way *out* of pain is often *through* it. This is shown in the story as happening instantaneously, but the real process is often difficult and may take a long time. Sometimes, resistance to healing includes resistance to *real* pain, and it is essential that we know that this may occur. The defensive "structures" inside us were acquired or built for a purpose, and even if their purpose lies in the past we cannot destroy or eject them without attending to how we are to live afterward. Healing often requires the continuing presence of loving, patient, discerning, strong support— and this must occur in prayer and communion with the Spirit.

FAITH

The presence of this episode right after the mountain scene of transfiguration suggests that the trip up the spiritual mountain may actually expose dark feelings that will only become apparent when we return to "normal" life, where the power of the Spirit must be called upon in faith to work for healing.

♦ ♦ ♦

- What is the relationship between reality, facts, doubt, and faith — in your life?
- When does doubt lead to faith? When does doubt undermine faith?
- When may it be better for you neither to doubt nor to trust, but to wait?
- What does it mean to you personally when Jesus says, "all powers come to the one who has faith?"
- What (or who) can draw out your own faith?
- Come back to this section and these questions whenever you encounter an apparently intractable problem, or when your faith seems to become weak.

***WALKING OUT THE GOSPEL: TO EXPLORE THIS FURTHER, DO EXERCISE 13 IN PART III, PAGE 418.***

## 24. A PRIVATE TEACHING

# A PRIVATE TEACHING

> ⁹:³⁰ And they went on from there and were traveling through Galilee. He did not want anyone to know it, for he was teaching his disciples, telling them, "The Son of Man is delivered into the hands of men, and they will kill him, and three days after being killed he will rise again." But they did not understand what he was saying, and were afraid to question him.

Jesus and the disciples passed through Galilee in secret, for he wished to teach his disciples only. There are times when it is helpful to be somewhat apart from the cares of the world if this is possible, so that the spiritually oriented parts of the person can be taught and nourished. We may not be able to physically separate ourselves or go on a retreat, but it is often possible for us to take some time to be quiet, to temporarily set aside our current activities and thoughts to reflect, pray, meditate, or just to be still. In such a quiet time we may then allow ourselves to focus on the inner teaching.

The nature of the teaching is an extension of what he announced earlier: the Son of Man is delivered up, killed, and rises again. The teaching must be repeated and explained, for it is helpful to have an overall idea of the journey before we embark. The teaching is a preparation for a transition that may appear, in advance, to be frightening, awful —maybe even impossible. The spiritually oriented parts of us are being prepared to lose their focus, to lose their center, to lose their leading and the only connection with God they have known so far. In the story the disciples *know* what he has *said*, they heard the words, but they were unable to understand the meaning of what he said. And they were afraid to ask.

This is an important stopping place; for we must ask, Why would the disciples be afraid to ask? Jesus has been repeating this teaching ever since Peter said, "You are the Christ." This is the third time Jesus has spoken of it in the Gospel story. It seems that the disciples are afraid to know the truth, which is that Jesus must leave and they will have nobody to follow, but must walk on their

## REALIZATION

own. We have seen that they repeatedly are shown in the Gospel not grasping the truth that Jesus presents to them—they miss the meaning of parables, they miss the significance of events, they get caught up in arguments with spiritual gate keepers. They seem to be getting stretched spiritually to the point where they are overwhelmed by the amount of change they are experiencing. This is not unusual when a person is confronted with advance notice of something terrifying. A person may get mentally numb for a time, trying to integrate the news and to recover from the shock. But Jesus needs them to understand, and the writer of the Gospel wants *us* to understand.

The teaching that the Son of Man must be killed and rise again was not for "public" consumption at this time, yet it is so important that Jesus has taken more than one occasion to teach it to the disciples. The teaching, then, is something that is only summarized in the phrase "The Son of Man is delivered into the hands of men, and they will kill him, and three days after being killed he will rise again." For it takes less than a minute to say these words, but Jesus has taken his disciples aside, on an untraveled path by themselves, to teach this to them when no one else is present. Why?

Because the outward form of the teaching—his death and resurrection—would most likely be misunderstood if it became "public." There is more to this than may be grasped on first reading, and we may easily misunderstand it, too— if it could be fully understood in a sentence there would be nothing to *teach*. For if all Jesus was doing was announcing a coming event, there is nothing more to understand. But there is much more, and it is a difficult teaching.

"The Son of Man is delivered into the hands of men." Jesus was perfectly willing to use the word "I" referring to himself, for when people asked him to heal them, he has answered, "I will." So if he is simply talking about himself, why does he not say "I will be turned over to my enemies and killed?" It seems that Jesus is talking about himself, yet also more, for he is more than the man who speaks to them. When he refers to "the Son of Man" the writer of the Gospel calls our attention, not just to Jesus in the story, but also most particularly to the Christ within us. Understanding this teaching is the central task of the rest of the Gospel.

## A PRIVATE TEACHING

This will also become clearer to the disciples, and to us, as the story unfolds.

> - Is Jesus raised from the dead, or is it the Son of Man who is raised from the dead? Is this a matter of "either-or?"
> - What is the relationship between Jesus and The Son of Man? What are the connections? What are the differences? When does an event pertain to Jesus only, or to The Son of Man only, and when does the Gospel refer to both at the same time?
> - How can this relationship become important for you in a practical way?

♦ ♦ ♦

There is another aspect of this vignette that highlights a feeling that we may all experience many times along our spiritual path, shown to us in the phrase "they were afraid to question him"—which might be rendered "they were afraid to ask." We encounter a situation that our minds cannot fathom or figure out, and we find that we may do nearly anything *except* ask within ourselves for guidance. We may not ask within because we are afraid of what may be given to us, or we are not confident that the spirit within us *knows* when our minds do not. And here is one of the greatest challenges we may face along our way: we do not ask, and then when we do ask, we may find ourselves saying within, like the father in the vignette earlier in the story, something like, "If you can help, please do something!" The gospel is a tool to help us with the task of growing through this stage.

## 25. LEADERSHIP

# LEADERSHIP

> 9:33 And they came to Capernaum, and when he was in the house he asked them, "What were you arguing about on the way?" But they were silent, for on the way they had been arguing with one another who was the greatest. And he sat down and called the Twelve, and says to them, "Whoever wants to be first must be last of all and servant of all." And he took a small child and stood it in their midst, and taking it in his arms he said to them, "Whoever receives one such child in my name[1] receives me, and whoever receives me receives not me, but the one who sent me."

The disciples do have an inkling of what they have been taught, and they think that in the absence of Jesus one of them may be looked to as the leader of the group. Since their concept of leadership relies on "greatness," they argue over which of them is the greatest, yet instinctively fall silent when Jesus asks them what they were talking about. Do we ever get the "what's in it for me" out of our aspirations? When we aspire to the spiritual life, it is difficult to admit that we may still compete out of pure egotism. But this question *is* very important: in the absence of personal spiritual guidance, what leads us? Do we follow our minds, our feelings, our bodies? Do we rely on courage, daring, strength, cleverness? Do we lean on patience or hard work? It is hard to look within us and see that a part of us yearns to jump up and yell, "I'm number one! *I* will lead you!" for there *is* in most of us one part that usually leads: for some, our intellects, for others our emotions, for some the body.

---

[1] This is the first instance of the use of this phrase "in my name" in the Gospel According to Mark, but not the last. While this book is not focused on this issue, it still may be helpful for you to consider, now or later, two things: first, what is the original meaning of the name *Jesus*? Jesus is the Greek rendition of a Hebrew name which could be rendered, "God saves." But what does *doing something* in that name (asking, receiving, healing, etc.) mean? In particular, what does it mean when applied personally, to your own life and to events and qualities within you?

## REALIZATION

While egotism may *move* us, its motion is not leadership so much as a response to a craving for stability, for familiarity, for comfort, for direction— or for getting our own way. Jesus then provides a model of spiritual leadership by saying that one who leads is one who serves, whose spiritual fullness allows him to meet the needs of others rather than push forward to be "first." People who feel the need for "greatness" often surround themselves with the trappings of wealth and power, they often "receive" into their presence only those who are willing to acknowledge their greatness and power in some way, whose presence supports or yields to their power. The gathering of outward power over others is often the sign of a lack of inner power. Jesus shows the model of spiritual greatness by taking a child in the middle of them, saying whoever receives such a child in his name receives him.

What does this mean? A child has no wealth, no power. A child cannot acknowledge or support the "greatness" of another, for a child has nothing but needs; so for us to "receive" a child in Christ's name is to imitate Jesus' relationship to those in need, which is that of helper and healer to all—this is his leadership, and this is the example we are to follow.

And, he says, when we act in this way, we do receive him. Helping those in need opens us to the power of the Spirit in our lives, which comes from the Source of all power. Jesus is teaching us that power flows through us whenever we direct our actions—with conscious intention—toward helping and healing. This is the essence of leadership, and so it is within us also. The part that shall really lead us into the spiritual life is the one that serves all other parts of us, the aspect that allows no part of our lives to be lost or written off but sees what is needed and uses all our qualities to meet the inner need.

- **What qualities within you are oriented toward helping and healing? Are these present and active often in your life?**
- **How can some of your "ordinary" activities, such as exercise, playing or singing music, walking, playing games, working at your job or profession,**

become opportunities to help and heal either your own inner subpersonalities or other people?
- Is there a quality within you that serves all other qualities?
- How can this service become leadership?
- How can this quality within you open to receive the Spirit?

♦ ♦ ♦

- Come back to this section and these questions whenever you feel confidant and self-assertive.

♦ ♦ ♦

## 26. THE TEMPTATIONS OF THE CHOSEN

> ⁹:³⁸ John said to him, "Teacher, we saw someone casting out demons in your name, and we stopped him because he was not following us." But Jesus said, "Do not stop him; for no one who does a work of power in my name can then speak ill of me. For whoever is not against us, is for us. For whoever gives you a cup of water because you bear the name of Christ—truly I tell you, he will surely not lose his reward. And whoever trips up one of these little ones who have faith, it would be better if he had a millstone hung around his neck and he were thrown into the sea. And if your hand trips you up, cut it off; for it is better for you to enter life maimed than with two hands go to the dump,[1] to the fire that is not quenched. And if your foot trips you up, cut it off; for it is better for you to enter life crippled, than with two feet to be thrown in the dump. And if your eye trips you up, throw it out; for it is better for you to enter the kingdom of God with one eye than with two eyes be thrown in the dump, where the maggots do not die and the fire is not quenched. For everyone will be salted with fire. Salt is good, but if salt has lost its saltiness, how will you season it? Have salt within yourselves, and be at peace with one another."

John picks up on the theme of healing "in your name" and remarks that the disciples have forbidden someone to use the name of Christ to heal, because he was not in fact a member of this inner group that has actually followed Jesus. The disciples feel the need to "protect the message," so to speak, the way modern writers copyright their work. They want to prevent "unauthorized" persons

---

[1] The dump is "gehenna" in the Greek— the valley of Hinnom, south of Jerusalem, where the filth and dead animals of the city were thrown out and burned. It was so well known that it became proverbial. See discussion on page 237.

## REALIZATION

from using it their own way.[2] They also want to affirm their own greatness again, as *genuine* followers of Jesus. They need to feel special, blessed, "number one." They want some assurance that if spiritual work is being done, it is being done *right,* and in the absence of the Spirit they have taken it upon themselves to *defend* it.

Jesus responds by taking down all of the disciples' pretension to greatness and specialness. No one, he says, can do a powerful work with spiritual intention, and be against the Spirit. The *works* do not lie, and it is in *action* that we show ourselves to be "spiritual" or not. The "work of power" that Jesus refers to is not just any action. Jesus could, if he chose, help people carry their groceries. But what distinguished his spiritual action from other actions is that there is always healing or empowerment of some kind in his actions. Needs are met, infirmities are released, freedom is gained. Jesus is explaining that real spiritual action *cannot be counterfeited.* Real spiritual power flows, regardless of outward allegiance, creed or association. Therefore, he shows us, whoever does real spiritual work is *in fact* "one of us," and we must help and support that work, for that support and help is part of the work itself. He says to the disciples, whoever helps you in your work in the least way—even giving you a cup of water—shares in the work, which is a cooperative venture, not a competition for "greatness" nor a patented "method" nor an exclusive association.

Within ourselves, too, healing cannot be counterfeited in the way a pill can mask pain and deceive us into believing that feeling well is the same is *being* well. When any part of us works for healing without striving for personal advantage or priority over another, spiritual power flows there, and the power accumulates in any part of us that supports the healing work. Some of us will attempt to suppress non-conforming parts of ourselves, and the zeal with which our inner judges attempt to make us "get it right" can amount to self-abuse.

Another side of this vignette concerns our expectations. We, like the disciples, may easily conclude that we *know* what healing looks like and where it comes from, and conclude that activity that does

---

[2] Compare this section with the discussion in Section 5, especially the healing of the paralytic on pages 72-77.

not conform to our knowledge is fraudulent, wrong, misguided, or even dangerous. The question of "authority" keeps cropping up in the Gospel, and here we see the disciples claiming some for themselves, based upon their *genuine* knowledge and experience with Jesus. People who advance on the spiritual path *do* acquire genuine knowledge and experience, and yet the Gospel is showing us that in the blink of an eye that same knowledge and experience may stop serving the Spirit when mixed with fear, egotism, exclusivity, or some other quality.

The Gospel's message is clear: do not interfere with the healing work of the Spirit! The child he speaks of is the same child of whom he said, "Whoever receives one such child in my name receives me, and whoever receives me receives not me, but the one who sent me." When we receive a child, we are giving to those in need, to those without power, to those without knowledge or experience— we support and lead and heal. The "child" who receives this work— whether it is a living child or needy person in our experience or an inner child that is a needy and immature part of ourselves—will place faith in the source of the help and teaching and healing. Jesus is talking to his *disciples*: the very ones who follow him but just forbade someone from healing because he wasn't "authorized." Jesus gives them the same lesson that he gave to the Pharisees. His warning is strong and graphic: the "authority" is *in* the healing power. Do not interfere with the work of the Spirit, or you yourself will suffer as a result. This warning is *not* meant for "unbelievers," or for "worldly" people, or for anyone who is not spiritually inclined— it is for the disciples, for the people on the path, for those who are trying to learn and grow, for people of conscience. Uncaring people have no fear of their consciences, but caring people may sometimes feel they would rather die than endure the burning conviction by their conscience that they have committed a violation of some kind.

Again there is another side to the parable, for when we "receive the child" in ourselves in Jesus' name, we are *giving up* our own claim to "adult" authority in order to follow, as a child would, the Spirit who lives within us— a Spirit who has no predetermined paths of "correctness," genuineness or authority, but simply *acts* with love and compassion.

REALIZATION

♦ ♦ ♦

- o How can your expectations get in the way of your ability to respond to the needs of the moment, or of the flow of the Spirit in your life?
- o Have you ever witnessed or heard of a noble action performed by someone who had no resemblance to "nobility?" A healing act done by someone who didn't care about healing? A seemingly spiritual response by someone who did not "believe" in spirit? A good deed done by someone you do not think of as "good?" The "right" action done by the "wrong" person?
- o What is the relation between the person and the action? How does the action affect your attitude toward the person? Why?
- o What can you do to learn and accept that "good" things may appear where they do not "belong?"
- o Is it possible that if something "good" appears in a "wrong" place, you may not see its "goodness" because of its context? What can you do to see things as they are?
- o What can you do to cultivate the habit of expecting the unexpected?
- o What can you do to acquire an attitude of allowing life to exceed your expectations?
- o Come back to these questions whenever you feel offended or angry about what some other people believe, or whenever you are afraid of being led down a "wrong path."

The Gospel shows us the disciples becoming protective because judgment and exclusivity and the need to "get it right" are particular temptations of people on the spiritual path. We are trying to learn, working to improve, seeking light, trying to change, reaching out to help, and it is all too easy to lose our balance. He says it is better to enter life maimed, crippled, one-eyed, than with two hands, two feet, two eyes go to *gehenna,* "where the maggots do not die and the fire is not quenched." This is a graphic—and accurate—description of a deeply guilty conscience. People who are striving for "perfection"— healing, growth, and transformation, and who strive to help others are most sensitive to errors, to failure, to conflict. Their focus on the goal and on others may make such people blind to their own real shortcomings, which may be projected onto others: the problems in ourselves may actually be things that are so cherished that we do not recognize them for what they are— obstacles. They seem to be as much a part of us as our arms, our legs, our eyes.

And what are these: our *eyes* are the way we perceive, the way we look at things; our *feet* are what we stand for, or walk toward—our principles and our goals; our *hands* are how we apply ourselves and what we grasp something with. All these are foundations of character and we may unknowingly cling to them as we do to parts of our bodies, even if they are misguided. It is precisely these parts of our *selves* that may lead us to stop the progress or healing of others while we blame the others for not being "right," or "true" or "authorized." This is yet another way in which Jesus teaches us to look to ourselves before we try to correct the "errors" in others, for the pain of self-pruning can be life-supporting, and it is preferable to the pain of conscience.

These symbolic eyes, hands and feet are not *essential*[3] parts of ourselves, and if they lead us— or others— astray Jesus tells us to be willing to give them up in order to "enter life," for in the Spirit all things are healed. Later, in Section 27, Jesus will tell us what the essential parts of us are, parts that cannot be given up.

> o **How might a cherished part of your life become an obstacle to spiritual growth, forgiveness, love?**

---

[3] For example, you can live without an eye or without both eyes, but you cannot live without a heart, or a brain, or skin, which are *essential* to your life. What inner parts are essential to you?

REALIZATION

*Gehenna*, the word often translated as "hell," was a place where a fire was always kept burning to take care of the trash, garbage and dead bodies that were discarded from the city.[4] Jesus is telling us that if we will not give up the things that hold us back, we will be as miserable as if we were thrown into a burning trash heap, and our suffering will be like a fire that will not cease— until we *do* give up the things that cause us to stumble.

♦♦♦

> o  What kind of pain feels like "gehenna" to you?
> o  What would get you into such pain?
> o  What would get you out of it?

Jesus then tells us that such suffering serves a purpose— for everyone, not just those who do "wrong." *Everyone* will be salted — with fire! Jesus compares us to food that is to be "salted"— prepared and seasoned. A good cook *cures* food to remove the undesirable elements and flavors, and *seasons* the food to enhance its favorable properties. In ancient times as in modern times, salt was used to perform both curing and seasoning functions, but it is the *functions* that he is emphasizing when he says, "everyone will be salted with fire." Everyone will undergo hardship, difficulty and pain, and everyone will be "cooked" and prepared until the undesirable is removed and desirable is encouraged and enhanced.

---

[4] I translate the term Greek word *gehenna* as "the dump," since it specifically refers to the Jerusalem city dump (see note on page 232) and I allow the reader any metaphorical associations that come to mind. Those who translate this term as "hell" (the English word "hell" is derived from a Germanic root meaning "a concealed place" or "the underworld") are choosing their own interpretation of the metaphor and then treating the metaphor as if it were a literal translation. "Dump" has connotations of "trash" whereas "hell" has a connotation of "death" or even "punishment." Jesus uses a specific metaphor, and I let it stand as such. Perhaps the best personal interpretation of this metaphor is simply "misery" or "suffering."

He says, if the "salt" that prepares and seasons you is outside of yourself, it will eventually lose its effectiveness. But if the "seasoning" is within you, its effect will continue until you are at one with yourself and with God, and at peace with others. The nature of our inner preparation, our curing and seasoning, will be unique to each of us, and it is important that we learn to recognize what kind of experience is our "salt," how it "cures" and "seasons" us, and realize that we are salted with *fire*—which burns and cooks out the undesirable qualities and brings forth a wonderful flavor, *and* which is also painful. If we try to escape this kind of pain, we end up with the pain of the trash dump—a different kind of fire—which, in the end, will lead us by a different route to the same result: "curing" and "seasoning."

♦ ♦ ♦

- What is the difference between the "fire" of salt—curing and seasoning—and the "fire" of conscience—"gehenna?"
- What people, events, experiences have served as "salt" in your life?
- Which ones "cured" you? Which ones "seasoned you?"
- If they did not seem to be either, is that because they were not actually useful in your life, or because you are not looking for how they could be useful?
- Is there a "salt" within you?
- Do you see a need for more curing, more seasoning? In what way?

- Come back to this section and to these questions whenever you have endured a painful experience.

## 27. WHOLENESS

## WHOLENESS

> <sup>10:1</sup> And standing up, he goes from there into the territory of Judea, across the Jordan, and again crowds gathered around him, and again, as was his custom, he was teaching them. And some Pharisees came, and to test him they asked, "Is it lawful for a man to divorce his wife?" He answered them, "What did Moses command you?" They said, "Moses allowed a man to write a certificate of divorce, and put her away." But Jesus said to them, "For your hardness of heart he wrote you this commandment. But from the beginning of creation, 'male and female he created them;' for this reason a man shall leave his father and mother and be joined to his wife, and the two become one flesh. So they are no longer two, but one flesh. Therefore, what God has joined[1] together, let man not pull apart." And in the house, the disciples asked him again about this. And he says to them, "Whoever divorces his wife and marries another, commits adultery against her; and if she divorces her husband and marries another, she commits adultery."

This section of the Gospel takes the story for the first time into Judea, an area where there was perhaps more focus on the law than elsewhere. It begins with consideration of social rules concerning marriage, but from the inner perspective these connections have great and important meaning. People, Jesus teaches, are created male *and* female, and even though we are born with physical gender, we are in our maturity joined with our opposite to become one whole person. In the inner interpretation of the Gospel we see this vignette as a continuation of the last lesson about what is to be "cut out" of our lives. The Pharisees, zealous for what they believe is "right," suggest that we can cut out whatever we don't like, or what doesn't seem suitable, just as a man in ancient Judea was allowed to simply write a "bill of divorce" and put away his wife. In this interpretation we see an "inner marriage" as representing essential but apparently

---
[1] Literally "yoked"

## REALIZATION

opposing traits that make us whole when joined together, just as a marriage makes two people of opposite genders one and whole.

Any person, whether man or woman, who "divorces" undesirable or "opposite" inner characteristics casts part of himself or herself out, creating a storm of conflict and imbalance, indicated by the word "adultery." Adultery is a disconnection, a violation against self *and* other, against wholeness —for one cannot violate self and *not* violate others. Here we are considering only essential characteristics, "what God has joined," for there are parts of ourselves that appear to be in direct opposition to each other, but which are in truth opposing expressions of a common root impulse, drive, characteristic, or inspiration that is basic and essential to our being human. Most of us "tilt" toward one mode of expression or another; for example being introverted or extroverted, intellectual or emotional, organized or spontaneous, and abandon any attempt at the "contrary" expression. In fact we may view the supposedly contrary expression as inimical, like the hand that causes us to stumble, and want to "cut it off," or "divorce" it.

It is vital that we learn which characteristics are essential or native to us and which are not, for one we keep, we "marry," we cherish like a spouse; and the other we "cut off," we eliminate as we would a stumbling block. Much of our pain and suffering are self-inflicted when we attempt to stifle or eliminate what is essential to us, and when we cling to characteristics that are not really ours but that have been grafted onto us by others.

How do we tell the difference? The Gospel makes a clear distinction: in the story, the essential aspects are represented as people, who are to be loved, "married," cherished, encouraged, healed and forgiven. The characteristics that are not native or essential to us but have been grafted onto or injected into our lives, are represented as spirits, and the undesirable characteristics are represented as "unclean spirits," or "demons," to be "driven out." If the non-native characteristics have become bonded to us, Jesus refers to them as an eye or an arm or a leg, which are to be "cut off" if they are harmful.

We noted earlier how often in the story the people who came to Jesus for healing did not understand, did not recognize Jesus for who he is, and did not obey his instructions. By contrast, the "unclean spirits" all knew him *and* obeyed him. This gives us some insight into the difference between the essential parts of us and the "alien" characteristics. In the story both people and demons have awareness—the demons' awareness is often superior, in fact—and both have desires. Both can act, but only the people in the story have *will*— the power to weigh alternatives and make conscious decisions of choice. The "unclean spirits" just do what Jesus commands. They are like viruses, in that they appear to have direction and intent, but their responses are always determined, automatic, or unconscious. Even something as close to us as an arm or a leg has no independent will. In the story a person represents an essential human aspect, a real part of us that always has the power of will, of deliberate decision and choice. In our own lives we can see that this power of will and choice is an essential aspect of what makes us human, and it is through our will that we heal what is human within us.

We notice in society around us that people who are caught up in obsessive or compulsive behavior, addictions, habits, prejudices or fears often have an impaired ability to make choices or decisions. They feel that in certain ways they have no choice, and they often work (usually unconsciously) to actively limit, prevent or control the choices of others. They speak with the voices of others and live behaviors that are not freely chosen.

When you find within yourself a voice, an inner quality or aspect that does not choose or decide, but only reacts (even if it claims that its reaction is "by choice"),[2] you may have discovered a characteristic that is not native or essentially a part of your true self, and you may choose whether or not to keep it in your life (even though the choice may be very difficult). When you find an inner part, an aspect of yourself or a subpersonality that is capable of reflection and deliberate choice—even if it often makes the "wrong" choice—then you have found a part of your true self, part of you that you are "married" to, that you cannot "divorce" without self-violation.

Aspects of our essential being can be viewed as "male" and "female," and these are joined in us to make our wholeness. A loving

---

[2] For example, many regular cigarette smokers insist that they smoke by choice (I did, for many years) but that sense of free will evaporates when their habit is denied or cut off. Such smokers cannot recognize that their "choice" was an illusion until after they have quit. Other behaviors also maintain an illusion of freedom.

REALIZATION

acceptance of the seemingly opposite aspects of ourselves can be among the greatest challenges of our lives. We may use different terms to describe them: male and female, dominant and submissive, inclusive or exclusive, rational or emotional, intellectual or physical, aggressive or passive, social or individualistic, and so on. These terms are not necessarily descriptive of basic reality, but they can be helpful as tools to "map" our inner terrain.

---

- Take some time to reflect on your own essential but apparently opposite characteristics and qualities. (You may want to use Table C on page 246 as a starting point)
- When do you tend to want to keep one and "divorce" the other?
- How do you work for harmony and "marriage," or synthesis?
- Are there some areas where you seem to have one quality but not its opposite? Is that because the opposite quality does not exist, or because it has been suppressed or "divorced?" What does such separation do to your personality, your life?
- Is there a way that a synthesis of the opposites is possible for you?
- Come back to this section and these questions whenever you feel an inner separation, or a desire to get rid of disagreeable parts of your personality.

---

♦♦♦

**WALKING OUT THE GOSPEL: TO EXPLORE THIS FURTHER, DO EXERCISES 14A AND 14B IN PART III, PAGES 419-421.**

Any person who tries to purge inconvenient or disagreeable but essential aspects from their lives does violence to themselves. We sometimes try to disown or divorce parts of ourselves to follow some idea, agenda, or teaching that urges us to separate the "good" from the "bad" without distinguishing what is to be separated. If we separate out essential parts of ourselves into "good" and "bad," desirable or undesirable, we begin a process of inner rejection that alienates us from ourselves as well as from God.

For example, I was brought up in an environment that encouraged boys to be "tough" and self-assertive, and that discouraged boys from expressing pain or showing compassion for others. So I unconsciously labeled the first qualities "good" and the second qualities "bad," and made every effort to do the "good" and avoid the "bad." The result of course was a young man who felt free to be angry and selfish, who was unaware of his own pain and hurt (except his frustration at not getting what he wanted) and of the pain that he inflicted on others. The few friends he had tended to be like himself and so could not help him much. As that young man grew older the inner divorce became dangerous, because the process of rejection became dominant both inwardly and outwardly, and the "invisible" inner pain made itself visible as a series of shattered relationships and, eventually, as cancer. My healing involved an inner marriage that brought together the qualities of strength and compassion, of acceptance of both and a joining of the two into a synthesis in which each quality carried some of its opposite— strength *with* compassion, empathy *with* discrimination. The inner marriage allowed me to get married in outer life, yet my wife and I are making some of the breakthroughs into real union after living together (as of this writing) for over 28 years.

Jesus, in the Gospel, is the embodiment and manifestation of God's creating Spirit, and all aspects of our being respond to the Spirit, feel the attraction of it and are healed by it. But even our inner disciples tend to develop their own agendas to separate the good from the bad, the desirable from the undesirable, and they tend to separate the "high" and the "spiritual" and the "mature" from the "low," "earthly," and "immature." The critical lesson here is to learn where such discrimination is helpful, and where it is not.

> 10:13 And they were bringing little children to him, that he might touch them, but the disciples rebuked them. But

REALIZATION

> when Jesus saw it he was very displeased, and said to them, "Let the little children come to me, do not stop them; for the kingdom of God belongs to such as these. Truly I say to you, whoever does not receive the kingdom of God as a small child would, will not enter it." And he took them in his arms and blessed them, laying his hands upon them.

Here is a continuation of the previous lesson. Jesus teaches that in examining ourselves, discrimination is important and necessary; but in opening ourselves to the Spirit of God within us, discrimination can be a hindrance. Do not, he says, keep the "low" or "immature" aspects of ourselves—our inner children—away from the presence of the Spirit, and do not attempt to inject our own agendas into our contact with the Spirit, for total receptivity is needed for the Spirit of God to fill our lives. "Childlike" and "spiritually mature" are two apparently opposite qualities that our inner disciples are eager to separate, but Jesus tells us that the *union* of these qualities is necessary for anyone who would "enter the kingdom of God."

Those who would enter it, he says, *receive* it. They do not create it, get it, deserve it, accomplish it, or arrive at it. Jesus is doing a lot of teaching, and here he challenges us. He tells the disciples to "step aside" for a moment so that the children may come to him. If our inner disciples cannot step aside for our inner children, then *they too become inner gatekeepers.* Again we see the process alternating between work and rest, between aspiration and acceptance as we move toward wholeness.

One way of looking at the qualities in our lives is to see the seemingly opposite aspects to be included, instead of excesses and deficiencies to be avoided. Here are some examples of qualities that can be looked at as qualities that seem to be opposites in their fullness, but when brought together in a "synthesis" form something new and wonderful. The synthesis is not a "compromise" that leaves qualities out, but a joining that includes all aspects of each of the apparent opposites.

I have chosen to call the seemingly opposing qualities "masculine" and "feminine" for convenience, and the Asian ideas of "yin" and "yang" are a good basis for going forward. Many western

# WHOLENESS

languages like French still retain the use of "feminine" and "masculine" nouns (not the same as "female" and "male") to indicate the sense of polarity, and even though the English language has dropped these usages centuries ago and made all generic nouns neutral, our language was rooted in an awareness of seemingly opposing qualities within us. In many ways the "marriage" or synthesis of some of these qualities in us may allow us to live the fullest life. I have filled the "synthesis" column with the word "And" to indicate the joining of qualities, because in English we seem not to have developed distinct words to express the "married" state. For people we refer to a couple, and Jesus speaks of the two becoming one flesh. Within us I speak of being balanced or whole.

## Table C:
## Balanced Qualities From
## a "Synthesis or Marriage of Opposites"

| "Feminine or Yin Quality" | Synthesis | "Masculine or Yang Quality" |
|---|---|---|
| Detail-Oriented | And | Generalist |
| Introverted | And | Extroverted |
| Non-linear | And | Linear |
| Open | And | Selective |
| Spontaneous | And | Structured |
| Playful | And | Purposeful |
| Accepting | And | Aspiring |
| Compassionate | And | Discriminating |
| Humble | And | Dignified |
| Committed | And | Detached |
| Respectful | And | Assertive |
| Tolerant | And | Decisive |
| Empathic | And | Discerning |
| Contemplative | And | Active |
| Intuitive | And | Reasoning |
| Sensitive | And | Resilient |
| Timeless | And | Time-sensitive |

REALIZATION

These qualities are easily adapted to the tables of qualities presented earlier, for we can see that each of these qualities also has an extreme associated with it; for example in the first column the extreme to the left of "detail-oriented" might be called "myopic," and the extreme to the right of "generalist" might be called "dreaminess." The extreme to the left of "compassionate" might be "gullible" and to the right of 'discriminating" might be "judgmental." So each quality may have a "far-left" quality that we need to avoid, and a "near-left" quality that we want to include, a "far-right" quality to avoid and a "near-right" quality to include, and a synthesis in the middle where the "near" qualities can be "married" to produce the inner wholeness.

This list is only intended to give you an idea of qualities that could be "married" within you, in a spiritual inner marriage that includes both qualities to produce a balanced inner and outer life. Feel free to work with your own qualities to develop some personal aspirations about the nature of wholeness and harmony in your life.

- Which qualities do you see in yourself? Do you see within yourself both the yin and yang qualities?
- What pressures move your qualities toward one side or another?
- Are there some qualities that are "married" within you, that you are sometimes tempted to separate?
- What helps you to move into synthesis in each area? What makes it difficult?

♦♦♦

# Table D:
# Expanded Qualities From a "Synthesis or Marriage of Opposites"

Now we will expand the qualities listed above into a hybrid list that includes both the extremes and the synthesis, suggesting that the qualities that we engage in our lives may tip into deficiency or excess and yet also contain elements that are necessary and must be joined, so that the full synthesis incorporates both balance and the marriage of seemingly opposing qualities.

| Extreme | Yin | Synthesis | Yang | Extreme |
|---|---|---|---|---|
| Myopic | Detail-Oriented | And | Generalist | Dreamy |
| Self-preoccupied | Introverted | And | Extroverted | Unselfaware |
| Scattered | Non-linear | And | Linear | Regimented |
| Indiscriminate | Open | And | Selective | Exclusive |
| Impulsive | Spontaneous | And | Structured | Rigid |
| Frivolous | Playful | And | Purposeful | Fanatic |
| Licentious | Accepting | And | Aspiring | Greedy |
| Gullible | Compassionate | And | Discriminating | Judgmental |
| Self-abusive | Humble | And | Dignified | Pompous |
| Dependent | Committed | And | Detached | Uncaring |
| Sycophantic | Respectful | And | Assertive | Aggressive |
| Indecisive | Tolerant | And | Decisive | Compulsive |
| Oversensitive | Empathic | And | Discerning | Opinionated |
| Obsessive | Contemplative | And | Active | Frenetic |
| Speculative | Intuitive | And | Reasoning | Over-intellectual |
| Squeamish | Sensitive | And | Resilient | Insensitive |
| Unreliable | Timeless | And | Aware | Driven |

You may see this continuum in various aspects of your personality and your experience. Notice that the balance that we seek is often a balance of the Yin and a balance of the Yang, and a marriage of the two balanced qualities. Feel free to explore how this framework fits within your own life.

## 28. SPIRITUAL POWER

# SPIRITUAL POWER

> 10:17 And as he was going out to the road, a man ran up and knelt before him, and asked him, "Good teacher, what shall I do to inherit the life of the ages?" But Jesus said to him, "Why do you call me good? No one is good but God alone. You know the commandments: you shall not kill, you shall not commit adultery, you shall not steal, you shall not bear false witness, you shall not defraud, honor your father and mother." He said to him, "Teacher, I have kept all these since my youth." Jesus, looking at him, loved him, and said, "You lack one thing: go, sell what you have and give the money to the poor, and you will have treasure in heaven; and come, follow me." At these words his countenance fell, and he went away sorrowful, for he had great possessions. And looking around, Jesus says to his disciples, "How hard it will be for those who have wealth to enter the kingdom of God." But the disciples were perplexed at these words, and Jesus says to them again, "Children, how hard it is to enter the kingdom of God. It is easier for a camel to go through the eye of a needle than for a rich person to enter the kingdom of God." They were greatly astounded, and said to one another, "Then who can be saved?" Jesus looked at them and says, "For people it is impossible, but not for God. For all things are possible with God." Peter began to say to him, "Look, we have left everything and followed you!" Jesus said, "Truly I say to you, there is no one who has left house or brothers or sisters or mother or father or children or fields for my sake and for the sake of the joyous message, who will not receive a hundredfold, now in this time, houses, brothers and sisters, mothers and children, and fields, in the midst of persecutions; and in the age to come, the life of the ages. But many who are first will be last, and the last first."

The vignette between Jesus and the rich man brings us back to the level of priorities. A man of great wealth kneels before the one

## REALIZATION

who lives in the Spirit, hails him as "good," and wants to share in the spiritual life. This is a man who is good at "schmoozing" to get what he wants, and he knows that it is politic to flatter one who has what he wants. He represents a part of us that is accomplished or prosperous in some way, and who is spiritually ambitious, yet fundamentally misunderstands the nature of spiritual life. He is under the impression that spiritual life is something that you can "get," and intends to do what he needs to do to get it. Jesus deflects his compliment by directing it to the Source of goodness, of which he is only a representative. But since the man needs to feel like he is "good," Jesus reminds him of all the standard ethical values that comprise ordinary "good" behavior. The man says that he wants more than just "being good," and Jesus sees this and loves him for this desire.

I'd like to stop our discussion for a moment to note this phrase: "Jesus, looking at him, loved him." I feel that this phrase captures an important detail, because the wording suggests that Jesus is not just "seeing" someone standing in front of him. He is looking deeper, appreciating something in this person that may not be apparent to others, who see the man's affluent surface. Jesus has often called his disciples— and us— to "Look!" at something, to "Hear!" something. In this scene with the rich man the Gospel is showing us that we can really look deeper and love someone. Awareness enables love. Love then issues an invitation, appealing to the man's will, his freedom to choose. And the lesson continues as Jesus shows us what to consider when we choose.

The vignette between Jesus and the rich man is a clarification of Section 10 on page 123, where Jesus said, "for to whomever has will more be given, and from him who has not, even what he has will be taken away," which could be taken by some people to be an endorsement of wealth as a normal adjunct of the spiritual life. Here is a wealthy man who seems to "have it all," except, Jesus tells him, that he lacks one thing. He learns that to "have" that one thing he must give up all the rest— not exactly a "prosperity gospel." This section also can be compared to Section 17 (page 176) where Jesus told everyone that what comes into the body is not his focus, but rather what comes out of the heart. The wealthy man has all the means to "get" things for himself, and he has done all the actions necessary to be able to be called a "good" man, but he lacks the one thing needed for spiritual life. He knows that he lacks something, for he comes asking for the life of the ages, but he doesn't really know what he is trying to get.

> o **Do you think you are a good person? or that you try to be a good person? Regardless of how you answer, how does it make you *feel* to know this about yourself?**

The life you are asking for, Jesus says, cannot be "obtained" by bargaining or by *any* specific virtuous activity. It is an *orientation.* If you completely renounce your allegiance and your focus on *things,* on attainment, on controlling your own agenda, and open yourself completely to the Spirit, you will "get" the desire of your heart—that is, by giving up your desire to "get" altogether. This is a different kind of "having" altogether.

He emphasizes this teaching with a graphic metaphor: it is easier for a camel to pass through the eye of a needle than for a person who trusts in riches and possessions to live the life of the Spirit. The life of the Spirit is an orientation toward the Spirit of God within us, a complete reliance upon and trust in inner resources—the exact opposite of a trust in outer possessions or circumstances, the attitude of "rich" people and many others also, for the poor who yearn for riches have the same orientation and reliance. This is also *our* orientation whenever we give the material world—"things"—more trust and focus than is appropriate. All that really matters to us—love, safety, beauty, joy, faith, compassion, awareness, kindness, and so on—come *through* things, not *from* things. Jesus is teaching us that *focusing* on the things— even as a byproduct of "the spiritual life" — is not going to bring us spiritual life.

In the story the man has tried to adjust his behavior to become virtuous, and he has obeyed the law in all things. But even obedience to law represents a focus on outer things, another kind of getting in return for giving. Jesus is offering more than "feeling good about being good," and the rich man inside us knows this. He would like to build upon the success that has marked his life so far, for "spiritual

## REALIZATION

life" would be the pinnacle of accomplishment. But Jesus is not showing us the way to peak performance.

Jesus describes a relationship in which power flows *one way*— from God, from the inner dimension, outward to and through the person. The power to establish this relationship does not come from us; it comes *to* us, from God, and he says, with God all things are possible because "God" is our name for the Source of all Power.

Peter is at this point feeling a little insecure, perhaps, for he says, "well, *we* have left everything and followed you," but he is not at all sure of himself, because in following Jesus he and the other disciples *do* want to "get" something, and it sounds like what the rich man has asked for is exactly the same as what the disciples want. They have given up everything, haven't they? In the ancient Near East as in modern times, people with wealth were considered blessed; it is often assumed that their wealth is to be admired, and is evidence that they are doing something "right," and that "to whomever has will more be given." Jesus has turned this around, telling people that what is commonly admired is in fact a liability and a spiritual handicap, for there are few wealthy people whose values are not integrated with and depend upon their wealth, so most of them cannot help but focus on the things instead of the spirit.[1] It is not that "wealth" is "bad," but rather that a spiritual or psychological *reliance* upon wealth is a misplaced expectation, sort of like hoping for warmth to come from the light of the moon. It turns our attention in the wrong direction.

It's easy to miss the bend in this road, because we all live in a material world and rely on material things. This is why the disciples are so perplexed— who can avoid this problem? Jesus is trying to show them— and us— the difference between using something and relying on it. If I rely on a hammer to build my house then I cannot build my house if I don't have my hammer; but if I am only *using* the hammer, then I focus on the project and use whatever tool I need— a hammer, maybe, or something else. Similarly there is a world of difference between using our material possessions as tools for living, and relying on them to provide the focus for our lives.

---

[1] This of course is an illustration of the third part of the parable of the sower in Section 10 on page 121. Wealth— material possessions and reliance on them— can fill our attention and become a focus for our actions, and choke out the word.

## SPIRITUAL POWER

Entering the kingdom of God is getting oriented to the way that spiritual power really flows and "going with" that flow. Since nearly everyone has some material possessions and has to pay attention to getting material food, shelter, and so on, the disciples are wondering if everyone is handicapped. Jesus affirms that yes, everyone *is* handicapped and nobody can walk this road without help, but he also makes it clear that a greater power is really in control of peoples' lives— *our* lives.

He reassures Peter and the disciples that their commitment is recognized, that there is a response to it. But Jesus also recognized that there is fear in Peter's question as well as egotism. Peter's question recalls the child's plea for a reward, "what about me, I've been good!" The disciples are demonstrating that there is often an element of spiritual greed in what appear to be the most sincere and enlightened pursuits. It can be a difficult matter to understand the nature of the "getting" and "having" that characterize the spiritual life. Jesus avoids a simple answer but hands the disciples a two-edged response, saying that they *will* be handsomely rewarded for their commitment, which will also bring persecutions to their lives before they enter a state of being in which the spiritual life is the norm rather than the exception. And finally he pricks their egotism with the saying, "many who are first will be last, and the last first."

> o **What does this mean for you—"many who are first will be last, and the last first?"**
> o **How might this be important within you, between the parts and subpersonalities of your life?**
> o **What kind of "having" is essential to the spiritual life, and what kind of "having" is a hindrance?**

◆ ◆ ◆

This entire section has dealt with the question of what one must *do* to live a spiritual life, to become a truly spiritual person. Jesus is trying to help people realize that what they do is often a hindrance to the spiritual life, that more *doing* will not alter that fact. Peoples'

## REALIZATION

actions are often a type of conditional transaction, "I will do this if you will do that," or "I will agree to this if such and such is the case;" and these actions are all a kind of giving in order to get something. The rich man's ethical propriety is marked by his desire to *get* spiritual life, and if there is no chance of him getting what he wants, perhaps he will abandon his ethics. It appears in the story that if he doesn't get the spiritual life in the manner to which he is accustomed (that is, comfortably), then perhaps he doesn't want it. The disciples, too, have given up things to get what they want, and Jesus assures them that actions do in fact have effects, but not always what they are expecting.

People on the spiritual path may give up house and family and land, and what they may receive may include a spiritual house and family and lands a hundredfold—and also persecution and spiritual life.[2] No one, he says, who embarks on the spiritual path will not receive these things, but it is not a "transaction" in which one gives (or gives up) in order to get. The dynamic at work can be difficult to understand. Spiritual life is not a "state" but a *love relationship*, and the reciprocal actions of a love relationship do not operate as "cause and effect," for while there is action on both sides, the connection is not mechanical, nor is it bound by rigid, specific rules. Trying harder, giving more, does not necessarily mean that more "results" will be forthcoming at any given time. It means nothing to be "first," best, brightest, most devout, or worst, laziest, poorest — for there *are no comparisons*. The kind of priorities that help us to succeed in the world are not useful in the spiritual life, for as he says, many who are first will be last, and the last first.[3]

> o **What priorities are spiritually helpful to you right now?**
> o **What qualities do you apply to these priorities?**
> o **Where do "things" fit into this process?**

---

[2] Recall the discussion on "cooking" in Section 26, pages 23ff, especially pp.237-238.
[3] You may find it helpful to compare this section with the discussion of the reciprocal relationship in Section 21 on page 202ff. especially p.207-210.

> o Come back to this section and to these questions whenever you have been trying to receive the gifts of the spirit, to live a good life, but feel that something is still missing.

♦♦♦

> 10:32 They were on the road going up to Jerusalem, and Jesus was walking in the lead; and they were amazed, and those who followed were afraid. Again he took the Twelve aside and began to tell them what was to happen to him, saying, "Look! We are going up into Jerusalem, and the Son of Man will be handed over to the chief priests and to the scribes, and they will condemn him to death and they will hand him over to the foreigners, and they will mock him and spit on him, and whip him, and they will kill him; and after three days he will rise."

This section elaborates on the theme begun above. Jesus tells his followers—for the fourth time—that the Son of Man, their leader, their guide, the one who is "first" in their group, will be brought to the lowest level, executed like a despised criminal, only to rise again.

♦♦♦

> o How does Jesus' telling them about the coming events fit into what he has said about "first" and "last?"
> o What does it suggest about spiritual leadership? What does it say about spiritual power?

REALIZATION

- Again Jesus does not use the word "I" in describing the coming events. He speaks of the "Son of Man" in the third person, "he." Why?

- Does his speaking this way say something to you about the Spirit of God within you? What?

# 29. SPIRITUAL POWER, PART 2

## REALIZATION

> ¹⁰:³⁵ James and John, the sons of Zebedee, came to him and said, "Teacher, we want you to do for us whatever we ask of you." And he said to them, "What do you want me to do for you?" And they said to him, "Grant us that we may sit in your glory, one on your right hand and one on your left." But Jesus said to them, "You do not know what you ask. Are you able to drink the cup that I drink, or be baptized with the baptism that I am baptized with?" They answered him, "We are able." Jesus said to them, "The cup I drink you will drink, and you will be baptized with the baptism with which I am baptized. But to sit at my right hand or my left is not mine to give, but it is for those for whom it has been prepared." And having heard this, the ten began to be angry with James and John. And Jesus called them to him and says to them, "You know that among the foreigners, those who rule subjugate them, and their great ones are tyrants over them. But it is not so with you: whoever desires to be great among you must be your servant, and whoever desires to be first among you must be slave of all. For the Son of Man came not to be served, but to serve, and to give his life as a ransom for many."[1]

Again there is an elaboration of the themes of relationship, self-advancement and the spiritual life. The brothers James and John have fastened on the idea of Jesus' "rising again" as indicating a final priority and prominence, and they are willing to go into the depths if it means that they will end up on the heights— they are willing to give a great deal if they can be assured of "getting" what they want in the end. They understand that spiritual life is a relation-

---

[1] The term which in English is translated *many* may have a use as an exclusionary term, as in "many but not all." The ancients, on the other hand, often used this word cumulatively, as in "there are *many* raindrops now, and there will be more and more until the rain barrel is full." We read the term in this cumulative sense here.

ship and they want the benefits of the special relationship they have with Jesus. This seems to be going the rich man one better, as the two disciples not only want to "get" something, they want guaranteed results![2] Taking up Jesus' saying about the first and the last, they are willing to be last if they can end up first. Jesus confirms to them that their spiritual walk will lead them through the depths, but once again he emphasizes that their spiritual work will not be a "transaction" in which either their work or their connection will "buy" them a place on the heights—he cannot promise them a place or position or a specific result in advance, in return for their commitment, devotion and sacrifice.

The other disciples become angry when they learn that two of them strive for preferment, and Jesus uses this reaction as an opportunity to show them all something about "advancement" in spiritual life. Preferment, he tells them, is what others use to *take* power, but the spiritual life is about *giving* power, giving life, about freeing others from their bondage. The "having" is what makes the "giving" possible, and yet without the "giving" there is no "having." The Son of Man has the life of the ages, and having that life is synonymous with giving it.

From the inner perspective we can observe that many of us are dominated by one aspect of our personalities—some are impulsive, some intellectual, some emotional, some brave, some timid, and so on. Many of us do not realize that we live under a kind of inner tyranny until we begin to seek balance within ourselves and discover that the part of us that "rules" our lives has no intention of sharing or giving up control. On that road to balance, we may work to attain a more spiritual life and perspective only to become discouraged because spiritual life and freedom do not descend upon us in direct proportion to the effort and investment we have made. When we are stuck at a particular stage, sometimes it seems that the harder we try the more stuck we get. Jesus shows us that the key to liberation is service, which has a different quality than attainment. Many of us have no difficulty serving what we see as good, or high, or worthy,

---

[2] But as Jesus has said, they truly do not know what they are asking for, and if they did they would not ask so blithely and confidently. But they *do* ask, and they do reach for something that is more difficult than they can imagine.

## REALIZATION

especially if there is some "reward;" but Jesus says that the Spirit of God serves *all*.[3] But "serving" is not simply a particular kind of "doing." Sometimes serving is not-doing; sometimes it is compassion, or presence; serving may *include* doing, but sometimes serving is to cease doing.

Jesus amplifies the nature of his own service, saying that the Son of Man came to give his life for many. In this last sentence Jesus sweeps all the issues about transactions, preferment, relationship and spiritual life into a single focus. In this sentence is a brief summary of the transformation that the Gospel is leading us to: the liberation of our inner disciples — and all the parts of us — is "bought" with the death of our inner Jesus, which makes possible the birth of the unlimited Spirit of God within us. All the previous issues will be worked out in this death. Jesus within us takes to himself all who come to him, whether they be happy or unhealed, healthy or diseased, honest or unethical— even those who are criminal and have committed atrocities— and he will endure all that is sent to him, all that is demanded of him, all that is perpetrated against him. This *radical acceptance* of all and everyone is how he gives his life, and this liberates many— as many as themselves open themselves to this total acceptance.

---

- **Is there one part of you— your intellect, your emotions, your profession, your sexual identity, your spiritual aspirations— that plays a dominant role in your life?**
- **How can that dominant part of you become servant of all?**
- **What are you hoping to attain in your spiritual life?**
- **How do you work for God? What do you "get" out of it?**

---

[3] Notice that Jesus says that whoever desires to be first must be a slave —not a slave of "all of *you*," nor of "all of the chosen," nor of "all believers" — but slave of *all*. What does this mean for you?

## SPIRITUAL POWER, Part 2

- Whom do you serve?
- When does your serving involve "doing," or "not-doing?" "giving" or "not-giving?"
- Picture where you are now in your spiritual walk— see how much you are able to discern about this place that has been prepared for you. How much of the preparation can you see? (You may ask someone who is familiar with your spiritual life to give you some insight into this, if that is comfortable for you) What and who else has been involved —or used— in this preparation?
- Can you sense within you one who will truly *accept* all and everyone, and everything in your life?
- How may accepting all lead you to give of yourself?
- Can you open yourself to radical acceptance in your own life?

- Come back to this section and to these questions whenever you do not feel appreciated or loved for what you do, or whenever you believe that some things or position or circumstance will enable you to finally achieve your goal.

# 30. FAITH, PART 2

## FAITH, Part 2

> **10:46** And they came into Jericho. As he and his disciples and a large crowd were leaving Jericho, Bar-Timaeus (son of Timaeus), a blind beggar, was sitting beside the road. When he heard it was Jesus of Nazareth, he began to shout out, "Jesus, son of David, have pity on me!" And many told him to be quiet, but he cried out even more loudly, "Son of David! Have pity on me!" And Jesus stopped and said, "Call him." And they called the blind man, saying to him, "Take heart! Get up, he is calling you." And throwing off his cloak, he sprang up and went to Jesus. And Jesus said to him, "What do you want me to do for you?" The blind man said to him, "My Master, let me see again." Jesus said to him, "Go; your faith has made you well." And immediately he could see again, and followed him on the road.

Here is one model of how spiritual freedom is attained—not by *doing* anything, but by focusing all attention and effort on the power of the Spirit of God, from whom the power of healing and restoration flows. Bartimaeus has to get himself to the right place at the right time— that is what he is called upon to *do*. He *asks* until he is heard. After that he is called to respond, to state *specifically* what he wants, to trust, and to receive. These are not the actions of someone who is attaining something. Rather they are attitudes of one who is cooperating in a process in which the power comes from another source. They are not *actions*, but neither are they passive attitudes. There is a brief but powerful interlude in which a relationship is established, and the relationship is founded on faith. Bartimaeus was already personally committed to Jesus in his heart the moment he opened his mouth, for he calls Jesus not teacher, but *"My Master."* Jesus tells Bartimaeus, "your faith has made you well." This faith is not an intellectual belief, but a driving desire to be healed that is acted upon, combined with a determined *personal* focus on the source of the power, an asking for wholeness and a complete trust in the efficacy of the Spirit, and an openness to receive what is given. And it is more than these.

REALIZATION

There is something in this interaction that is not present in the vignettes with the rich man and the disciples, for Bartimaeus does not seek advantage, position, preferment, or power, but restoration. What is restored is his ability to discern, which many with sight do not have. Unlike some people who have been healed by Jesus earlier in the Gospel, Bartimaeus now has the discernment to know that his next step is to follow Christ after he is healed, to learn more. For those who have been following him, Jesus shows that the work lies in restoring those who are in need, in serving with power. Here is another aspect added to the question we have asked earlier, "What is faith?"

♦ ♦ ♦

- **Come back to this section and to these questions whenever you feel that your own efforts are not very effective.**

♦ ♦ ♦

*WALKING OUT THE GOSPEL: TO EXPLORE THIS FURTHER, DO EXERCISE 15 IN PART III, PAGE 422.*

# NOTES

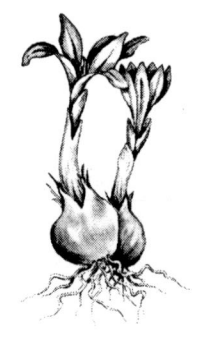

# **CONFRONTATION**

All of the aspects of inner realization that have gone on before have been leading to a decisive movement by the Spirit in our lives. So far the Gospel has led us to understand the role of the Spirit in our lives, to see the living Spirit in a greater context than our individual lives, to learn how the Spirit's power is to applied to practical reality, and to adjust our self-attitudes toward leadership, authenticity and wholeness. We were then given lessons that clarify the nature of spiritual power and our relationship to it, leading to the next aspect of how spiritual power is applied in life— faith.

Now the Gospel will illustrate how the Spirit begins the great transformation in our lives with a confrontation with the commanding ego— the one within us that calls itself "I" and rules for its own ends. The lessons of faith are clarified into four steps which serve as a practical guide for most circumstances. The practically-oriented aspects of our personality that line up behind the ego are shown to resist the inflowing of the Spirit with a series of tactics that highlight the major difference between ego-life and spiritual life: the commanding ego lives on conflict and thrives in the atmosphere of conflict, especially the polarity between "good" and "evil" which it uses as a counterfeit of spiritual life. The Spirit is inclusive and works for wholeness rather than division and conflict, and even its confrontation with the ego is not based upon conflict or polarity.

Finally the Gospel holds up the scriptures to scrutiny as Jesus responds to challenges from the "scribes," or keepers of the book. He shows that love is the basic commandment of God, and that the priorities of those who "keep the book" are not always the priorities of God. This part begins with Mark 11:1 and goes as far as Mark 12:40.

## 31. CONFRONTATION

## CONFRONTATION

> ¹¹:¹ And when they were approaching Jerusalem, at Bethphage and Bethany, near the Mount of Olives, he calls two of his disciples and says to them, "Go into the village ahead of you, and immediately as you enter it, you will find tied there a colt that has never been ridden; untie it and bring it. If anyone says to you, 'Why are you doing this?' say 'The Lord has need of it and will send it back here immediately.'" And they went away and found a colt tied at a door in the street, and they untied it. And some of the bystanders said to them, "What are you doing, untying the colt?" They told them what Jesus had said and they let them go. And they brought the colt to Jesus and threw their cloaks on it, and he sat on it. And many spread their cloaks on the road, and others spread rushes they had cut in the fields. And those who went ahead and those who followed cried out, "Hosanna! Blessed is the one who comes in the name of the Lord! Blessed is the kingdom of our father David that is coming! Hosanna in the highest!" And he entered Jerusalem and went into the temple; and when he had looked around at everything, as it was already late, he went out to Bethany with the Twelve.

In this section we begin Jesus' final week with the entry into Jerusalem. From the inner perspective, this is the beginning of the challenge of the Spirit to the commanding self, the ego, for the sovereignty of the person. This is a point in the spiritual process that occurs only after a long journey. Our "walk from Galilee to Jerusalem" may take months, years, decades. All that has gone before is a preparation for this process, and it begins with a symbolic act that puts Jesus' life into the context of the spiritual history of ancient Israel: the entry of Jesus into Jerusalem on a colt is meant to recall the passage from the prophet Zechariah in which the king comes victorious, humble, into the city riding on the foal of an ass, ending strife and war, commanding "peace to all nations, his dominion shall

## CONFRONTATION

be from sea to sea, and from the River to the ends of the earth."[1] The entrance of Jesus signifies the overt entry of the Spirit into the ruling part of our personality, in such a way as to give a clear signal that its rule will end inner strife and will include all parts of the person and all of the person's experience.

Here is a continuation of the previous lesson in which Jesus showed us how dominating rulers behave— manipulating their position for their own advantage, just as James and John try to do— and how the purpose of the Spirit is not to take power but to give it. Jesus, like Zechariah's king, does not enter the city in a golden chariot, but riding a colt like a poor person. His aim is not to destroy or subdue, but to bring peace. And this is his role within us as well.

> 11:12 And on the following day, when they came from Bethany, he was hungry. Seeing in the distance a fig tree in leaf, he went to see if he could find anything on it. And when he came to it he found nothing but leaves, for there were no figs at the time. And he said to it, "No one may eat fruit from you ever again." And his disciples heard him.

The entry of the Spirit into our "inner Jerusalem" will occur in stages, the first of which is marked by a modest awareness of spirit in our consciousness. There follows a symbolic vignette in which Jesus goes to the fig tree.[2] In the Gospel Jesus represents the Source of Life, and he withdraws the flow of life from this tree, which is all signs but no nourishment—like the Pharisees earlier in the story.

---

[1] Zechariah 9:9 - 10. Compare how Jesus is placed in this larger context in Section 22, page 214ff.

[2] In some translations the story contains some apparently contradictory elements: on the one hand, Jesus approaches the tree because it is in leaf, and fig trees normally bear fruit when they are in leaf; but on the other hand, some translations say that it was not the season for figs, which would suggest that the tree was in leaf out of season. I have rendered the section that there were simply "no figs at the time." In either case the spiritual sense of the story remains: that the tree gave the signs of fruit when no fruit was to be had.

The following day (below, in the story) the disciples see that the tree has withered away to its roots. This vignette is meant to focus our attention on the overall theme of what is to follow, for it will be easy to miss this theme in the back-and-forth action between Jesus and the others.

> 11:15 And they came into Jerusalem. And he entered the temple and began to drive out those who were selling and those who were buying in the temple, and he overturned the tables of the money changers and the seats of those who sold doves; and he would not allow people to carry merchandise through the temple. And he was teaching, and saying, "Is it not written, 'my house shall be called a house of prayer for all the nations,' but you have made it a den of robbers!" And the chief priests and the scribes heard it and were seeking a way to destroy him; for they feared him, because the whole crowd was struck with amazement by his teaching. And when evening came they went out of the city.

In the second day at the temple, Jesus finds it infested with people who use it as a market rather than as a place of prayer and worship. Here we find people who buy and sell, for whom the work of holiness has explicitly become a transaction. Is Jesus implying that all people who trade are thieves? No. But the presence of "transactional" *quid pro quo* behavior robs the temple of its essential qualities: giving from the heart, open-handed reverence, surrender to the will of God, and humble, whole-hearted receiving of the gifts of God. Here we see the "giving to get" mentality institutionalized in the central locus of public worship. When Jesus saw this mentality in his disciples he taught them the difference between the spiritual life and the aspirations that drive us in our worldly concerns, but here he finds the same mentality backed by the leaders of religious life and all the power of the state. These powers are not open to teaching, nor are their minions.

## CONFRONTATION

Jesus drives out those who use the temple as a cover for their greed and those who use it as a short-cut across town, and his doing so is a rebuke to those in the temple who have allowed or profited from this behavior.

The temple is an apt symbol for the physical doors to spiritual life. For all of us, spiritual life comes through and into physical life in a variety of ways, but for most of us there are certain places, practices, ideas, beliefs, associations that focus our spiritual connections. For some of us it is nature; for some of us it is church, synagogue or mosque; for some it is belief or ritual; for some it is a holy book or place. These are all meant to be means of access to the spiritual life, to help us connect to what is greater than ourselves. But for some, these are not doors to the spirit, but simply entrenched patterns that take the *form* of spirituality, but that actually serve other purposes— material gain, convenience, or power.

In this vignette Jesus illustrates the reaction of the Spirit in our lives when it discovers the physical door to spiritual life being used to thwart the spiritual process. Like the fig tree, the temple shows all the signs of life, but has no nourishment to offer. If we realize that this is happening in our lives, we may expect some (perhaps dramatic) inner movement to correct the situation.

---

- **For you, what are the physical doors to spiritual life?**
- **What do they open to?**
- **Do you have any "traders" in your inner temple? If you do, what do they offer? What do they serve?**
- **Are there gatekeepers in your temple? If so, what are they? —ideas, rituals, beliefs, stories, traditions, behaviors?**

---

♦ ♦ ♦

At some point in our lives, when our Spirit overtly enters our daily lives and finds that some supposedly "spiritually" oriented parts

## CONFRONTATION

of our lives are in fact choking off spiritual practice and deep spiritual contact, it will, if possible, provoke confrontation within us as it moves to shut down practices that do not support spiritual life.[3]

The confrontation will be real, for these other aspects of our life will not just docilely pack up and disappear. Like the priests and scribes in the temple, they have a system and a way of life to protect, and they will work to thwart or destroy whatever threatens them.

> o  **What aspects of your religious or spiritual life might not welcome the free-flowing life of the Spirit? What part of your life might be disrupted or disorganized if you respond to the Spirit?**

---

[3] Yet, as Jesus has indicated in the parable of the sower in Section 10 on page 121, sometimes the "thorns" succeed in choking off the word and no harvest is available for a time.

## 32. SPIRITUAL POWER, PART 3

# SPIRITUAL POWER, PART 3

> 11:20 In the morning as they passed by, they saw the fig tree withered away to its roots. And Peter remembered and said to him, "Master, look! The fig tree that you cursed has withered." Jesus answered him and says, "Have faith in God. Truly I say to you, whoever says to this mountain, 'Be taken up and cast into the sea,' and does not hold back in his heart but trusts that what he says happens, it will be so for him. This is why I say to you, in all that you pray and ask, trust that you have received, and it will be so for you. And whenever you stand praying, forgive, if you have anything against anyone, so that your father who is in the heavens[1] will also forgive the wrongs you have done."

While there will be real confrontation on one level of our lives when the Spirit enters, on another level of our being there is no battle, for the power of the Spirit sends life where it will and withdraws it where it does not bear fruit. And the fruitless fig tree, withered away to its roots, is the witness in the story. Jesus takes this opportunity to explain some key elements of how spiritual power is manifested through a person. First, he says, "have faith in God." The awareness of our inner source is the starting point, and "having faith" suggests not only an awareness, not merely an acknowledgement or intellectual assent, but a deep personal relationship of the kind that allows complete trust; a level of confidence that is as basic as our trust that we are living and breathing. This is a trust on so deep a level that we would not even think about it most of the time, for it is the foundation upon which our awareness of "facts" is built. It is a trust built on

---

[1] "The heavens" was a common term in ancient times used to denote a region above the sidereal heavens — essentially a realm "above" the physical universe— where God dwells. This term essentially means "beyond any specific place." There have been many other attempts to describe the "location" of God with words, including the term "eternal," which has evolved until it now means "beyond or out of all relation to time." Yet Jesus clearly is also saying that God is *in* the world, because forgiveness and healing are experienced in the here and now.

## CONFRONTATION

experience of connection and relationship, not on theory, theology, doctrine or intention. God is the One who sends light and life into all without regard to person, place or any other factor, so having faith in God is not only trust, but a trust in the One who provides for *all*. Here is another aspect of faith, adding to those illustrated in previous vignettes.

The second step is to apply the power of this relationship *to* the "facts," to allow the deep connection to inform our intention with a knowing trust that the intention will be manifested as surely as, for most of us, the air comes into our lungs when we take a breath.

Third, he says, believe that what you intend is already accomplished. This is, again, not merely acknowledgement or intellectual affirmation, but an inner experience of the intended result as *done*, accomplished and completed, with all the attendant results and effects.

Finally, he says, clear your heart and mind of all anger, bitterness, and resentment, and forgive any and all those whom you have anything against. As you become one with the Spirit within you, there is less and less room for inner division, and what comes into you becomes aligned with what goes out of you. If hurt or anger goes out, then hurt or anger comes in; if forgiveness goes out, then forgiveness comes in.

Anger, for example, is an emotion that may seek to stop something or to destroy something, and it may respond to a wound or to an attack. Of itself, anger cannot be the positive channel of spiritual life, but only at best a response to something negative, itself a negation that may pave the way for something positive through which the life and power may flow. That power can only flow after forgiveness has removed the blocks and obstacles that provoked the anger, for spiritual power is a species of love. The love can only flow when there is alignment of inner attitude and outer attitude—sort of like a valve in a water pipe: water will flow only if the valve is opened. Forgiveness is the only way to open our spiritual valves.

Forgiveness is the projection or extension of the trust in the One who provides for *all* into a specific relationship between you and another person, for forgiveness is a way for us to mirror the attitude of God and to follow Jesus in his radical acceptance by not withholding love from anyone. Forgiveness, then, is not an act done once, twice, twenty times. It is an attitude we develop toward all things, all people—including ourselves—inwardly *and* outwardly.

> - Do you hold hurt, resentment, bitterness, anger or hatred in your life toward someone or something?
> - Is there bitterness or anger directed toward parts of yourself?
> - Where is forgiveness needed in your life?
> - What will you do to make it—or allow it—to happen?

♦ ♦ ♦

> **You may want to refer again to Exercise 15 in Section IV, and recall what your response to the question, "What do you want? What is the desire of your heart?" as you review:**
>
> **The Four Steps of Faith:**
>
> **1. Have faith in God that what is really needed for *all* shall occur;**
> **2. Pray, and allow your relationship with God to provide an intention for you in your situation; allow your intention to include "what is truly best for *everyone* involved," even if you do not know what that "best" is;**
> **3. Use your inner senses and your imagination to see and experience the result of your intention as already accomplished; act as if it is done;**
> **4. Forgive any and all people in your life if you have anything against them, and allow the power of God to flow through you.**

CONFRONTATION

- o Meditate on the meaning of these steps for you: how you will engage your Spirit, your mind, your soul, your body in the process of faith, and of bringing your faith into reality.
- o Scan your awareness for any sense of the need for forgiveness, for yourself or for others. If you notice any anger, regret, shame, bitterness, sadness, or fear, these may lead you to where forgiveness is needed. Allow yourself, when you are ready, to follow these emotions to a part of your own reality or history that evokes the feelings.
- o First, the reality of the situation must be seen and acknowledged as deeply and completely as possible; then, choose to forgive, to release all negative, harmful connections between yourself and with anyone else, anywhere, at any time, even if the person is no longer alive in this life.
- o What is the relationship between "what you want" and "what is really needed that is best for all?"
- o What will you do to include "what is truly best for everyone involved" into your intention?
- o After you mentally see the result as accomplished, conceive, plan and carry out some action (even a symbolic action) that tells you and the world, "it is done."

- o Come back to this section and to these questions regularly.

***WALKING OUT THE GOSPEL: IF IT SEEMS APPROPRIATE, RETURN TO EXERCISE 15 IN PART III, PAGE 422.***

***WALKING OUT THE GOSPEL: TO EXPLORE THIS FURTHER, DO EXERCISE 16 IN PART III, PAGE 423.***

## 33. AUTHORITY AND POWER

## CONFRONTATION

> 11:27 And they come again into Jerusalem. As he was walking around in the temple, the chief priests and the scribes and the elders come to him, and they say to him, "By what authority are you doing these things? Or who gave you this authority to do them?" Jesus said to them, "I will ask you one question; answer me, and I will tell you by what authority I do these things. Was the baptism of John from heaven or from men? Answer me." And they argued with one another, "If we say, 'from heaven,' he will say, 'why then did you not believe him?' but if we say 'from men'—they were afraid of the crowd, for all regarded John as truly a prophet. So they answer Jesus, "We do not know." And Jesus says to them, "Neither will I tell you by what authority I am doing these things."

The third day marks the beginning of a series of challenges between Jesus and the priests, scribes and elders of the temple. This is the beginning of open confrontation between the Spirit and the spiritual gatekeepers—they challenge him to name the authority by which he acts. Spiritual gatekeepers are usually careful not to claim ultimate authority and power for themselves, but they often claim exclusive *access* to ultimate authority and power, for their experience of reality is profoundly political in the sense that they perceive all power as either restrictive, controlling, or permissive. When they witness a challenge to their own power they can only understand it politically, as coercive. They themselves use scripture and tradition and political organization as the basis of their authority, yielding only to the superior military power of Rome. They cannot comprehend an authority that is *not* political, that arises from creative, life-giving, healing power, instead of coercive power.

There is an inner analogy to these gatekeepers for many of us. If we examine the structure of our own personality we will find that our lives are usually organized around the teachings we have absorbed, the habits we have formed, the associations that connect us to others, and the restraints imposed on us by law and custom,

## AUTHORITY AND POWER

which are ultimately enforced by raw physical power by the state. These are our inner priests, scribes, elders, and Romans. For most of us there is not a direct unrestricted flow of spiritual power to our awareness and behavior, but the power of life is controlled by teachings, habits, associations, custom and law. If a creative power enters our lives that does not conform to any of these, the first reaction within us will be to try to control the new power, to bring it under the influence of the organizing principles that make our lives stable, profitable, or satisfying. Our instinctive reaction is to view the new force from the same point of view that informs the rest of our lives: "by what authority do you do these things?"

Many of us may be willing to entertain new ideas and practices, but only if the new force "fits in" with what we already believe and harmonizes with how we have chosen to live. If it does not, we are likely to dismiss it; or if we are willing to still consider it, we may find ourselves challenging its source and validity.

Jesus returns the challenge, in effect asking them—and us—"what is the source of the authority of your conscience? Is it divine, or just something that you picked up from others?" For when the voice of conscience—the voice that cries out, "Change!"—is suppressed or overridden by "practical" considerations, we have a strong impulse to justify ourselves and to stifle anything that might defend the voice of conscience. Jesus is the voice of Spirit acknowledging the conscience, asking us, "was it from God, or just something made up—from men?" to force the parts of us that suppress or ignore conscience, that want to stop the work of the Spirit, to make a choice.

Just as he asked his disciples, "Who do you say I am?" in Section 21 (page 202 ff.) to provoke them into providing a context for their experience, now he asks the temple establishment, "Who do you say John was?" For a person's "position" on the identity of John (conscience) is a reliable indicator of whether they support the work of the Spirit. Similarly, their question of what authority Jesus has is, for them, a reliable indicator of whether he can be controlled by them. Jesus responds with the reciprocity of the Spirit: if they will declare their position, he will respond in kind. The Spirit meets us where we are, mirroring us in a way that amplifies our responses and provides us with opportunities—if we listen and see.

But they realize that if they declare that conscience (John) is from God then they have no defense in their suppression of it; if they declare it is from men, (just made up) they risk the open opposition of all parts of us that *know* that the voice of conscience is not something arbitrary, self-serving or capricious, but a voice that arises from a deeper source of truth. Whether they answered "yes" or "no" they would be moved to acknowledge truth in one way or another. So the opposition forces within us prefer to take no stand, to remain agnostic, for the refusal to commit oneself allows the maximum flexibility for defense. At some times, "I don't know" can be the ultimate defense within ourselves, too; a defense against awareness and the need for action, which would lead us toward truth.

Jesus is "smoking out" the opposition, exposing not genuine doubt but the appearance of uncertainty. The opposition does want their "truth" tampered with— they want no interference with their system and their program.

Contemporary examples of similar confrontations can be found in the annals of modern science. Einstein's theories at first provoked reactions ranging from dismissal to scorn to disbelief to hatred, before the evidence led most people to accept them. Einstein, in turn, later rejected quantum theory because it did not conform to his belief in God and how the universe operates. Later, many physicists initially rejected newer findings and theories, which have sometimes taken decades to be recognized. As of this writing, several new approaches in other disciplines, such as the "new biology" and spiritual psychology, are largely ignored, dismissed or attacked by mainstream "established" thinkers, who have a lot to lose if the new theories are accepted. The accepted "system" of thought or behavior is often connected to a huge amount of academic work, economic investment, government policy, and personal pride on the part of many people, and the human condition is such that we usually defend what we have when so much is riding with and on it.

Something similar may happen when a new inspiration enters our own lives. We will find out for ourselves that we too have a system for our lives, and that a program determines our attitudes—it matters little whether our program is "positive" and "constructive," or "negative" and "destructive," or whether it is theoretical or theological, or practical and economic. A system may organize our thoughts or beliefs; a kind of program may organize and control the life of a drug addict around self-hatred, drug highs, crime, and fear; just as a program may organize and control the life of a nun around

## AUTHORITY AND POWER

devotion, prayer, work, and self-sacrifice. One of us may organize life around constructive work, another in a life of contemplation, a third in high-stakes gambling, another in playing bingo, another in a life of the mind in an academic setting. Our established beliefs may be religious, scientific, or practical. Our system may have strict rules or no rules; it may have a goal or no goal, it may be self-serving or dedicated to others. It may be dominated by habits or by reason, instinct or passion. The common element is a repetitive pattern that seems to be resistant to change.

> - **What is your program, your system? Or do you have no system of your own? Or do you follow someone else's program?**
> - **Take a brief inventory of your habits, your attitudes, your regular way of being yourself.**
> - **Describe yourself as you are right now, the overall pattern—or lack of pattern—of your life as you live from day to day, as if you had to describe yourself to someone in five minutes or less. Does your life have a "theme?"**
> - **Are these patterns permanent? Have they always been there?**
> - **What happens when people or events interfere with the way you are, or try to move you to do something or to stop doing something?**
> - **Do you see yourself as remaining basically the same as you are now for the rest of your life? Do you want your life to remain essentially as it is?**

When the wind of the Spirit begins to blow through our lives, it works for a level of freedom and responsiveness that will exceed anything we have previously experienced and it may severely disrupt our systems and programs. If this happens, the parts of us that live by the program may well resist the interference with all the power at their disposal, and for some of us this resistance may actually be life-threatening at times.

## CONFRONTATION

The first strategy these parts of ourselves—our inner spiritual gatekeepers—use is to attempt to get the Spirit to name its "authority" and thereby put itself at the same level as themselves. For the Spirit to name an "authority" would be to accept a position, an interpretation, a doctrine, or a dogma, something that is arguable and rebuttable. Control could then be exercised by its accusers in the name of what is "true" or "right." But their objective is not "rightness," but coercive, controlling *power*. Argument can be an effective way to create polarities, to shift the focus away from creativity and life toward "right and wrong."

Our commanding ego will attempt to find ways to challenge the Spirit's legitimacy as it begins to move in our lives. It will present ideas, theology, doctrine, logic, church, scripture, tradition, community, scientific facts or law as "authorities" against which to measure the Spirit within us, and if possible to discredit it and divert us from following it. The ego will easily find support for its resistance in the teachings of churches and religious institutions or in the "correct" interpretation of scriptures, in science, statistics and in "practical realism."

If your spiritual walk is led by what is actually an ambitious "spiritual" subpersonality within you, then the ego may be able to derail your spiritual journey, at least for a time. We can challenge ourselves to discover the basis of our resistance to spiritual freedom. If we decide to follow the Spirit, it will give us what we need to go on.

◆ ◆ ◆

- What authority does your own "conscience" have in your life? What weight does it carry for you?
- Does it have the same authority as, say, a parent, or a preacher, or a friend, or an advisor? Or is it a goad and a nuisance?
- Does it have the authority of God? If you feel that the authority of your conscience comes from God, does that mean that you *must* respond to it?

## AUTHORITY AND POWER

- If you feel that it does not come from God, then is it still important? Why or why not?
- How do you respond to it?
- What does your response to it tell you about the "authority" that you recognize in your life?
- How do you know "who is this, really?"
- What is the relationship between power and authority in your life?
- Where does power arise from? Where does spiritual authority arise from?

- Come back to this section regularly, to see whether there is any confrontation between the Spirit and your way of life.

## 34. RECOGNITION

## RECOGNITION

The question about authority is really about power, for the priests, scribes and elders are afraid that Jesus may be able to *force* them to change—for this is really the only kind of power they recognize or authority they respect. Jesus understands them well, and proceeds to tell a story that exposes them.

> 12:1 And he began to speak to them in parables. "A man planted a vineyard, set a hedge around it, dug a pit for the wine press, and built a watch tower; then he leased it to farmers and went abroad. When the season came, he sent a slave to the farmers to collect some of the produce of the vineyard from them. But they grabbed him and beat him, and sent him away empty-handed. And again he sent another slave to them; this one they beat on the head and insulted. And he sent another, and this one they killed; and so with many others, some they beat and some they killed. He still had one other, a beloved son; finally he sent him to them, saying, 'They will respect my son.' But the farmers said to one another, 'This is the heir! Come, let us kill him, and the inheritance will be ours.' So they seized him and killed him, and threw him out of the vineyard. What will the lord of the vineyard do? He will come and destroy the farmers and give the vineyard to others. Have you not read the scripture, 'The stone that the builders rejected has become the cornerstone; this is the Lord's doing, and it is amazing in our eyes.'" And they wanted to arrest him, for they knew that he had told this parable about them, but they were afraid of the crowd. So they left him and went away.

Jesus has told a parable that makes plain that he understands their true intentions, and that makes plain to all his listeners that the opposition is out to destroy him. His parable tells of people who are commissioned to grow fruit, to produce results, for the service of God. But the farmers grow to serve themselves.

## CONFRONTATION

In the inner interpretation we see the vineyard as our lives, for we did not plant ourselves or guide our early growth, but we have been shaped by a wide variety of forces outside ourselves in such a way that is accurate to say that we ourselves are "God's vineyard." A basic impulse to life was planted in us, and at some point in time the direction of our lives is "handed over" to us to be the farmers of this "plot." We arrive at maturity and the ability to make decisions and choose the direction our lives will take, and Jesus' parable is indicating that the normal response is that we devote a portion of our energies to serving the larger Life out of which we have sprung. If we are ruled by our inner gatekeepers, then we are probably like the farmers in Jesus' parable who find a way to keep all of their "produce" and ignore the Source out of which life has arisen. The parable indicates that God makes repeated efforts to reach us, not to make us "tithe" a portion of our income—remember that this is a parable. The "produce" of our lives is more than income: it is our care and concern, our interest, our minds and emotions, our energy and action. The parable says that God wants us to give some our "produce" to God, yet we must remember that God is All-in-All, and will speak to us individually as to how that produce is to be conveyed—in the parable, God sends messengers and finally his own son to draw the tenants out of their self-centeredness. If we are dominated by entrenched gatekeepers, the messengers will be sent away, maybe even "killed."

In this parable we have the message that the Spirit is openly challenging our self-centered egos and making it clear that the Spirit will prevail even against the ego's work of inner murder, for One who is Lord and Master created the vineyard and still controls it. But again the scribes and Pharisees and elders are afraid that Jesus will unleash some physical, coercive power upon them—as they would do to him if they believed that they could succeed. Here, perhaps, lies our own fear of the Spirit—that it will force us against our will, just as we might use our will to compel ourselves and others.

> o **Do you have an "inner vineyard?"**
> o **Who built it? Who is tending it? Who controls it? What are its fruits?**

# RECOGNITION

- Who has a right to the fruits? Are they all yours, or does someone else have a claim to some?
- Does someone else have some control over your life? If so, who?
- What would your life be like if you were never compelled—by people or by circumstances—against your will?
- Are you afraid of the Spirit coming into your life?
- Can there be a synthesis of some kind between your will and the will of God? Why might you want—or not want—such a synthesis?

♦ ♦ ♦

- Come back to this section and to these questions whenever you feel comfortable with your spiritual life. Check on your "inner farmers" and see who they are working for.

## 35. POLARITIES AND CONFLICTS

## POLARITIES AND CONFLICTS

> 12:13 And they send some Pharisees and some Herodians to him to trap him in his words. And they come and say to him, "Teacher, we know that you are true and give preference to no one, for you do not regard the faces of men, but in truth you teach the way of God. Is it lawful to pay taxes to Caesar or not? Should we pay them, or should we not?" But knowing their hypocrisy, he said to them, "Why do you test me? Bring me a denarius, and let me see it." And they brought him one. And he said to them, "Whose image and title is this?" They answered, "Caesar's." Jesus said to them, "The things of Caesar, give to Caesar; the things of God, to God." And they were amazed at him.

The strategy of the opposition now is to shift the ground a little, but is essentially the same—to try to get Jesus to take a position on one side of a polarity (it doesn't matter which side) that they can attack. One such polarity is setting the focus of spiritual life in opposition to practical reality, and they goad Jesus to favor one side against the other. But the Spirit refuses to support any inner conflict, instead insisting that practical effort be made for practical goals, and spiritual effort be made for spiritual goals, and no conflict arises. The Spirit is resolutely inclusive, rejecting the invitation to conflict.

This part of the Gospel is equivalent to an inner activity in which we think we see a clear dichotomy between "spiritual life" and "practical life," and we find ourselves resisting the life of the Spirit because we think it will get us into practical trouble or urge us to resist the demands of practical life. Any honest "practical" person will refuse to shirk the normal practical demands of life, and we may find that this kind of thinking appears in our minds when the demands of the spiritual life become more rigorous. We may find ourselves embracing this kind of dichotomy as a reason why we turn away from spiritual life.

# CONFRONTATION

> 12:18 Some Sadducees, who say there is no resurrection, come to him asking a question, saying, "Teacher, Moses wrote for us that if a man's brother dies, leaving a wife but no child, his brother shall marry the widow and raise up children for his brother. There were seven brothers; the first married a woman and died with no children. And the second married her and died with no children; and the third likewise. And the seven left no children. Last of all, the woman also died. In the resurrection, whose wife will she be? For the seven had her as wife." Jesus said to them, "Is not this why you are deceived, because you know neither the scriptures nor the power of God? For when they rise from the dead, they neither marry nor are they given in marriage, but are like angels in heaven. And as for the dead being raised, have you not read in the book of Moses in the story about the bush, how God said to him, 'I am the God of Abraham and the God of Isaac and the God of Jacob?' He is not the God of the dead, but of the living. You have wandered far from the truth."

The opposition then presents a parody of faith in life, for they do not take it seriously. They try to trap him on an absurd point of religious doctrine into supporting some kind of conflict, but he responds by saying that in the spiritual life the bases for conflict are removed. He refuses to accept the mockery. He also points out that those who invent conflicts based upon far-fetched examples actually have no understanding of the reality of the spiritual life, any more than do people who believe that physical death is the end of a person's life.

The forces of opposition need Jesus to accept some position that they can *oppose*, and they cannot tolerate someone who does not live *against* something—against Caesar, against women, against a brother, against sinners, against death—against something or someone. Polarity is built into their outlook.

## POLARITIES AND CONFLICTS

This vignette represents yet another tactic that we may find ourselves using, knowingly or unconsciously, to resist the life of the spirit. Our practical minds may easily find a religious doctrine that seems excessive and use this as a pretext to debunk the spiritual life in general.

All the opposing forces have tried to get Jesus to take a position of limitation, of conflict, of death, just as within us the forces of opposition attempt to induce us to accept laws, dogmas, doctrines, precepts and practices that are closed, limited, and fixed, or that lead to inner conflict—something that can be judged and rejected—and in this way shut down the free flow of the Spirit of God in our lives. Jesus speaks for the Spirit, saying that God is the source and root of living *people*, not dead things, dead ideas, or dead practices. What is "dead" may not be "deceased," and "gone," but merely stiff, inflexible, incurious, unresponsive, and not growing anymore. But the dead can be raised.

♦ ♦ ♦

- How does your mind react to polarities, to opposites like right-wrong, good-bad, success-failure, correct-incorrect?
- Are you more comfortable if you believe that what you are reading, or what you are thinking, is either right or wrong? Are you more—or less—comfortable if there is no polarity? Why? Does your feeling influence your thinking?
- What place do polarities have in your life? Where do they belong, and where do they not belong?
- Where do judgments of right and wrong belong in your life?
- Notice whether you feel a non-acceptance or a resistance to an active spiritual life, and what form your non-acceptance or resistance takes. If you experience such resistance, become aware of the reasons you have for maintaining this resistance.

CONFRONTATION

♦ ♦ ♦

> ○ Come back to this section and to these questions whenever you find your thoughts, feelings or experience are on one side of a polarity or a judgment.

## 36. THREE RESPONSES TO SCRIBES

## CONFRONTATION

> 12:28 And one of the scribes came and heard them disputing with one another, and seeing that he answered them well, he asked him, "Which commandment is first of all?" Jesus answered, "The first is, 'Hear, O Israel! The Lord our God, the Lord is One; and you shall love the Lord your God with all your heart, and with all your soul, and with all your mind, and with all your strength!' The second is this: 'You shall love your neighbor as yourself.' There is no commandment greater than these." And the scribe said to him, "Well, Teacher! In truth you have spoken that he is one, and there is no other but he; and to love him with all the heart, and with all the understanding, and with all the strength, and to love one's neighbor as oneself is *much* more than all the whole burnt offerings and sacrifices." And when Jesus saw that he answered with understanding, he said to him, "You are not far from the kingdom of God." And after that, no one dared ask him any question.

In the context of our inner interpretation of the Gospel the scribe's question is meant to move us beyond polarities and judgments, beyond doctrines and ideas, to what is truly basic and essential: What comes *first* in the spiritual life? Jesus answers directly to us: first, the Source of your being is One; it is not scattered or polarized, in conflict or divided. It is One and it is God. You are to *love* the Lord your God—not half-heartedly or in a limited way, not only with "right" thinking or "good" behavior, but with *all* your heart, *all* your mind, *all* your strength, *all* your soul, with all you have and all your are. *And* you are to love all people, and all of yourself, and others *as* yourself. Using the inner interpretation of the Gospel is one way to see others as yourself, and to love both. Jesus walks out the role of the Spirit in our lives, loving all people, healing all who come to him, bringing all people together in harmony before the One who is our Source.

## THREE RESPONSES TO SCRIBES

The scribe recognizes that Jesus has spoken a basic truth, and adds that the love of God is more important and more basic than any other practice, no matter how venerable and accepted.

> o **What happens to your life when the first, second and third most important things in your life are "love?"**
> o **How are Jesus' healings and teachings examples of how these commandments can be carried out?**
> o **How would you carry them out today?**

Commandments have to do with basic questions of right and wrong, and Jesus answers the scribe's question to tell us what is most basic of all: The first commandment is to love, and the second commandment is to love. The judgments of rightness or correctness or truth may have a place in our lives, but only if they follow these first two commandments.[1] In the story it is a scribe who poses the question, "which commandment is first of all?" This man represents a part of us that has studied and learned the teachings that are accepted in our culture as the truth, and we see that this vignette shows another part of us that is looking for a way to reject the Spirit—in this case, to compare the teaching of the Law and the Bible with the promptings of the Spirit. The Gospel is emphasizing that the core of the Law and the teaching of the Spirit are the same, so when Jesus hears the scribe agree with him on first principles—that the love of God is the first commandment, and the love of neighbor as ourselves is second—Jesus acknowledges their proximity.

But why does he say, "you are not *far* from the kingdom?" Does the scribe acknowledge the truth because it is written in his heart and informs all his actions, or because it is written in a sacred book and is therefore "the law?" The understanding and belief of truth is only one part of life, but the kingdom of God is a state of being in which

---

[1] We notice that Jesus does *not* say "love your neighbor if he is good, or if he behaves well, or if he does what is right." Just "love your neighbor as yourself."

CONFRONTATION

we *live* the truth and we become the truth. The scribe teaches the truth, but as a scribe in the temple he may not be fully living the truth, and Jesus subsequently warns of scribes who are saluted and honored for the truth that they believe and teach, while the truth that they *live* is that of hypocrite and predator.

Similarly we may find that we can easily *agree* with many or all of the teachings of Jesus, but what does this say about how we live? Do we live by what we believe?

> 12:35 And as Jesus was teaching in the temple, he said, "How can the scribes say that the Christ is the son of David? David himself, in the Holy Spirit, declared, 'The Lord said to my lord, sit at my right hand, 'til I put your enemies under your feet.' David himself calls him 'Lord,' so how can he be his son?" And the large crowd was listening to him with delight.

Jesus takes a moment to talk about the Christ, explaining that the *real* Christ is not a descendent of King David, for the Christ lived in David's awareness and David called him "Lord." He is showing that while he himself is walking out the role of Christ on earth, the Christ is not merely human—not the son of David, but the son of humankind, the Son of Man whose life is far greater than that of a human lifespan; a Spirit whose life was available to King David and is available to us. Therefore any attempt to show that Jesus is literally the descendant of King David misses the significance of Jesus' life and also ignores Jesus' own words. This teaching is to show *us* where to look for the Christ—not in history, but within ourselves, where, like King David, we may talk with him and listen and learn.

Jesus is explicitly challenging scripture for the second time. The scribes were those who did the writing, and when Jesus challenges what "the scribes say" about the Christ and about David, he is challenging scripture. Jesus walks in the Spirit, and in the Gospel story he represents the Spirit within us, which is not bound by anything dead, or fixed, or written.

## THREE RESPONSES TO SCRIBES

> 12:38 And as he taught, he said, "Beware of the scribes, who like to walk around in long robes, and to be greeted with respect in the market places, and to have the best seats in the synagogues and the places of honor at the banquets. They devour widows' houses and say long prayers for the sake of appearance. They will receive much greater judgment."

The scribes have the words and signs of holiness, and Jesus is showing us that the part of us that loves recognition for being right, saying the right things, looking right, may be a predator that gives no heed to genuine needs. Here we have the third successive vignette concerning the scribes—the writers, keepers and interpreters of the scriptures. In the first, Jesus satisfies the scribes' insistence upon scriptural priorities; in the second, he shows that these spiritual gatekeepers do not understand who Christ is, and in the third he shows that the priorities of the scribes are not the priorities of the Christ or of God.

He has presented direct responses to the challenges of some spiritual gatekeepers as a way of directing our attention to the parts of our own lives that are most prominent, most successful, and most respected only to warn us that these parts of ourselves may prop themselves up at the expense of "poor" parts of us, who are as defenseless as a poor widow. Why? Because this leads us directly to the next section, in which the individual—the very victim of the scribes' predatory behavior—provides the example of true godliness.

- **Who are your "inner scribes?" What traditions and teachings do they interpret and protect (these may be scientific, religious, political or other varieties)?**
- **How might you find yourself more focused on scripture, teaching or tradition than on the Spirit?**
- **What would you do if that occurs?**

# NOTES

# TRANSFORMATION

In this part of the Gospel we leave the concerns of the scribes behind and focus on the great inner action that the Spirit has initiated. We begin with a vignette which shows the power of focus in the application of spiritual power. This is followed by a remarkable account of a great upheaval, in which a great and painful new birth is described in apocalyptic terms as a prelude to the final episodes of the Gospel. We are shown that the violence of the commanding ego's reaction to the great transformation is expressed in terms of betrayal and hatred and sows such confusion that many of us are tempted to abandon the process— which is what our ego structures most want. But those who endure to the end will be delivered.

Throughout the Gospel process our disciple parts may have had only a dim understanding of what has been happening despite their commitment to Jesus. But here we will find that an unknown, anonymous part does understand and acts appropriately, recognizing the truth that Jesus represents. But this action provokes another part within us to rush forward with a personal agenda, to force the transformation process in a particular way. We will discover that the transformation process may be too difficult for our conscious awareness, and even our most devoted inner disciples may be pushed to denial or abandonment.

We will discover that the triumph of the commanding ego in its quest to wipe out the influence of the spirit ultimately cannot last, for the death of Jesus is not the end, but the beginning of a new life in us. This part begins with Mark 12:41 and goes to the end at Mark 16:8.

## 37. SPIRITUAL POWER, PART 4

## TRANSFORMATION

> <sup>12:41</sup> He sat down opposite the treasury and was watching the crowd putting money into the treasury, and many rich people put in large amounts. A poor widow came and put in two small copper coins, which are worth a quarter. And he called his disciples and said to them, "Truly I tell you, this poor widow has put more into the treasury than all the others. For all of the others gave of their surplus, but she out of her poverty has put in everything she had, all she had to live on."

Our response to the Spirit cannot be measured against or compared to the response of any other person, for the response to the Spirit of God is not an objective, quantifiable phenomenon. Just as the invisible intelligence that organizes and grows our bodies does not rely upon any outer, "objective" criteria as our bones, nerves, muscles, and brains are developed in the womb or as we grow up, so our responses to Spirit are proportional to our inner development. Outside forces shape our physical circumstances, just as the circumstances of life have made some people rich and some widows poor. Jesus shows that subjective proportionality of our spiritual responses is most important to our spiritual condition and growth—the contribution of vast sums by the wealthy are proportionately lower than the contribution of the widow, which was all that she had. Compare her to the scribes mentioned above: the scribes devour the widow's house to build them*selves* up; the widow, deprived of nearly everything, gives all she has left to the service of God.

The focus here is not on contributions to the temple, for Jesus has already made it plain that he opposes all of the commercialization of religious life when he turned the money-changers out of the temple. In earlier teachings he has directed our attention to what comes out of our mouths rather than what goes in.[1] Now he directs our focus to what comes out of our hands, rather than on what comes in. For he is teaching about the source and direction of power, not

---
[1] See Section 17, page 176.

## SPIRITUAL POWER, PART 4

about objective measurements of the *effects* of power. When we commit only a portion of our inner resources, we divide our will and we scatter the power in many directions, so that even immense power has relatively little effect. When we commit all that we have in a single direction, then even scanty resources can have great effect. The effect is realized in the one who makes the commitment as well as in the recipient. Proportion matters. This is a direct continuation of the teaching contained in the feedings of the thousands.

♦ ♦ ♦

- **What proportion of your focus and energy is in the Spirit?**
- **Go back to Section 32 on pages 275-279 and compare the lessons there with this vignette.**
- **Why is a total commitment important? What difference does it make?**

## 38. THE GREAT TRANSFORMATION

## THE GREAT TRANSFORMATION

> 13:1 And as he came out of the temple, one of his disciples says to him, "Look, Teacher! What stones! And what buildings!" And Jesus said to him, "Do you see these great buildings? There may not be one stone upon another left here, that will not be thrown down."

These great buildings are the edifice of our self-serving, self-centered ego—devoted to using all the resources available to build itself up. It builds a grand structure of traditions—a temple of ideas, beliefs, scriptures, laws and behaviors—to create a reality for itself that pays lip service to the worship of God, but is actually devoted to human busy-ness with the self as its object. Without the Spirit at its source, the whole endeavor is futile and ultimately empty. It must come down so that the Spirit may operate freely in our lives, and the self assume its rightful place as servant, not ruler.[1]

> 13:3 And when he was sitting on the Mount of Olives opposite the temple, Peter, James, John and Andrew asked him privately, "Tell us, when will this be, and what will be the sign that all these things are about to be fulfilled?" Then Jesus began to say to them, "Take heed that no one deceive you. Many will come in my name, and say, "I am,"[2] and they will lead many astray. But when you hear of wars and rumors of wars, do not panic; these must happen, but they are not the end. For nation will rise against nation, and kingdom against kingdom; there will be earthquakes in

---
[1] With this in mind, it may be helpful to go back and review Section 25 on page 227, where the egotism of the disciples prompted Jesus' teaching about leadership.
[2] Once again Jesus uses the formula for God's self-revealing from Exodus: " I am"

## TRANSFORMATION

various places; there will be famines—these are the beginning of the birth pains. But look out for yourselves. They will hand you over to councils, and you will be beaten in synagogues, and you will be stood before governors and kings because of me, as a witness to them. First, the joyous message must be proclaimed in all the nations. And when they might lead you to betrayal, be not anxious about what you might say, but say whatever is given to you in that hour, for it is not you who speak, but the Holy Spirit. Brother will betray brother to death, and a father his child, children will rise up against their parents and put them to death; and you will be hated by all because of my name. But the one who endures to the end will be delivered. When you see the loathsomeness that destroys and lays waste, set up where it ought not to be (let the reader understand!), then let those in Judea flee to the mountains; let the one on the roof not go down into the house to take something up; and let the one in the field not turn back to pick up his coat; but woe to those who are pregnant or nursing in those days! Pray that it will not happen in winter. For in those days there will be suffering such as has not been from the beginning of creation that God created until now, and never will be. And if the Lord had not cut short the days, no one would be saved; but for the sake of the chosen ones, whom he chose, he cut short those days. And then if someone says to you, "Look! Here is the Christ!' or 'Look! There he is!' do not believe it. False christs and false prophets will appear, and give signs and wonders to deceive, if possible, the chosen ones. But you see—I have told you all beforehand. But in those days, after that suffering, the sun will be darkened and the moon will not give its light, and the stars will be falling from heaven, and the powers in the heavens will be shaken. And then they will see the Son of Man coming in clouds with great power and glory. And then he will send the messengers and he will gather his chosen ones from the four winds, from the ends of the earth to the

> ends of heaven. But from the fig tree learn the parable: as soon as its branch becomes tender and the leaves sprout, you know that summer is near. So also, when you see these things happening, you know that it is near, right at the door. Truly I say to you, this generation will not pass away until all these things have taken place. Heaven and earth will pass away, but my words will not pass away. But about that day or hour, no one knows, neither the angels in heaven nor the Son, but only the Father. Watch! Stay awake! For you do not know when the time comes. It is like a man going on a journey, when he leaves home and puts each of his slaves in charge of his own work, and commands the gatekeeper to stay awake. Stay awake, then! For you do not know when the master of the house comes—in the evening, or at midnight, or at cockcrow, or at dawn; or he might come suddenly and find you asleep! What I say to you, I say to all: Stay awake!"

This section is unique in Mark's Gospel because it dwells upon what appear to be future events, prophesying wars and disasters, persecution, the coming of false christs and false prophets, followed by the coming of the Son of Man in power and glory. From the inner perspective we have seen all along that sequential time is not an issue, for things may happen "immediately" in the spiritual dimension without regard to the kind of cause and effect that we look for in physical reality. A spiritual event may happen in "real time" either very quickly or very slowly—in minutes or in years.

In our inner interpretation this section is pointing toward a tumultuous transformation that is to occur in our inner future. The short account comes first: there will not be one stone of the temple that will not be thrown down; our inner temple—the structure of the commanding ego—will be completely overturned. Jesus is telling his disciples and those of us who follow him that the transformation he is leading us into will involve a transition time in which our understanding of God and our trust in the Spirit will be assaulted, as well as our self-identities and our devotion to the spiritual path. We

## TRANSFORMATION

will find ourselves in the midst of conflicts and be threatened with more conflict. The systems and programs that have governed our lives, whether "positive" or "negative," will accuse us and haul us to account to answer *in their terms* for what is happening.

Our desire for spiritual transformation is what will provoke all the violence, conflict, deceit, and hunger. As Jesus says, these are but the beginning of the birth pains. The spiritual transformation that Jesus is leading us toward is a new birth, the birth of a new person out of our present selves. The emergence of our new selves will not go smoothly and painlessly, but will demand that we answer for what we have brought upon ourselves and the others who are part of our lives. The transformation itself is a changing of what moves us as well how we are moved, and Jesus coaches us not to try to "figure out" what is going on, for this is like asking someone caught at one point in the middle of a hurricane to describe the overall weather patterns of the world—he cannot describe anything except the storm that surrounds him.

Let go, he counsels, and do not worry about what you are to say, but trust the Holy Spirit within you to answer, for that source has the perspective that is needed.

There *will* be pressure on us to betray the truth, to give up the cause of transformation, and it may come from all directions, including our own family and closest loved ones, and from parts within ourselves. The inner community that supports the edifice of the commanding ego wants the death of the Spirit, and that community may include the inner father, brother and child—some of the most intimate and central parts of the life we know. They will try to undermine or betray any parts of us that work for the freedom of the Spirit. This is something to be *expected*, for the commanding ego in each of us resists the Spirit and will try to kill or neutralize its influence. This is not simply the work of an adversary, but as we have seen it is the work of qualities within us that tip from balance into polarity, and even the qualities of holiness, praise and worship—our inner Judas—can be pressured into betrayal. If we respond to this pressure out of our own ego-resources, we will be overcome. But if we surrender and trust the Spirit with our responses, we will say and do what is needed.

The joyous message—the Gospel—he says, must be proclaimed in all nations. In this interpretation the good news is that you are

## THE GREAT TRANSFORMATION

transforming from a helpless, unconscious being, torn by conflicting impulses and at the mercy of the forces of the world around you[3]—which is full of fear, anger and hatred— into a person whose parts and aspects and subpersonalities are all in harmony, unified under the direction of a Self who is open to the continual flow of the spiritual power of God, at peace internally and with the world. On this level, proclaiming the Gospel to all nations has nothing to do with converting other people to our beliefs. The meaning of the Greek text is, "announcing the joyous message," which is essentially an act of *affirming* and confirming a wonderful reality—the process by which we ourselves are transforming into spiritually-oriented and spirit-filled persons. This in itself will bring benefits to all people in our lives because—as Jesus has demonstrated—the work of the Spirit is to heal, to reconcile, and to bring life.

But we live in a network of relationships, and our life's closest connections—with parents, siblings, and children—have been built upon and reinforced by the judgments, conflicts, impulses, fears, hatred, needs and loves of the world around us. People who are immersed in such networks invest their identities in them just as the rich person invests in possessions. When we begin to dis-identify from all these fragmenting forces and connections, we may arouse resentment, resistance or intense hatred, because our transformation will have a disruptive impact on the identifications of others, which have depended on our support or at least our cooperation.

Our change may well be resisted by those we love and who love us. We will also disorient others when we cease to identify ourselves as victims as much as when we stop being oppressors, and when we change we may be resisted consciously or unconsciously by people whom we formerly hurt as well as by those who formerly hurt us—for it was the system and the program that we had been reinforcing and validating by remaining ego-centered. The mutually supporting "co-dependent" ego-networks cross the lines of love and hate, and the dissolving of the webwork of ego connections may arouse negative reactions from all around us—Jesus says, "You will

---

[3] A condition that many of us will deny, as our definitions of "helpless" and "unconscious" may not find correspondence with what we perceive to be the facts and judgments of our everyday lives; but I suspect that these words nevertheless do in fact describe many of us on a deeper level .

## TRANSFORMATION

be hated by all because of my name. But the one who endures to the end will be delivered." Keeping our "eyes on the prize," staying true to the transformation we are undergoing, we will be transformed in the end and our new state of being will make all our trials worthwhile.

He warns, however, that there is one particular danger that stands out in the whole process. We shall be tempted sorely to *force* the process, to attempt to overwhelm the apparent chaos and impose order for the sake of our stability, our sanity and our identity, for the process we are undergoing is one of profound disintegration of ego-power prior to the final integration. Any such attempt by the commanding ego to impose order, once the spiritual transformation has begun, is equivalent to domination by our "inner Romans," who will desecrate all and attempt to stifle the spiritual transformation in the name of "order"—a false peace. What is the "desolating sacrilege"—the loathsomeness that destroys and lays waste, set up where it ought not to be? Not merely an idol in the temple, but within ourselves, it is the belief in *force* accepted and respected in the place of God in our hearts and minds. This is the inner Roman—the desire to *make* things happen, by force if necessary, not only physically in the world, but also within ourselves. Inner coercion and violence may seem to be invisible to others, but they lie at the root of all outer violence. If the belief in and practice of spiritual violence and coercion rule us when the Spirit enters into our lives, the result will be an elemental conflict in which many parts of us (and others) may be severely damaged; an inner conflict such as we have never before experienced, and never will again experience, that might destroy us except, the Gospel says, that God will set a limit to it for the sake of those whom he has chosen.

Whom has God chosen? He has chosen *you*.

◆ ◆ ◆

In such a conflict, incredible things may happen to us, and we will see things outside ourselves that would deceive even the most dedicated of us, and tempt us to see powers outside that would lead us to abandon the quest for inner transformation. But Jesus tells us, Remember that I have warned you of this ahead of time: our task is to restrain the impulse to identify with any of these outside influences, and endure to the end by keeping ourselves, our identities, free

## THE GREAT TRANSFORMATION

from outer entanglements and focused on the inner source from which all power, love and peace flows. He is not urging anyone to cut off contact with loved ones or other people. In the story he urges people, when the time comes, to flee *Judea.* Judea represents the home of accepted religion and orthodoxy, but it is also a hotbed of conflict between religion and worldly power. In the end, raw physical force wins that conflict, both historically and within us. Jesus advises us to *get out!* Do not allow ourselves to be drawn into this conflict, or allow such a conflict to arise within us.[4]

Even though this process is a signal of a new birth, it will be accompanied by much destruction and suffering. He says, pray that it not happen in winter, and woe to those who are pregnant or nursing when it happens. What does this mean within us? Inner transformations follow timing and patterns that do not necessarily make sense to our minds, and that may not fit neatly into the sequence of our lives. They sometimes erupt into our lives like volcanoes spewing ash and lava from an unknown source. Whether or not we are aware or prepared for such transformations, they require us to respond with all of our personal resources of strength, patience, openness, faith and love. Someone who is already in a "winter" will need much help to undergo it. Someone who is pregnant or nursing—devoting inner resources to the life or care of another—will be unable to undergo the transformation without a lot of help, and the "child"—or whomever is being supported—will also need help and healing.

This kind of healing transformation may look like a major life disaster to anyone who is not aware of what is really happening—it is a "healing crisis," and those who do not perceive its true nature may try to stop it.[5] They may unknowingly try to stop the healing as well as the crisis. In particular, some modern medical and psychiatric professionals do not recognize the reality of spiritual crisis—spiritual emergency—and treat the evidence of spiritual transformation as symptoms of disease to be stopped, eradicated, or suppressed

---

[4] This section is an amplification of the teaching in Section 35 on pages 291-295. Here the polarities become violent opposition, and again we are told to stay away from the polarity, which becomes destructive.

[5] Often with some kind of force: either psychological, physical, or pharmacological.

## TRANSFORMATION

with medication. Some spiritual emergencies are so severe that they do require medical support and psychological therapy, but it is important that the symptoms of spiritual crisis (which often manifest physically in some way) not be confused with organic, physical disease.

Jesus knows that each person who is on the path is eager to know how things will work out, and when things will occur. But we notice that he never urges people to rush into transformation. Even though he has been teaching people how to move in the direction of change, he specifically warns us against forcing it on our own schedule. The process that leads to the great transformation in our lives begins with our repentance and moves us through the healings that have been the subject of the Gospel, but once the process is underway we do not take the initiative—rather we allow the Spirit to lead us. We *follow* Christ. Watch! he says; be aware of what is happening in your life. There are signs that will tell you. Just as the tree coming into leaf tells you that summer is approaching, the kind of conflict he has described is the sign of approaching change. Be not afraid of such disorder and apparent chaos; be not deterred by the inner violence and outer resistance (that may take the form of resentments and hatreds), but know that these are the signs that your transformation is underway, and that the resolution of your struggle is near. But as to when this will occur *for you*, no one knows beforehand, for part of the process depends upon your own choices and responses, and part is governed by events which we cannot be aware or in control of—none of which are "determined" beforehand. And yet Jesus can say with certainty that it *will* occur, for this is the way that creation has been organized.[6] The work of the Spirit is a more fundamental law of the universe than even the laws of physics that govern the heaven and the earth.

He repeats his encouragement to us to take up our own parts in the process, for while we cannot know in advance how or when the Spirit will come upon us, we must prepare ourselves as best we can. Watch! he says. Be aware!

---

[6] In a similar way, 60 years ago my mother could not tell exactly how I was going to grow and what kind of person I would be, but she could say with certainty that I would grow, for that is what children do.

## THE GREAT TRANSFORMATION

Who are the "false Christs?" When we are in the midst of the great transformation we are neither caterpillar nor butterfly, but something indeterminate, neither old nor new. This may be a time of stress and suffering on one level of our lives or another, and we may grasp at "solutions" (false Christs) that seem to promise relief, but that actually give all sign and no healing. There are some people who hear the "voice of God" within them, and follow that voice, which may in truth be only too human—sometimes tragically so. Much of the early part of the Gospel story asked "who is this?" and commanded people to be silent, because it is hard to discern the real voice of God, and easy to be misled. We each may find in ourselves (or in someone else, like a doctor or a preacher) something "authoritative" but we, like the disciples, only *know* the truth after much trial, much error, much learning, and even then only by the grace of God. The first half of the Gospel has explored how we know the inner voice, and we saw how even those closest to Jesus misunderstood him. But, he says, during this great upheaval, even the chosen ones—our inner Simon and Andrew, James and John—may be deceived, for the pressure is extraordinary and disorienting to the extreme. It is not those who understand, but rather those who *endure* who are saved—those who stay with the process, get the help they need, who "keep awake" and trust God.

Healing comes when we emerge from the chrysalis of transformation, when there is indeed "joy in the morning."

This entire vignette is a portrait in advance of the betrayal, arrest and crucifixion of Jesus—the "birth pangs" that accompany our inner transformation, which for some of us is accompanied by deep, profound suffering.

♦ ♦ ♦

> o **How would you describe your "inner temple?" What is your inner religious structure, your inner political structure? What part of you commands your life—"drives your inner car?" Or does the control get moved between several parts of you?**

# TRANSFORMATION

- Does your inner "I" that commands answer to another? Or does it make decisions without much regard to other parts of you?
- Have you ever experienced the beginning of changes in your life that were so frightening or difficult that you needed them to stop? If so, what made that necessary? Could some difficult changes be good, and worth undergoing? What kind of help and support would be needed to do this?
- Have you ever undergone a profound change in your life?—like a recovery from a serious disease, a divorce or death of a loved one, a conversion or change of basic beliefs, a change in basic life circumstances? If you have, was the pattern of how you felt about yourself (the "who I am") changed as a result? If so, how? Do you think that this change was part of your spiritual growth and transformation?
- Is it possible for you to undergo a profound change without major inner resistance or outer non-cooperation? Do you think your loved ones would support you if you were to undergo a fundamental change in your life?
- If you are following the Gospel process in your own life, look to see where you are right now in the process. Do you feel a transformation beginning or underway? If you do, what are you doing or what help and support are you getting, to endure the process? Who is there to help you? Do you seek help? Do you accept all the help that is available to you?
- If you sense a transformation unfolding in your life, are you able to wait for it to proceed at its own pace and time?

## THE GREAT TRANSFORMATION

> ○ Come back to this section if you feel that your life is undergoing some kind of profound change, if you feel unsure of your way, if you doubt whether you have chosen the right path, if you feel tempted to give it all up because it is too hard.

♦ ♦ ♦

## 39. THE ANOINTING

# THE ANOINTING

> 14:1 It was two days before the Passover and the Festival of Unleavened Bread, and the chief priests and the scribes were seeking how to arrest him by stealth and kill him, for they said, "Not during the festival, or there will be a riot among the people." And while he was at Bethany in the house of Simon the Leper, as he sat at the table, a woman came with an alabaster jar of very expensive genuine nard perfume, and she broke it open and poured it over his head. But there were some who said to themselves indignantly, "Why has this perfume been wasted like this? For this perfume could have been sold for more than three hundred denarii[1] and the money given to the poor." And they reproached her. But Jesus said, "Let her alone; why do you trouble her? She has performed a good service for me. For the poor you always have with you, and you can do good for them whenever you wish; but you will not always have me. She made do with what she had; she has anointed my body with perfume beforehand for burial. Truly I say to you, wherever the joyous message is proclaimed in the whole world, what she has done will be told in remembrance of her."

This section, from the inner perspective, is the beginning of the transformation that Jesus has been preparing us for since his revelation as the Christ. We begin with a woman who anoints him with very expensive perfume.[2]

This unnamed woman is remembered because she is the only person in the story who acts as if she knows and understands what is happening, and who acts appropriately on her knowledge. The story tells us that within us there is one who does recognize the Spirit and who acts out of deep love, even though we may not know

---
[1] About ten months' wages for an average worker at that time and place.
[2] Clearly some of Jesus' followers were very wealthy! What does this wealth signify from an inner perspective?

## TRANSFORMATION

who she is or why she acts as she does. This is important, because here, as in the vignette above, understanding is not the prime requirement. She is remembered because of her love and for what she did to express this love within the realm of her ability. None of the disciples *understands* what she is doing, and they are still walking in judgment, while Jesus sees what we are meant to see and explains her action to the disciples—and to us.

Jesus' body is anointed before his death, for it will not be anointed after death. The Spirit will lead the way in the transformation, and it is time to change focus. The change may be recognized only by some "anonymous"[3] part of us, whose action may seem to make no sense to us. But the Gospel is alerting us to look for a response within ourselves that is like the anointing of Jesus in some way, an indication that some part of us is not panicked, not judging, not confused. We may become aware that some part of us is calm and joyful, that rejoices in the midst of our trouble, and Jesus is telling us to become aware and remember this when it happens. This is a special moment for us.

We have had a physical person in Jesus before us all this time, and he uses this vignette to drive his point home—the perfume is to anoint his body for burial. "The Christ" means "the anointed one." This vignette creates a new meaning for the word—for Jesus is anointed not to "rule" as the foreign tyrants rule, but to serve all and to die in the bodily incarnation and image so that the Spirit may rule all. It is only after this incident that Judas goes to the priests and offers to cooperate with their efforts to arrest Jesus. This episode is the signal to Judas to proceed, for Jesus has now accepted homage from a person, he has behaved like a king: this was what Judas was waiting for. Similarly an inner action arising from a knowing calm or rejoicing at our impending transformation may trigger a response of some kind within us, as some part of us reacts to force the process, as will become plain in the next section.

---

[3] And unrecognized, just as women were mostly unrecognized in Jesus' time.

## 40. SPIRITUAL WARFARE: THE BEGINNING OF THE BETRAYAL

## TRANSFORMATION

> ¹⁴:¹⁰ And Judas Iscariot, who was one of the Twelve, went to the chief priests in order to hand him over to them. When they heard it, they were glad and promised to give him money. So he sought a good opportunity to hand him over.

Judas represents the part of us that sincerely seeks the spiritual life, but who believes that it is only natural and right that the Spirit *overcome* the flesh.[1] The spiritual perspectives of many of us are founded on beliefs in spiritual warfare and conquest, on the absolute certainty that the Spirit will overcome and *defeat* all opposition. From such a perspective, conflict is welcome, for it will result in victory. Judas is the personification of this belief, and when he decides to betray Jesus to the priests, it is with the firm conviction that Jesus will emerge from the confrontation (after three days) as the unchallenged ruler of all. Judas, like the others, cannot conceive of a God without opposition, he cannot envision life or God without conflict and polarity. He cannot fathom the kind of radical inclusiveness that Jesus teaches and embodies.[2]

This is a part of ourselves that cannot wait for things to unfold, but must work to ensure that our spiritual agenda is achieved; a part of us that dislikes being patient, that cannot give up control—and that cannot understand the talk of death. He needs something to *happen*, and is certain that his champion, the Spirit, will prevail. The Gospel shows Judas going to the priests because this is a way for the story to show us that here is an instance of one of our own inner disciples abandoning its commitment to *follow* the Spirit, because the going has gotten too tough to sit through. Waiting feels like passivity to a part of us, it makes us feel helpless and victimized

---

[1] Or that one form of worship will overcome another. The anointing of Jesus can be seen as a direct challenge to those whose worship is performed through the channels approved by the temple priests and elders. Judas' actions can be seen as championing a more spiritual worship over a more worldly one. The effect is the same in both interpretations.

[2] The other disciples cannot fathom it either, yet. But it is Judas who acts.

# SPIRITUAL WARFARE

when we undergo a troubling experience and do not *act* to relieve the difficulty.

Jesus has foretold the betrayal of Judas when he spoke of the loathsomeness that destroys and lays waste being set up where it ought not to be (that is, the belief in the power of brute force set up in the heart of a disciple of the prince of peace), for in those words he anticipated the tendency that Judas now acts out: doing it in our own way, on our own terms, at a time of our choosing, believing that *power over others* is what gets things done and that calling up that power will accomplish what is desired. But that kind of power is not healing or restorative, and the true power of God will not—*cannot*—be drawn into competition with "earthly" power.

Judas is acting out the very thing that Jesus warned against earlier: he cannot *wait*—he is not able to limit what he says or does to what he is given by the Spirit, but is *led* to betrayal by his need to act, and by his own innermost ideals—which become polarized and extreme when he holds them to himself instead of surrendering them to the Spirit. Judas is an inner *disciple*—he is not a planted saboteur. The story shows us that our spiritual quest may be undermined or attacked by some of the very parts of ourselves that are committed to that very quest—parts that do not understand what is really going on within us.

- **Recall our discussion of qualities earlier in this work (also see Table A on page 51 and Table B on page 104 ). A small shift can move a balanced quality into an extreme of excess or deficiency.**
- **Re-examine your own qualities. Which of them still tend to move into an extreme or polarity when you are provoked or pressured in an emergency?**
- **How can you maintain your balance?**
- **What kind of pressure or emergency in your life would create a situation in which you would find it hardest to "wait" to allow inner and outer events to unfold?**

TRANSFORMATION

♦ ♦ ♦

Many people on the spiritual path believe that understanding the dynamics of our souls—our "psychology"—is not important for spiritual growth. But many of the crimes committed by "spiritual people" from Judas Iscariot to the European Grand Inquisitors and the leaders of the Crusades in the middle ages, down to modern practitioners of "holy war" and *jihad*, have been committed by people whose spiritual outlooks were rooted in the belief in "spiritual warfare" in which the Spirit of God is one polarity that is pitted against another, evil, polarity—or, in other terms, that heaven is pitted against earth, or some other variation on this theme. This belief in elemental conflict often leads people into an "us against them" mentality and eventually may be used to justify unjust or even violent means for the sake of a totally polarized end—personally, socially, or politically. The wounding that results from such conflict is the kind "soul wounding" that therapists in spiritual psychology are trained to help heal. [3]

Jesus represents God, who is both within and beyond all polarities. Jesus comes with love and compassion to heal the sick, because it is the sick who spread disease. He comes to the deranged, because a sound mind is essential to spiritual life. He even comes to the people who do not accept his inclusiveness, for he comes for all and to all. Care of the soul and care of mind and body are essential aspects of spiritual life (which is itself the foundation of a *whole* life), and psychology is also an essential aspect of spirituality. Jesus has been teaching this from the beginning of his ministry, by reaching out to *all*, just as God reaches out to all creation to heal our collective insanity.

---

[3] The basic character of "spiritual warfare" is not affected by whether its practitioners claim to understand that "true" spiritual warfare is to be waged exclusively with weapons of spirit and peace, for historically the imagery of warfare has widely been taken literally in all eras, resulting in both inner and outer violence.

SPIRITUAL WARFARE

> 14:12 On the first day of Unleavened Bread, when the Passover Lamb is sacrificed, his disciples say to him, "Where do you want us to go to prepare for you to eat the Passover?" And he calls two of his disciples, saying to them, "Go into the city, and a man carrying a jar of water[4] will meet you. Follow him, and where he enters, say to the master of the house that the Teacher says, 'Where is the guest room where I may eat the Passover with my disciples?' He will show you a large room upstairs, furnished and ready; and there make preparations for us." And the disciples set out and went into the city, and found it just as he had told them, and they prepared the Passover. When it was evening, he comes with the Twelve.

The Spirit proceeds with the process of transformation. Passover was a celebration of the people being "passed over" centuries earlier by the plagues that were sent to Egypt by God to induce Pharaoh to set the people free. Lamb's blood was the sign that protected the people from the plague of death. Jesus and the Twelve will eat in celebration of the deliverance of the people, and during the meal he will present the Twelve with a great challenge. For there is a new kind of "passing over" that Jesus is to represent to the disciples and to us, and the symbolism of the sacrifice of the paschal lamb is to lead us to understanding the new freedom which Jesus is teaching.

♦ ♦ ♦

---

[4] The New American Bible's online note for this verse (http://www.usccb.org/nab/bible/mark/mark14.htm ) points out that carrying jars of water was normally considered "women's work" in ancient times, so that a man doing this work would have stood out. Perhaps this is an early evidence of the early Christian practice of not segregating men and women in traditional ways. Many other Gospel lessons point in the direction of overcoming polarities for the sake of wholeness and unity, including those in Sections 27 (p.260) and 38 (p.318).

## 41. LOVE AND BETRAYAL

# LOVE AND BETRAYAL

> 14:18 And as they were at table eating, Jesus said, "Truly I say to you, one of you will betray me, one who is eating with me." They began to grieve, and to say to him one after another, "Not I?" But he said to them, "One of the Twelve, one who is dipping in the bowl with me. For the Son of Man goes as it is written of him, but woe to the one by whom the Son of Man is betrayed. It would have been better for that one not to have been born."

Why does he announce this, and why does he announce it *this way*? He does not accuse or expose one person, but says, "*one* of you will betray me." Is this meant to make all of them squirm? For they all *do*. I think that he is helping the Twelve to come awake to the reality within each of them.

Judas is one of the Twelve, and is not to be considered separate in any way from the others in this vignette or at any other time. He has followed Jesus, he has taught and anointed and healed along with the others. They *all* grieve, and they *all* consider whether in some way they might betray him, and he intends for them to respond this way. We mentioned earlier that Judas was introduced as the betrayer when the Twelve were first named. Any of the Twelve could have been named as the betrayer, because *any* of the Twelve could have "overshot the mark" before the others. Each of the disciples represents qualities of inner seeking that are used by the Spirit to begin the great transformation, and each of them is, by itself, fragmented and separate. Jesus knows that his own transformation is to take place, "for the Son of Man goes as it is written of him," and he also knows that one of the disciples will play a pivotal part in his going. Because the disciples represent inner qualities that are doing all they can for him, the Spirit knows that one of them will not be able to restrain itself—it will try too hard—because before the transformation none of them is *whole*. All of them are dedicated, and yet none understands what is really happening, and all of them are likely to cross boundaries; all will be pushed into the extreme of polarity. *All* of them will fall away, as he says just a few moments later. But

## TRANSFORMATION

knowing that all will fail and that one will fail *first*, he proceeds to eat with them all and bless them all equally and remind them of their mission, for he knows that "failure" is not the end of things, but the beginning.

What does this mean for us? Those who will "see the kingdom of God come with power" throw all their effort, all their concentration, all their focus and energy into the spiritual transformation. We "sell all that we own" and follow Christ. And yet we find that inevitably there is some part of us that is not content to follow, but must be taking some kind of action. There are times when God's work does not go fast enough for us.[1] We need his will to be *done*, and we set about doing it—not *with* him, but *for* him. We inevitably fail to do it. When we fail, we suffer.

His warning of woe to the betrayer is not a threat of punishment, but a statement that Jesus knows what suffering *any* of them will endure if they realize that they have betrayed him. One of them *will* endure it. Here is a hint of the nature of the great transformation that Jesus is to embody. The transformation of Jesus to the risen Christ, of man to Spirit, can *only* seem as a betrayal[2] if it is seen from a worldly viewpoint, but from a spiritual vantage point the coming transformation is just one step in a larger process.

The Spirit cannot flow freely and fully within our lives until our focus relinquishes the limited image of "God" represented in "man." There is an unwitting alliance between the parts of us that resist the Spirit—our inner scribes, Pharisees and priests—and the uncomprehending inner disciples who want to follow the Spirit but don't know how. All the disciples swear they will not desert Jesus, and all of them do desert him nevertheless, despite themselves. The most devoted follower, Peter, seems to fail the most. But in truth the most

---

[1] And our impatience may arise from a very practical issue: it is exceedingly difficult to go slowly in our transformation, because the change can be *painful*. We may want to instinctively hurry things to try to reduce the pain.

[2] The Greek work that is translated as "betray" means literally "to deliver" or "to hand over." Translating this word as "betray" adds a connotation with an intensity that may or may not be in the original. The antagonism and polarity represented in our English word "betray" is not present when we view the overall situation from the vantage of the Spirit. Some translations like Young's Literal render it "deliver."

## LOVE AND BETRAYAL

eager one, who fails most spectacularly, is Judas Iscariot, who consciously adopts the means used by Jesus' enemies. They *all* "betray" Jesus, only one does so first—and the first will be last.

But again, the "failure" is only on one level—but this is the level on which we live before the transformation is complete. In the Spirit there is no betrayal and no failure—"the Son of Man goes as it is written of him." The earthly image of Christ *must* perish, the limited concept of God *must* die, so that the true, unlimited Spirit of God may live within us. For this reason, Jesus can love *all* of the disciples and have communion with all of them, knowing that one will play a special, painful role in the coming events.

- **If you are willing, and if it seems right for you, respond to the following exercise. Do not respond to this exercise if it does not seem right for you.**
  - **Allow yourself to imagine, or hear within yourself, the Christ—the Spirit of God within you—say to you, "One part of you will betray me."**
  - **Then ask, "How might I betray the Spirit of God within me? By doing something? By not doing something? By saying, or not saying, by believing or not believing?"**
  - **There might grow within you a fear of this betrayal, but allow yourself to *accept* this statement, "one part of you will betray me," without trying to prevent it, or to correct it, or to analyze it, or to do anything about it.**
- **Receive this statement not as a condemnation, but as a statement that some part of you will not know that its actions are no longer in balance, that its efforts to help will in fact be harmful.**
- **Watch! Keep awake! Notice what is happening within you and outside of you.**
- **Know that it will be painful when you realize that this has occurred, and know that your work is to go on with the process of transformation anyway.**

## TRANSFORMATION

♦ ♦ ♦

Here, as in all of his life and ministry, Jesus embraces all—including the ones who may seem to us to be lowest and most repulsive. He eats and drinks with all, he forgives all, so the last may be first. Judas remains beloved, even after the betrayal—he is forgiven more for having sinned ("missed the mark") more.

> o  **In what ways do you strive hardest for growth, for learning, for wholeness?**
> o  **What do you want most in your spiritual walk?**
> o  **How might your striving hinder your transformation?**
> o  **How can this striving be harmonized with the total surrender that leads to transformation?**
> o  **Can you forgive all?**

♦ ♦ ♦

> o  **Come back to this section and to these questions whenever you feel that you have fallen short in your spiritual walk.**

♦ ♦ ♦

> 14:22 And as they were eating, he took a loaf bread, and after blessing he broke it and gave it to them, saying, "Take; this is my body." And he took a cup, and when he

> had given thanks, he gave it to them, and all of them drank from it. He said to them, "This is my blood of the covenant, which is poured out for many.[3] Truly I say to you, I will no longer drink of the fruit of the vine until that day when I drink it new in the kingdom of God." And when they had celebrated with song, they went out to the Mount of Olives.

This Passover meal is the symbol of the Great Transformation, for in sharing the communion meal Jesus *shows* the disciples what their work is: to internalize the Spirit of God. Thus far they have had a flesh and blood teacher to guide them on the spiritual path, but as Jesus has told them, "you will not always have me." In his absence, they are to take the body of what he has been to them and taught them and eat it, digest it, make it their own flesh and blood, to allow the Spirit to guide their bodies and their minds in all they do.

What is the covenant? This is the first time in the Gospel that this word is used, although it has a rich history in Old and New Testament and elsewhere. The blood of the covenant is poured out for many, and the Twelve are the first to drink of it. The Hebrew tradition of covenant was to seal the relationship between God and His people, and Passover blood is a sign of liberation. This new covenant is to seal the relationship between Christ and those who follow him—a new relationship of liberation. For us, this is a covenant of relationship between our conscious selves and the Spirit of God within us, so that we may commit ourselves to an awareness of our inner Source and to an alignment of our will with that Source. The traditional language used to describe this relationship is worship and obedience, and the Source is God.

♦ ♦ ♦

---

[3] See note 85 on page 259; we emphasize the *cumulative* connotation of the word "many."

TRANSFORMATION

> - If you are willing,[4] and if it seems right for you, respond to the following exercise. Do not respond to this if it does not seem right for you.
>   - Alone or with others, contemplate Jesus as representing the Spirit of God within you—drink from a cup of wine (or fruit juice) and let it be for you the blood of Jesus, of the covenant between you and God. Eat a piece of bread, and allow it to be for you the body of Jesus. Allow this blood and body of Christ, the Spirit of God, to flow into your blood and body as the bread and wine flow into your body, until there is no wine or bread left on the outside, but all is brought within you.
>   - Feel yourself become open to the Spirit and receive it.
>   - Allow this body and blood to flow into your disciple qualities, into the parts of yourself that seek God.
>   - What changes in your disciple qualities after you eat and drink of Christ?
>   - What flows into you? What can flow out of you?
>   - Reflect upon this experience, and describe to yourself or to others what you have experienced.

◆ ◆ ◆

> 14:27 And Jesus says to them, "All of you will fall away; for it is written, 'I will strike the shepherd, and the sheep will

---

[4] This is a personal spiritual exercise and is not meant to be a substitute for the sacrament of communion for those who belong to Christian churches.

## LOVE AND BETRAYAL

> be scattered.' But after I am raised up, I will go before you into Galilee." Then Peter said to him, "Even if they all fall away, I will not." And Jesus said to him, "Truly I say to you, today—this very night—before the cock crows twice you will deny me three times." But he said vehemently, "Even if I must die with you, I will not deny you." And they all said the same.

---

- **If you have eaten and drunk of the body and blood of Christ within you, now contemplate the empty cup and plate—your life with no outward Jesus, no human Master, no Teacher, no Gospels, no Bible.**
- **Contemplate Jesus saying to you, personally, "You will fall away."**
- **If you are not a follower of Jesus, contemplate the source of wisdom and inspiration in your life leaving you.**

---

The task of the disciples is to leave Jesus—or more precisely, to remain in their work and accept the fact that he will physically leave them. He knows that they will not do this willingly, and he knows that the coming events will force the separation. He tells them that he will be cut off from them, and that they will leave him and go their way, back to their homes in Galilee, led by the Spirit. They are able to see this possibility only as a complete disaster, as a separation from the source of their teaching and leadership and inspiration, and since they have dedicated their lives to him they all assert that they will die rather than renounce Jesus.

They are in Judea now, and Jesus tells them that after the transformation he will return before them to Galilee. What does this mean to us? Jesus' entire life and ministry has been centered in and around Galilee; he comes to Judea to the final confrontation, and he tells the disciples that he, and they, will return to Galilee. "Judea" is the place of belief, tradition, ritual and law; it is also the place of

## TRANSFORMATION

confrontation, the place of transformation, the place where great violence and upheaval are to occur. When the time comes, the disciples are to flee from here without hesitation. Something will be destroyed in us, and when the time comes our disciple qualities are to turn back to their work, for we will discover that the Spirit will lead us even when we were sure that it had been extinguished. But before that time it is impossible for us to really understand.

It is difficult for us to see that we must give up Jesus—our limited image of God, for this is truly the only God we know. To "fall away" from this feels like a betrayal of all that is sacred, of all that we live for—and we would rather die than do this willingly. But again, the limited viewpoint is all we have at this time. We must be brought to the transformation by events beyond our conscious control.

Jesus has told the disciples the apocalyptic story of disaster to prepare them for what is coming, telling them to flee Judea when the time comes. But they cannot see what is coming, so he urged them to "stay awake!" They have not yet made the connection between that story and what has begun to unfold. The writer of the Gospel is showing us this process, for we too may fail to recognize the transformation when it begins to happen—we may join in the battle between the polarities, or try to "save" our inner Jesus, as Peter did, by stopping the transformation.[5]

♦ ♦ ♦

---
[5] See Section 21, pages 209-210.

## 42. SURRENDER

## TRANSFORMATION

> 14:32 And they went to a small field called "the oil press" [Gethsemane], and he said to his disciples, "Sit here while I pray." He took Peter and James and John with him, and he began to be greatly distressed and troubled. And he said to them, "My soul is greatly grieved until death [comes]. Remain here and stay awake." And going a little farther, he fell on the ground, praying that if it were possible, the hour might pass from him. He said, "Father [Abba], all things are possible for you; remove this cup from me; yet, not what I want, but what you want."

Jesus may represent the Spirit of God within us, yet he is a very personal aspect of that Spirit, and he responds with a personal will. He also has made the choice to align his personal will with the Will of God, and if they differ he surrenders himself to God. Even the holiest aspects of our personal will have a loyalty to physical life, and only the greater perspective of God can lead him to yield.

Within us, too, we may discover a deep impulse to refuse the transformation. Our will must be strong and aligned with our deepest purpose in life in order to go forward. And we will need support. He takes the same three disciples whom he has singled out on previous occasions—Simon, James and John, who represent inner hearing, the strength and will to overcome obstacles, and the favor of God. These have been the most important qualities right from the start, and they can play a crucial role now in our agreeing to go forward, if we are able and if God wills it so.

> 14:37 And he comes and finds them sleeping, and he says to Peter, "Simon, are you asleep? Could you not stay awake one hour? Stay awake, and pray that you not be put to the test; the spirit is really willing, but the flesh is weak." And again he went off and prayed, saying the same

> words. And again he came and found them sleeping, for their eyes were very heavy, and they did not know what to say to him.

For all of us on the spiritual path, even the thought of giving up our ideas of God, our images of spiritual reality, our way of believing and relating in a spiritual way, is profoundly traumatic. We do not do it willingly. The disciples do not understand what will happen, and they are in denial. Even the most spiritual personal aspect, our spiritual umbilical, our inner Jesus, is reluctant to undergo this metamorphosis and prays to be relieved of the task, for our transformation means his death. This momentary inner conflict is far too intense for the disciple parts of us to bear: in the story, even the most devoted disciples (and these essential qualities within us) cannot remain awake during this time—they fall asleep despite their best effort to support Jesus.

Similarly, when we undergo this shift, the core of the change may occur without our conscious knowledge of it, for our conscious awareness has too deep an allegiance to our spiritual symbols, ideas, practices and beliefs to willingly give them up. The change in allegiance—from the physical image of Jesus (outside of us) to the invisible presence of the Holy Spirit (within us)— will occur unconsciously. When the disciples are awakened, it has begun and the betrayer is at hand.

> 14:41 And he comes a third time, and says to them, "Sleep on now, and rest away! . . . . let it be. The hour has come. See, the Son of Man is delivered into the hands of sinners. Get up! Let us be going. Look! The one who delivers me up has come."

## TRANSFORMATION

> - If Jesus in your life is going to leave—to die—can you be awake to this?
> - If Jesus within you is willing to give up his mission, can you be awake to this?
> - What are you called to be awake to?
> - What if there is a tap at your shoulder and a voice says to you, "Nevertheless, you have slept through it. Now rise up and live through what is to happen next."
> - Be ready for this possibility, for you will do the best that you can do, yet still parts of you may sleep, and later awaken.

♦ ♦ ♦

Why does Jesus take his three "first" disciples within him and ask them to watch, while he prays to be spared the coming ordeal? These are the same disciples he has taken with him to awaken Jairus' daughter, and to the mountain top: they witness the miraculous. They are also the ones who want to be "number one," and whose first reaction is to stop the transformation. These are the greatest potentials within us—to succeed, and to fail. If these parts of us can be awake to the Spirit at this critical moment, the great transformation may occur without inner violence and trauma. Jesus does not pray that the transformation not occur ("for the Son of Man goes as it is written of him"), only that it occur without violence and trauma. The transformation is the awakening of parts of us to the Spirit, and thus far no event has been sufficient to fully awaken the inner disciples, who "sleep on" in ignorance and lack of understanding, despite all that has happened.

This is why Jesus says almost in the same breath, "sleep on," and "get up!"[1] For he is acknowledging that the shock of betrayal, of

---
[1] And yet these words are spoken on two levels of meaning: "sleep on" spiritually, for you cannot help that at this time; but "get up" physically, for events are upon us!

violent confrontation and separation, will be needed to awaken the disciples—and yet they will not gain a true awareness of what has happened until later, after "the Son of man has risen from the dead."[2]

The ministry of Jesus is a work to heal and to awaken the inner parts of our person. For the wounded parts to be healed, the "disciple" parts are to be awakened to do the work of the Spirit. The task of awakening the disciple parts is a formidable one, and the story indicates that the failures are many and profound. In fact, the disciples never do awaken within the story of Mark's Gospel. But the transformation proceeds with death and resurrection, rather than a slow awakening that is possible for some of us.

---
[2] See Section 22, page 214-217.

## 43. CAPTURE AND CONDEMNATION

> 14:43 And immediately, while he is still speaking, Judas—one of the Twelve—arrives, and with him a crowd with swords and clubs from the chief priests, the scribes and the elders. The betrayer had given them a sign, saying, "The one I kiss is the man; arrest him and lead him away under guard." And when he arrived, he immediately comes up to him and says, "Master!" and he kissed him. And they seized him and held him. But one of those who stood near drew his sword and struck the slave of the high priest and cut off his ear. And Jesus said to them, "Have you come out with swords and clubs to capture me as if I were a bandit? Every day I was with you in the temple, teaching, and you did not arrest me—but let the scriptures be fulfilled." And all of them deserted him and fled. A certain young man was following him, wearing nothing but a fine linen chiton. They caught hold of him, but he left the garment behind and fled, naked.[1]

Judas has aggressively provoked extreme spiritual confrontation. On the one hand, he probably has a deeper faith in spiritual power than the others do, and he is willing to unleash that power. But he also carries the mistaken belief that spiritual power works just like material or political power, and it is that belief that leads him to act as he does. He brings Jesus into the hands of material power with an expression of love—a kiss—confident that the Spirit, the true King of Israel, will prevail.

Many of the most important events of the Gospel occur at night. In our interpretation, this is the "night of the soul," and in this vignette the worldly parts of the person act to arrest the Spirit, just as earlier they acted to stop the work of the conscience. Jesus does

---
[1] This follower was covered with only a linen tunic, a common mode of Greek dress. Nakedness did not mean the same to Greeks as to Jews. It is important to know that Greeks as well as Galileans were with Jesus to the end, and that they all fled for their survival after he surrendered himself. Who are the Greeks and Galileans within us?

## TRANSFORMATION

not resist this action, but his followers do. He has been teaching them, preparing them for this event for a long time by now, but they still do not understand. They attempt to resist force with force and are put to flight. We see that the disciples are still carrying their defenses (swords) and do not hesitate to use them to protect what is important to them. Jesus, on the other hand, lives without defenses.

We may easily perceive inner discord as something to be quieted and find ourselves forcefully working to make ourselves calm in the face of uncertain inner turmoil. Not all inner turmoil is a sign that the spirit is working to heal us, and Jesus has indicated that even the turmoil that is a sign of healing will likely throw us into confusion. The story tells us that even many of our inner spiritual supports, our inner disciples, will resist genuine spiritual change. The kind of radical inner transformation that the Spirit brings about within us cannot be engineered by our minds, and may not be consciously supported as it reaches its climax in our lives. The Gospel is alerting us to these facts because our awareness of the overall process is a principal aid in our coming through it all into healing.

Judas is still one of the disciples, more confidant than the others in the outcome, but understanding no more than they. In the end, his action seems to set him apart as "the betrayer," but we can see that his betrayal is an act of love without understanding, not an act of hatred. His action resembles that of a child who goads or provokes a parent to get what he wants. In this essential respect, the fact that he acts out of love, he remains one of the Twelve, even though his actions and their consequences separate him from the others. Before the transformation occurs, no part of us really understands and all parts of us fail.

> o **How might you "push the envelope" in a spiritual way?**
> o **How do you work to make the spiritual transformation of your life happen?**
> o **How might a part of you do this, and with the greatest love and enthusiasm take one step too many, push too far?**

## CAPTURE AND CONDEMNATION

> - **Look for this, be prepared for it, and do not be dismayed if or when it occurs.**
> - **Watch for how parts of you may resist the transformation; keep awake to what is happening to you, allow the Spirit to guide you even in this hour, as your best qualities maybe seem to desert you and you feel desolate.**
> - **Stay with the process. Trust.**

The story of Judas is a portrayal of a part of us that is working to *engineer* the work of transformation. In the end the transformation does occur, but not in the manner he expected. This aspect of the Gospel is a cautionary tale, meant to urge us to refrain from devising our own paths to salvation, or from assuming that we can see the path that needs to be taken. If we could see the pathway that is needed in our lives, we would not need the transformation.

♦♦♦

The Gospel is preparing us to become witnesses to ourselves as well as witnesses to others, in the sense of being observers of what happens. It is essential that we keep aware of what is happening within us as this transformation process goes forward, just as the Gospel story continues on with the narrative even though the disciples have fled. We may discover at some times that our best qualities have deserted us as the inner transformation progresses—we do not watch or listen, do not try, have no courage, we are not generous or charitable, we may become so discouraged that we feel that we just don't care. Our inner Judas, who has brought about this seeming collapse, may still be present, along with one other: Peter, our inner listener, who is now the rock of our persistence.

> 14:53 And they led Jesus to the high priest; and all the chief priests, the elders and the scribes were assembled. Peter had followed him at a distance, right into the courtyard of

> the high priest, and he was sitting with the guards, warming himself at the fire. Now the chief priests and the whole council were seeking testimony against Jesus to put him to death, but they did not find it; for many gave false testimony against him, but their testimony did not agree. Some stood up and bore false witness against him, saying, "We heard him say, 'I will destroy the temple that is made with hands and in three days I will build another, not made with hands.'" But even on this point their testimony did not agree. And the high priest stood up in the middle and asked Jesus, "Have you no answer to what they testify against you?" But he was silent and did not answer. Again the high priest asked him, "Are you the Christ, the son of the Blessed?" Jesus said, "I am,[2] and you will see the Son of Man seated at the right hand of Power, and coming with the clouds of heaven." Then the high priest tore his robe and said, "Why do we still need witnesses? You heard the blasphemy! How do you see it?" And they all condemned him as deserving death. Some began to spit on him, and cover his face and strike him, saying to him, "Prophesy!" and the guards took him and slapped him.

The forces of material power, including the spiritual gatekeepers, take charge of the images and symbols and personification of Spirit, and find that the Spirit of God is an affront to their sense of religion, an outrage against all of their belief and practice. Jesus' answer to them is the answer of God out of the whirlwind: "I am." He quotes the prophet Daniel and the psalmist to tell them what confronts them. They do not understand and are merely insulted, and proceed with their condemnation.

---

[2] This is the third time Jesus has used the formula "I am," from Exodus 3:14. And we see him say "I" and also refer to the "Son of Man" in the third person in the same sentence. It may be helpful here to reflect again on his use of words.

Their image of Messiah, The Christ, is the ultimate extension of how they see themselves, which is why they—and Judas—envision the Christ as a political leader: the "good" side in the war of force between good and evil. Jesus is not on one side, however, but as the true spiritual leader he is the servant of all.

This section of the Gospel shows the confrontation between the Spirit of God within us on the one hand, and our religion, our theology, our sociology, our life values, our highest ideals and strongest beliefs—the mental and religious foundation on which the commanding ego's "temple" is built—on the other. The council has much to say, but its witnesses will not agree. The Spirit does not respond to accusation with anything more than its *being*,[3] for its power is not polarized, not divided; its victory will not vanquish, but include. For the Spirit, confrontation is not the same as conflict—confrontation is a *facing* another, while conflict is a battle against the other. In Jesus the Spirit confronts while refusing to engage in conflict. In the persons of the chief priests and the council, the commanding ego perceives confrontation *as* conflict, and looks for excuses to initiate violence. Even the forces of worldly power, Jesus says, *will* eventually *see* the relationship between the inner Spirit and the Universal Spirit—the Son of Man seated at the right hand of Power. In the end, it is the very *being* of the Spirit that the ego wants to extinguish, and any excuse will do.

How might our commanding ego work to snuff out the life of the Spirit? If we are sincere and open to such thoughts, we may wonder whether the impulse within us is more than just "an impulse," and ask the voice within us if it is God, and it will answer, "I am," and we (the commanding ego, which calls itself "I") may simply not believe it. Or we may ask the same question and an unhealed part of us may be the one that answers, "I am," and we *will* believe it. In either case our commanding self, our ego, will attempt to take charge and discredit "the phony voice of God," or if we do not get that far we will merely sense an "idiotic impulse" that we can easily dismiss. The need to ask the question, "Who is this, really?" never completely

---

[3] See my note on gender pronouns on page 34. I use the word "it" referring to the Spirit, but the Spirit includes both genders and is also beyond gender, so feel free to use the pronouns that you are comfortable with.

## TRANSFORMATION

leaves us at this stage in our lives. If we can remain awake and alert to what is happening within ourselves, we may see this in action, and act to stop the work of the ego, and listen again for the voice of the Spirit within us. The need to listen, to observe, to witness, to choose, never ends.

> - **Listen within yourself as you begin to exercise spiritual power. Ask again as often as necessary, "who is this *really*?"**
> - **Keep awake, watch. Observe inwardly and outwardly.**
> - **Listen within. Check your perceptions for the reality of the spirit. Look for arrogance, self-righteousness, intolerance, or any other sign that one of your own subpersonalities is trying to step into the shoes of the Spirit of God.**
> - **Be alert to parts of yourself that are willing to embrace one side of a polarity in the name of truth, goodness, holiness, or some other ideal, and condemn all that does not side with you.**
> - **Be open to allow the Spirit of God to make changes in you and in your life.**
>
> - **These changes may seem to "just happen," but watch for patterns that may tell you that something deeper is at work within you.**

◆ ◆ ◆

## 44. LOVE AND BETRAYAL, PART 2

# TRANSFORMATION

> 14:66 While Peter was in the courtyard, one of the servant girls of the high priest came by. When she saw Peter warming himself, she stared at him and said, "You also were with the Nazarene, Jesus." But he denied it, saying, "I don't know him. I don't understand what you're talking about." And he went out into the porch, and the cock crowed. And the servant girl saw him and began to say to the bystanders, "This man is one of them." But again he denied it. Then after a little while the bystanders again said to Peter, "You really are one of them, for you are a Galilean."[1] But he began to curse[2] and he swore an oath, "I do not know this man you are talking about." And immediately the cock crowed a second time. And Peter remembered that Jesus had said to him, "Before the cock crows twice, you will deny me three times." And he broke down and wept.

While the inner turmoil approaches its climax, the most persistent and devoted part of us, our inner Peter, stubbornly refuses to let go— and yet cannot follow all the way, either. The anguish we feel when this transformation begins is deep— for we must give up the one who is leading us before we feel we are ready. Our world is collapsing and no new world has dawned. All we have is our hope and our defenses, which lead us to denial. The cock crows to symbolize that dawn is imminent, yet Peter is not awakened—he is still in the mentality of fear and scarcity,[3] wanting somehow to stop the process if he could. Paradoxically, it is the very forces most opposed to the Spirit that bring about its

---

[1] The Judeans look at Galileans as outsiders. These people say, "you really are one of *them.*" See Section 17, especially note 63 on page 177, concerning Galileans and Judeans.

[2] Meaning that he would be cursed if he were not telling the truth.

[3] Jesus has taught the disciples about fear and scarcity earlier. See Section 20, pages 194-196. But in this emergency, Peter is not yet ready to call for help within himself, for he still sees Jesus outside of himself. We may do the same.

## LOVE AND BETRAYAL, PART 2

final emergence in our lives, and those that have supported its emergence that now fight and are scattered.

Why is the story about Peter here? Because even as the ego takes charge, the part of us that is dedicated to hearing with understanding continues to listen. Jesus has taught us this, saying, "Listen! Pay Attention! Keep Awake!" and now when the crisis comes, a part of us that is our inner Witness must follow the events within us, to discern, to understand the meaning of what is happening. But because our inner witness is not yet living in spiritual wholeness, it will not stand up to the ego and will vehemently deny the Spirit when challenged. Why? Because again the question has arisen: "Who is this, *really*?" How can the true Son of God allow himself to be led away by bureaucrats? How can the true Spirit of God who is All in All be squelched by our petty egos? Can this really be God?

But he has told us in advance: you will question, you will doubt, you will deny. This is all right. You are not lost, the effort is not futile. Continue to watch, use your judgment and discernment. Wait. Keep awake. Trust.

♦ ♦ ♦

## 45. GOOD AND EVIL

# GOOD AND EVIL

> ¹⁵:¹ And immediately, in the morning, the chief priests held a conference with the elders and scribes and the whole council. They bound Jesus and led him away and handed him over to Pilate. And Pilate asked him, "Are you the king of the Jews?" He answered him, "You are the one who says it." And the chief priests were accusing him of many things. Pilate asked him again, "Have you no answer? See how much they accuse you of." But Jesus made no further answer, so Pilate wondered. At the festival, he customarily released to them one prisoner, anyone they asked for. Now there was a man called Barabbas in the prison with the rebels who had committed murder during the insurrection. And the crowd came and began to ask that he act according to custom. And Pilate answered them, "Do you want me to release the king of the Jews to you?" For he knew that that the chief priests had handed him over out of envy. But the chief priests stirred up the crowd to have him release Barabbas to them instead. Pilate spoke to them again, "What do you want me to do with the man you call the king of the Jews?" They shouted back, "Crucify him!" Pilate asked them, "What evil has he done?" but they shouted all the more, "Crucify him!" So Pilate, willing to placate the crowd, released Barabbas to them; and he had Jesus whipped, and handed him over to be crucified.

Our thoughts and beliefs will continue to work their will, for the order and sense used by the Spirit is antithetical to the kind of order and sense that we normally adopt to live in the world—it is of an entirely different kind. Our inner Pilate exercises his power to maintain order (in the name of "peace") and will sooner unleash a terrorist (or "freedom fighter") than release the Spirit of God; for the terrorist is someone with whom the inner Pilate is familiar and can fight. The terrorist, like Pilate, is a man of polarities and of action. This kind of adversary is actually welcome by both Romans and priests, because the "war between good and evil"

## TRANSFORMATION

may be the favorite turf for many of our subpersonalities. The inner Pilate may appear to be an adversary to the inner high priest, but in the end they work for the same result—the pre-eminence of temporal worldly power and practical action, and the suppression of the inspiration that is the physical expression of the Spirit. The materially oriented parts of us have little or no respect for the Spirit, looking only for the practical gain to be had from any event. There is even an explicit acknowledgement by Pilate that the Spirit has done no evil. Their actions are not really taken to fight evil, but to maintain a system, a way of life. The "crowd" is manipulated to demand it.

The inner conflict is highlighted in a different way when we consider Barabbas, who is an essential part of this situation. "Barabbas" means "son of the father," and he is imprisoned at the same time as Jesus, the "son of God." Barabbas is a man of action—but what kind of action? The priests and Romans stand for the existing order, whereas Barabbas wants a new order, but it is still outward and political: the revolution he advocates is not the fundamental change of orientation that Jesus represents. The inner priests and Romans would rather deal with an inner Barabbas, for he is on the same level as they are. In our inner world, Jesus truly stands alone.

The Gospel is showing us that we may face confusion, polarities and conflict right up to the edge of our transformation, as the demands of the outer life try to crowd out inner change. Our inner Barabbas is a pseudo-Christ who carries nearly the same name, but none of the deep inner truth of Christ, and in the story the people are given the opportunity to choose between them. We too, as we move toward transformation, will have opportunities to choose—between struggle and surrender; between conflict and acceptance; between outer freedom and inner freedom. We may not see clearly what we are choosing between—they may look a lot alike in some ways. Or we may feel inward or outward pressure to choose action—the way of Barabbas, which *feels* liberating, but may in fact perpetuate the patterns of bondage.

The times of choosing are important moments in our journey. In particular, we may be pressured to choose between polarities as events seem to push us into extremes and "either-or" situations. Our inner priests, Pilate and Barabbas are all forces in our lives that push or pull us to temporary fixes instead of the healing and wholeness that Jesus leads us toward.

## GOOD AND EVIL

- Who is your "inner Pilate?" What part of you really rules, no matter what you think or believe?
- What kind of action does it take to keep the inner peace? Do you feel that sometimes you have to "enforce" inner peace?
- Observe the ways in which your "inner Pilate" may seem to be very useful and helpful to you.
- How can the inner self-discipline that creates inner peace and order, that is helpful when it is a balanced quality, become the extreme of control by force?
- What could move it back to balance?
- How can choosing to pursue practical activity (like gardening, going for a walk, chopping wood—or maybe even hitting something or destroying something) seem to help to relieve the inner pressure when you feel anxious or perplexed?
- How might such practical action, which provides a kind of relief from inner stress, divert you from a real resolution, healing, or transformation?
- Can practical action become a substitute for spiritual power instead of its expression? If so, how?
- When is inner turmoil a sign that you are "far from the kingdom of God," and when can it be a sign that you are approaching the kingdom?
- Is there an "inner Barabbas" in your life, who fights for outer freedom in your life without regard for inner freedom? What makes outer freedom so important, so attractive, that we may sacrifice inner freedom to get it?
- What choices lead you to the wholeness that Jesus represents? What awareness makes it possible for you to choose wholeness when outer events put you under pressure?

## 46. DEATH OF JESUS

# DEATH OF JESUS

> 15:16 Then the soldiers led him off into the courtyard—that is, the praetorium—and they call together the whole cohort. And they put a purple robe on him, and set a crown of twisted thorns on him. And they began to salute him, "Hail, King of the Jews!" And they struck his head with a reed, and spat on him and knelt down in homage to him. And after mocking him, they took off the purple robe and put his own clothes on him. And they led him out to crucify him. And they compel a passerby, Simon of Cyrene, the father of Alexander and Rufus, who was coming in from the country, to carry his cross.

The practical and active sides of our inner selves may have no respect for this "Spirit" that allows itself to be whipped and beaten, and may mock the inner spiritual "ruler" just as the soldiers mock Jesus in the story. There is a part of us that cannot see anything to be gained by such a "surrender." The parts of us that are accustomed to live in the day-and-night, good-and-evil world of polarities cannot understand why the spirit does not work to *get* what it wants and *fight* to accomplish its ends, and they simply cannot respect an impulse to wholeness that includes all and everything. For these parts of us (like the rulers that Jesus taught about in Section 29 on page 259) are tyrants, accustomed to living under tyranny[1] on one level and imposing tyranny on another. For some of us, it will be a tyranny of the mind, for others a tyranny of the body, but for those of us who do live in an

---

[1] In the sense of having absolute power vested in a single ruler. There is no "power sharing" in a tyranny. An inner tyranny is a condition in which one part of us is able to impose its will on other parts of us. I occasionally felt the sting of this as I was writing this book, as my inner drive to write overrode my body's protests as I sat for too many hours in front of my computer. The resulting manuscript that you have in front of you was bought with pain in my neck and shoulders. The need for inner healing and integration still remains on many levels even after we have an increased awareness of some of its processes.

## TRANSFORMATION

absolute power system, the ruling parts of ourselves usually do not willingly acquiesce to actions initiated by other parts. For those of us who live in an "inner power structure" that looks a little like the political tyrannies of history, inner cooperation may seem stupid or weak, because kings that try to rule by listening and cooperating have rarely succeeded, and often have been deposed. But this is the "practical" viewpoint of soldiers in the "war between good and evil" for whom the triumph of one side is the only goal. Within ourselves we will see that the parts of us that work against spiritual healing are interested in specific, limited goals such as academic or professional advancement or success, admiration by others, self-satisfaction, relief of pain or stress, accumulation of possessions, having one's wants and desires met or being served by others.

The apparent triumph of these parts of ourselves can only be temporary, for the part of us which works for the healing and prosperity of all parts of us is so basic to our being that it cannot be extinguished. This tense and graphic section of the Gospel is leading us toward the final resolution and realization.

In the story Jesus does not carry his own cross, but the burden of it is felt by another. And we may well find that the strain of our spiritual transformation will show up most obviously in unexpected ways—not in our Spirit, not in our inner disciples, but in a "passer by," perhaps in our bodies, maybe in another person. All parts of us, and those around us, need support in this process.

> 15:22 And they bring him to golgotha place (which means "skull place"), and they offered him wine mixed with myrrh,[2] but he did not take it. And they crucified him, and divided his clothes among them, casting lots to decide what each would take. It was nine o'clock in the morning when they crucified him. And the inscription of the charge against him read, "The King of the Jews." And with him they crucified two bandits, one on his right and one on his left.

---
[2] Possibly as a painkiller. See "Medicinal Myrrh" by Brett Leslie Freese, at www.archaeology.org.

> And those who passed by reviled him, shaking their heads and saying, "Ha! You who can destroy the temple and rebuild it in three days, save yourself and come down from the cross!" Likewise also the chief priests with the scribes were mocking him among themselves, saying, "He saved others; he cannot save himself. Let the Christ, the King of Israel,[3] come down from the cross now, so that we may see and believe." Those who were crucified with him also reviled him. At noon, darkness came over the whole land until three o'clock. At three o'clock in the afternoon Jesus cried out in a loud voice, "Eloi, Eloi, lema sabachthani?" which means, "My God, my God, why have you forsaken me?" When some of the bystanders heard it, they said, "Listen, he is calling Elijah."[4] And someone ran and filled a sponge with sour wine, and putting it on a stick, gave it to him to drink, saying, "Wait! Let us see if Elijah comes to take him down!" Then Jesus gave a loud cry and breathed his last.

What has happened? In the story Jesus, the human representative of the Spirit within us, has been killed, as if he were like any other small-time threat to inner order, "like a bandit." From the inner perspective, the power of Life has been withdrawn from the worldly, limited, representative of the Spirit of God. In the story the physical man Jesus feels abandoned by God, because, in a way (bodily), *he*

---

[3] Perhaps the priests called him this and not "King of the Jews," as the Romans did, because he was a Galilean, *not* a Judean, whereas to the Romans they are all "Judeans"—the word we now translate as "Jews." Inner politics and prejudice may also be a pretext for inner violence.

[4] "Elijah" would have been pronounced "el-ee-yah" and might easily have been heard instead of "el-a-ee" by scornful bystanders, full of stories about Jesus being John, or Elijah, or one of the prophets, who hear what they want to hear. So they give him some "soldiers' wine" to stimulate him to stay alive for their imaginary circus, but they are disappointed. We may find parts of ourselves remaining impassive or even joking in the face of the deep inner agony we may experience in the course of transformation.

## TRANSFORMATION

*has been.* He knew what was to happen, but even he did not fully understand until the event occurred. As Jesus himself has said earlier, there are some things about which neither the angels in heaven nor the Son know, but only the Father. He too, like John, has come before one greater than himself. The conscience opens the way for the greater Spirit of God to fill a human image in our lives; this image in turn opens the way for the Spirit of God itself to flow freely in all aspects of our lives.

Here is the completion of what Jesus has taught his disciples: the man who walks out the role of Christ on earth must die. This was his first teaching to them after they realized that he was the Christ. Within us, also, we may strain to come to the realization that we have within us one who represents the Spirit of God, and when we finally understand this we must also understand that the representative must "die" so that the Spirit itself may be born and live freely within us. The death makes the inner rebirth possible.

> 15:38 And the curtain of the temple was torn in two, from top to bottom. And when the centurion who stood facing him saw that he breathed his last, he said, "Truly, this man was son of God."

The curtain in the temple was a barrier that separated people from the most sacred space, the "holy of holies." "The death of Jesus" is the parable for The Great Transformation, which can be called "the birth of the spiritual life" from the inner perspective. This birth occurs as the barriers between our ordinary awareness and our spiritual awareness are removed, "torn from top to bottom."

And here also we find a symbolic portrayal of an inner part of us, an "inner centurion" who has been the commander of the soldiers who have actually crucified Jesus, coming at the last minute to a realization of *who* they have just killed. There is no indication in Mark's Gospel that this man was anyone other than the one whose subordinates mocked and scourged Jesus before nailing him to the cross. There is no indication in the story of *why* he comes to the realization that this man was not just another bandit, yet the Gospel says that he understood at the end.

In a historical story the only connection between the curtain in the temple and the centurion's realization would have been made by someone who had some relationship to both the temple and the Roman army, or by a reporter who gathered up disparate stories after the fact. In our inner interpretation these two events are connected by consciousness, for we remember that our "inner Peter" continued to follow what was happening after all our other inner disciples have been scattered. Within us, *all* parts are related and there is a communication between them. Before our healing, the communication is muted or covered over, but we are arriving at the point in the story where healing is emerging from the turmoil just as the legendary phoenix emerges from its own ashes.

Our inner witness is able to discern, even at the point of an inner death, the simultaneous inner birth of something else, symbolized by the temple curtain. The inner realization by our witness sparks an understanding by the practical aspect of ourselves, the "inner centurion," who previously was convinced that the "kingdom" and its "king" were so idiotic that all they merited was mockery.

---

o **How do you exercise your "inner witness?"**
o **Is there a difference between your conscience and your "inner witness?"**
o **Is your inner witness able to maintain awareness even during emotional or physical crises?**
o **Jesus' account of the "apocalypse" in Section 38 (see page 308) was a preparation for these events. How can that account provide you with a larger context in which to understand the crucifixion?**
o **What would be the inner equivalent, for you, of the tearing of the temple curtain?**
o **What kind of experience would provide a real connection between spiritual events and physical events in your life?**

## 47. BEYOND DEATH

# BEYOND DEATH

> **15:40** There were also women looking on from a distance, including Mary the Magdalene, and Mary the mother of James the younger and the mother of Joses, and Salome, who followed him and served him when he was in Galilee; and there were also many other women who had come up to Jerusalem with him.

The story indicates that there were other witnesses to the Gospel than the inner disciples, other supporters. We have seen Jesus teach that the essence of leadership is service (See Section 29 on page 258), and he himself was served by many women all through his ministry, from Galilee right to the end.

This is the second indication in the Gospel that Jesus was served by others—women who follow him and support his work, who have been present from the first day to the last, identified in the story mostly by the men to whom they have given birth. The role of what is female and feminine in the Gospel is foundational, for Jesus has told us that the struggles of spiritual transformation are *birth* pangs. This transformation has been prepared and supported by many mothers, and it is witnessed by many mothers. Who or what within us gives birth to the qualities that are chosen to support the spiritual life? We may feel the steadfastness of "the mothers" within us, even as our other qualities, our inner disciples, are scattered and driven to confusion, denial, fear. The mothers are one way the Gospel story lets us know that there are other inner witnesses to what has been happening within us, and that the role of these observers is actively supportive, and far more important than we at first may realize, particularly at this stage of our transformation.

- **What parts of you are "the inner mothers?"**
- **How do they support you?**
- **How do they serve you?**
- **How do they serve your Spirit?**
- **What have they given birth to in your life?**

TRANSFORMATION

> 15:42 And when evening had come, since it was the Day of Preparation—that is, the day before the Sabbath—Joseph of Arimathea, a respected member of the council, who was also himself seeking the kingdom of God, went boldly to Pilate and asked for the body of Jesus. But Pilate wondered whether he had died already, and summoning the centurion, he asked him whether he had been long dead. And having learned from the centurion, he granted the corpse to Joseph. And having bought a linen shroud, he took down the body and wrapped it in the linen, and laid it in a tomb that had been hewn out of rock, and rolled a stone against the door of the tomb. But Mary the Magdalene and Mary the mother of Joses were watching where he had been laid. When the Sabbath was past, Mary the Magdalene and Mary the mother of James and Salome bought spices, so that they might go and anoint him. And very early on the first day of the week, when the sun had risen, they come to the tomb. And they were saying to one another, "Who will roll away the stone for us from the entrance to the tomb?" When they looked up, they see that the stone, which was very large, had already been rolled away. As they entered the tomb, they saw a young man sitting on the right side, dressed in a long white robe, and they were very alarmed. But he says to them, "Do not be alarmed. You seek Jesus of Nazareth, who was crucified. He has been raised; he is not here. Look, there is the place they laid him. But go, tell the disciples, and also Peter, that he is going ahead of you to Galilee; there you will see him, just as he told you." And going out, they ran away from the tomb, for trembling and amazement had seized them, and they said nothing to anyone, for they were in awe. (End at 16:8) [1]

---

[1] See "About the English Version," page 21.

Here for the first and only time in the Gospel we find people who have experienced something miraculous, amazing, beyond their comprehension—and they have had the spiritual presence and awareness to remain silent. These are three of the women and mothers who have served, largely unnoticed and unacknowledged, throughout the Gospel process. It is these women who are the first witnesses to resurrection—the Great Transformation—and as we undergo a radical transformation, it is a deeply female or feminine aspect of each of us that is present in the beginnings of our new life, for it is only through this deeply receptive aspect of ourselves that a spiritual awareness is born.

Jesus has personified this awareness in its limited, human form. As our transformation unfolds, we begin to live with a very personal awareness of our spiritual source that infuses our daily life and outlook, receiving power and insight, relieving us of conflict, judgment, striving, and filling us with life and love, forgiveness and compassion. We have learned some of this by watching Jesus walk out his mission as Christ on earth, but his mission is completed only as each one of us gives up our limited images and *ideas* of holiness, ethics, salvation and God, and opens to the living presence of the Holy Spirit of God on a daily basis—when we are no longer led by "what comes into us" from outside ourselves, but live in the power of the Spirit that flows into us from within, and through us out into the world.

The climactic end of the Gospel story, the death and resurrection of Jesus, is outwardly a quiet affair in which small external events indicate great inner happenings. The great transformation may be invisible on the outside.

The "young man" in the tomb said to the women, "he is going ahead of you to Galilee." After the transformation of our spiritual orientation, we simply go home, back to our places and the activities that have been our lives—but now we go as we are led by the Spirit. We return transformed, and we approach these places and persons and activities with a new outlook—listening with the outer ear, but also listening with the inner ear for the promptings and direction of the Spirit. We do not get this from books, from events, or from people—and yet the Spirit can and does speak to us through books, events, and people. Something is added to their voices, and to us, which is not quantifiable, not "verifiable"—yet it is observable to those with "ears to hear, and eyes to see."

As the story ends, we are not left with any "neat and tidy" conclusions. The last we saw of the disciples was the scene of their scattering as Jesus was led away from the garden, and in the story the last we saw of Peter, the "rock," was his cursing and denying that he knew anything. In this Gospel we never see the disciples live or work in the fullness of the Spirit, yet we know that their work does not end, for the risen Jesus will "go before them" back to Galilee. As we experience the Deep Transformation, our work will go on, our inner disciples will have a new kind of leading, and God's work will be done.

Some people have remarked that the Gospel seems to show the disciples as dimwitted fools who do not recognize what is before their eyes despite Jesus' repeated explanations, demonstrations, rebukes and exhortations. It is hard to imagine real people being so opaque in the face of such overwhelming events. But it is here that we must go back to our original emphasis on the inner interpretation, for in this interpretation the disciples' behavior makes sense. The Gospel *uses* the story of Jesus to help us to see and to learn, and it makes very clear for us what in life is not clear at all. In the Gospel Jesus explains some things to us that we may not be open enough to see or understand in life, and the portrayal of the disciples in the Gospel provides a very accurate picture of inner parts of us who need prompting, teaching, rebuking, more teaching, correction, *practice* and more practice in order to understand the spiritual significance of the events of our lives. In my observation and experience the repetition of lessons that occurs in the Gospel is constantly needed for most of us, and the gradual evolution of spiritual awareness is a difficult path that is marked by setbacks, delays, misunderstandings, resistance and even sabotage.

We may, for example, witness an event in which scarcity and calamity yield to a surprising abundance with no apparent cause, yet how many of us will say to ourselves, "This is like the feeding of the multitudes in the Gospel" and ask ourselves what our attitudes are toward scarcity and abundance, and what unseen forces may have acted in our lives to produce this effect? The disciples are indeed the model for us to learn from, for their failings are our failings, and it is important that we take Jesus' instructions to them as instructions for us. If we are to follow Jesus in our lives, then we must follow the overall path of the disciples in the Gospel, looking for the meaning of the events of our lives, and knowing that we too may not understand something that is happening right in front of us.

♦ ♦ ♦

We notice again that the author of the Gospel According to Mark has left us a blank space to work with: he has not filled in the space after the empty tomb, with detailed accounts of what Jesus did, what he said, what the disciples did and said. The Gospel ends with the women running from the tomb, trembling with awe. Why the abrupt ending? A history would go right on and tell us the *story* of what happened next. But when we look at the Gospel from the inner perspective, we see that the great transformation will be different for each of us, and the Spirit will work in each life uniquely. So as we contemplate the approach of our own transformation we keep Jesus' words in mind: "Watch! Keep awake!" as we look for how the Spirit will work here, now, *in my life.*

♦ ♦ ♦

Here at the end of the Gospel we have God's response to Jesus' words in Section 8, the answer to our question, "Is God's forgiveness conditional?" As the Gospel story has progressed we have seen people put up ever stronger roadblocks to the work of Christ (God's Spirit in us): gatekeepers, accusations, slander, doubt, enmity, lies, diversions, misunderstanding, ignorance, deceit, unconsciousness, betrayal, abandonment, and finally murder. The resurrection at the end of the Gospel is God's answer to all of it: *nothing* that human beings can do stops God's work of forgiveness and healing.

Watch to see how the Spirit of God transcends the control of your own commanding ego, how the Spirit survives all attempts to stifle or kill it, how it will return again and again until you know *who this is* and what this Spirit is doing in your life. When it seems not to be present, this is only a reflection of your own present lack of awareness.

The Spirit may speak to you loudly so that you are shaken off your feet. It may whisper to you so softly that you mistake its voice

## TRANSFORMATION

for a rustle of leaves in a gentle breeze. It may speak to you in your own mind or in the impulses of your own body; out of the voices of others, older or younger, through the voices of the natural world or through synchronicities that seem to have no outward cause. It may speak to you in time or out of time.

You are only aware of the Spirit because it has moved in your life. Once the Spirit has entered your awareness it is always with you, whether you continue to be aware of it or not, so your own attention matters, for it will not force itself into your attention. It will mirror you in many ways—when you invite it in, it invites you in. The Spirit of God *will* invite you, but never coerce you. It will not excuse you, but it will heal you. It will challenge you, but never reject you. It will see you through to your core and forgive you, always.

> o **What will you do with this forgiveness?**

Your experience of the Spirit may lead you through pain and suffering, yet many of us have come to the realization that often the only way out of suffering is through it. The transformation of your inner life will, ultimately, lead you beyond suffering into freedom and wholeness.

Know that you belong in the Family of Mankind, which is the Family of God, and that God keeps you in the palm of His hand. As you listen for the inner voice, continue to ask *"Who is this, really?"* until the time when its response resonates so deeply in your being that you are filled with a deep, powerful sense of being loved and having love and good will for all being and all beings, that becomes a knowing, and the question needs to be asked no more.

Then, return to your own Galilee to do your work.

# 48. SUMMARY:
# THE PROCESS IN THE GOSPEL STORY

# SUMMARY

Can we put the Gospel process into a "nutshell?" I find that to be a difficult challenge. The Gospel provides something for us even when we approach it from a variety of vantage points, and it "keeps on giving," as the saying goes— the wealth that it contains has not been exhausted after two millennia's study and application, and it can offer something new for each reader. I think the reason for this is the Gospel's ability to draw on our individuality even as it points us toward what is universal. My own approach has focused on Jesus as healer and guide, a living representation of God whose mission was to provide a model and a means for us to open our own lives to the life of the Spirit.

The Gospel story tells of the ministry and transformation of Jesus, which I see as an invitation to be transformed ourselves. The "great" transformation is a process that includes many smaller transformations, and the Gospel story presents a series of steps to help us on our way. The Gospel holds many, perhaps innumerable layers of meaning and understanding its process is the work of a lifetime. This process could be discussed at greater length but that would take another book, or maybe two or three books—but no single book or any collection of books can claim to definitively explain it, for its meaning grows out of what we as individuals bring to it.

I hope that you will be able to use the Gospel and the foregoing discussion as a basis for understanding some of the work that God is doing in your own life, and the steps God is leading you on. The steps that I have covered in the Gospel do not necessarily appear in the same order in our lives, and we may revisit some steps many times in our lives. It may be helpful to go back and start over again, read the Gospel slowly, and see where it might speak to you personally, with these smaller transformations in mind. If the Gospel does not speak to your circumstances at a given time, you may find it helpful to remember the stories within the Gospel so that when you reach the right moment in your journey they will have something to say to you.

My interpretation of the Gospel is by no means exhaustive, and I certainly do not offer it as "the correct" one. There are many fascinating and important aspects of interpretation that I have passed over, for my intention has been to sketch the outlines of a process of spiritual growth, which the Gospel can be used to illuminate and encourage. You will no doubt find other questions that will help you to probe and explore as you walk your own spiritual path. Many spiritual guides, ministers, priests, teachers of spiritual psychology, therapists and healers have developed exercises to help the student and the traveler. I strongly suggest that you avail yourself of the resources that are to be found on your journey.

The Gospel of Mark has laid out for us the outline of a spiritual transformation that is available to anyone. The steps in the process are not linear, not a straight path from our Galilee to our Jerusalem and back. There is a lot of going back and forth, going over and over, learning again at a deeper level what we learned at first, and a responding to the inner guidance that we learn to do more as we go along.

Some walk alone, others with living teachers, others in groups. We each find our own unique path to arrive at a spiritual door through which we are created to go, just as caterpillars are born to transform into butterflies. None is left behind, even though no person knows the hour or the day when their own transformation will begin or end.

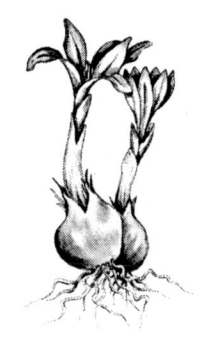

# Appendix A
# The Fruits of the Spirit

## FRUITS OF THE SPIRIT

Some qualities can be seen differently from the ones we considered in Tables A-D, not as a point of balance between extremes or synthesis of opposites, but as the presence of something. We can approach these qualities in a different way, noting their presence or absence. Maintaining balance in the "disciple" qualities listed in Tables A and B may lead us to manifest these, whose presence is often called the Fruits of the Spirit. This list is not the same as the one found in Paul's Letter to the Galatians Chapter 5, because we list the qualities that require learning and balance in Tables A and B among the "disciple" qualities. The Fruits listed below are not learned, but received as gifts from within.

**Love**

**Joy**

**Peace**

**Goodness**

**Faithfulness**

- **Do other qualities belong here for you?**

- **What is it to "have" these qualities present in your life, and how is it different "not to have" them present?**

- **How may working for balance in the "disciple" qualities lead us to these Fruits?**

- **Is it possible to manifest these qualities without having achieved the balance or synthesis of the "disciple" qualities in Tables A and B?**

## APPENDIX A

- What happens if we try?

- What is the relationship of the qualities that are given by God, and those that are the result of our own efforts?

- Can some qualities be achieved and yet also be given by God?

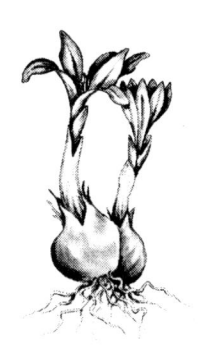

# INDEX OF STUDY QUESTION ISSUES

The following index lists some sections of this book that it may be helpful to review if a particular issue comes up for you, even though the issue may not seem to be the "subject" of the chapter that is indexed.

## STUDY INDEX

| Issue | Section | Page |
|---|---|---|
| Acceptance, radical | 29 | 258 |
| Acceptance of betrayal | 41 | 327 |
| Adversary | 2 | 36 |
|  | 8 | 109 |
| Anger | 32 | 275 |
| Aspiration | 40 | 322 |
| Attainment | 29 | 258 |
| Attention | 10 | 120 |
| Attitude of "having" | 10 | 120 |
| Attitude of "not having" | 10 | 120 |
| Attitude, negative | 21 | 202 |
| Attitudes that build your relationship with God | 21 | 202 |
| Attitudes | 9 | 117 |
| Authority | 33 | 280 |
| Automatic reactions | 20 | 191 |
| Avoiding people | 17 | 176 |
| Awakening | 2 | 36 |
| Balance | 40 | 322 |
|  | 3 | 44 |
| Barrenness, Inner | 12 | 139 |
| Betrayal | 41 | 327 |
|  | 43 | 341 |
| Birth | 47 | 361 |
| Bitterness | 32 | 275 |
| Body of Christ | 41 | 327 |
| Bread and Fish, Inner | 15 | 163 |
| Bread and wine | 41 | 327 |
| Centurion, Inner | 46 | 355 |
| Change | 1 | 28 |
| Change, Life | 3 | 44 |
| Change, Profound | 38 | 307 |
| Children, Inner | 12 | 139 |
|  | 14 | 154 |

# STUDY INDEX

| Issue | Section | Page |
|---|---|---|
| Choice, to respond to inner voice | 1 | 28 |
| Christ, identity of | 21 | 202 |
| Circumstances, power of | 20 | 191 |
| Coincidence | 16 | 169 |
| Comfortable, feeling | 34 | 287 |
| Commandments | 36 | 296 |
| Commitment, total | 37 | 304 |
| Condemnation | 8 | 109 |
| Confidence | 25 | 227 |
| Conflict between teachings and inspiration | 22 | 214 |
| Conflict, Inner | 8 | 109 |
| Confrontation | 33 | 280 |
| Connections between traditions and the Gospel | 22 | 214 |
| Conscience | 1 | 28 |
|  | 2 | 36 |
| Conscience, authority of | 33 | 280 |
| Control over your life | 34 | 287 |
| Control and discipline | 6 | 84 |
| Craving | 5 | 68 |
| Crisis | 3 | 44 |
| Critic, Inner | 2 | 36 |
| Crucifixion | 46 | 355 |
| Dancing Princess, Inner | 14 | 154 |
| Dead part, Inner | 12 | 139 |
| Death | 21 | 202 |
| Death of Jesus, being awake to | 42 | 336 |
| Death of Jesus | 46 | 355 |
| Demons | 4 | 57 |
| Denial | 44 | 348 |

STUDY INDEX

| Issue | Section | Page |
|---|---|---|
| Depth | 3 | 44 |
|  | 10 | 120 |
| Direction, change of | 14 | 154 |
| Disciples, Inner | 3 | 44 |
|  | 14 | 154 |
| Disciples, Inner, rejecting | 14 | 154 |
| Disciplines, spiritual | 6 | 84 |
| Disgust | 17 | 176 |
| Dislike | 17 | 176 |
| Dispute | 23 | 218 |
| Disruption of religious life | 31 | 269 |
| Divorce, inner | 27 | 239 |
| Doors, Physical, to spiritual life | 31 | 269 |
| Doubt and Faith | 23 | 218 |
| Doubt | 38 | 307 |
|  | 23 | 218 |
| Envelope, pushing | 43 | 341 |
| Error | 17 | 176 |
| Expectations | 26 | 231 |
| Experience, painful | 26 | 231 |
| Extremes of qualities | 40 | 322 |
| Failure | 41 | 327 |
| Faith and doubt | 23 | 218 |
| Faith and knowledge | 13 | 146 |
| Faith, Four Steps of | 32 | 275 |
| Faith, weak | 23 | 218 |
| Falling short, feeling | 41 | 327 |
| Family, Inner | 9 | 117 |
| Family, Spiritual | 9 | 117 |
| Farmers, Inner | 34 | 287 |
| Force, control by | 45 | 351 |
| Forgiveness | 5 | 68 |
|  | 8 | 109 |
|  | 32 | 275 |

# STUDY INDEX

| Issue | Section | Page |
|---|---|---|
| Forgiveness | 41 | 327 |
| Fruits of the inner vineyard | 34 | 287 |
| Galilee, returning to | 47 | 361 |
| Gatekeepers, Inner | 31 | 269 |
| Gatekeepers, spiritual | 5 | 68 |
| Gehenna | 26 | 231 |
| Gifts of the spirit, receiving | 28 | 249 |
| Goodness in context | 26 | 231 |
| Grounding | 10 | 120 |
| Growth, Inner, resisting | 14 | 154 |
| Growth, spiritual, hindering | 6 | 84 |
| Habit, self-destructive | 11 | 131 |
| Habits | 9 | 117 |
| "Having," attitude of | 28 | 249 |
| Healing | 4 | 57 |
|  | 5 | 68 |
| Healing, learning after | 19 | 188 |
| Heart, things of | 17 | 176 |
| Hell | 26 | 231 |
| Help, Unexpected | 2 | 36 |
| Herod, Inner | 14 | 154 |
| Hurdles, spiritual | 5 | 68 |
| Hurt | 32 | 275 |
| Ideals | 5 | 68 |
| Identity | 21 | 202 |
| Impossible, desiring the | 15 | 163 |
| Ineffective, feeling | 30 | 263 |
| Inferior, feeling | 18 | 184 |
| Influences, Outside | 6 | 84 |
|  | 17 | 176 |
| Inventory of self-observation | 10 | 120 |

378

# STUDY INDEX

| Issue | Section | Page |
|---|---|---|
| John the Baptist, Inner | 1 | 28 |
| Judgment | 35 | 291 |
| Judgment, Inner | 5 | 68 |
| Knowledge and Faith | 13 | 146 |
| Lack, feeling of | 20 | 191 |
| Leadership | 25 | 227 |
| Leadership, spiritual | 28 | 249 |
| Lessons, spiritual | 21 | 202 |
| Listening for the voice of the Spirit | 22 | 214 |
| Listening, Inner | 5 | 68 |
| Love | 36 | 296 |
| Marriage, inner | 27 | 239 |
| Mob, Inner | 5 | 68 |
|  | 7 | 97 |
| Mother-in-Law, Inner | 4 | 57 |
| Mothers, Inner | 47 | 361 |
| Neediness | 6 | 84 |
| Nobility | 26 | 231 |
| Obstacles to spiritual growth | 26 | 231 |
| Offended | 26 | 231 |
| Open to Spirit | 41 | 327 |
| Opposite qualities | 27 | 239 |
| Opposites, union of | 27 | 239 |
| Opposition, spiritual, to worldly things | 17 | 176 |
| Other side | 16 | 169 |
| Outsider, Inner | 18 | 184 |
| Painful experience | 26 | 231 |
| Parent, Inner | 12 | 139 |
| Parts, Inner, that need healing | 7 | 97 |
| Pattern of your life | 33 | 280 |
| Perceptions, strange | 16 | 169 |

## STUDY INDEX

| Issue | Section | Page |
| --- | --- | --- |
| Permission | 5 | 68 |
| Pharisees, Inner | 5 | 68 |
| Physical Doors to Spiritual life | 31 | 269 |
| Pilate, Inner | 45 | 351 |
| Polarities, Inner | 35 | 291 |
| Power and Authority | 33 | 280 |
| Practical action, to relieve inner pressure | 45 | 351 |
| Prayer – see "Faith" | | |
| Preconceptions. Spiritual | 22 | 214 |
| Preparation | 29 | 258 |
| Pressure | 3 | 44 |
| Priorities | 28 | 249 |
| Problem, intractable | 23 | 218 |
| Program that runs your life | 33 | 280 |
| Proportion | 37 | 304 |
| Provocation, pressure from | 40 | 322 |
| Pushing too far | 43 | 341 |
| Qualities that serve the Spirit | 7 | 97 |
| Qualities, balancing | 2 | 36 |
| | 3 | 44 |
| | 4 | 57 |
| | 6 | 84 |
| | 14 | 154 |
| Qualities, opposing | 6 | 84 |
| | 27 | 239 |
| Reacting to events | 17 | 176 |
| Reactions, automatic | 20 | 191 |
| Realization | 21 | 202 |
| Recognition | 39 | 319 |
| Regret | 14 | 154 |

# STUDY INDEX

| Issue | Section | Page |
|---|---|---|
| Relief | 45 | 351 |
| Relief and healing | 6 | 84 |
| Repentance | 1 | 28 |
| Resistance to change | 11 | 131 |
| Resources, Inner | 15 | 163 |
| Right Action | | |
|   by "wrong" person | 26 | 231 |
| Right and Wrong | 35 | 291 |
| Rising from the dead | 22 | 214 |
| Salt, Inner | 26 | 231 |
| Satan | 8 | 109 |
| Scribes, Inner | 36 | 296 |
| | 5 | 68 |
| Self-Assertive | 25 | 227 |
| Self-discipline | | |
|   and control by force | 45 | 351 |
| Separation, Inner | 27 | 239 |
| Service | 25 | 227 |
| | 29 | 258 |
| Silence | 5 | 68 |
| Simon, Inner | 4 | 57 |
| Sleep, spiritual | 42 | 336 |
| Son of Man | 24 | 223 |
| | 28 | 249 |
| Source | 21 | 202 |
| Spirit, Unclean | 4 | 57 |
| Spirit of God | 1 | 28 |
| Striving, spiritual | 41 | 327 |
| Strong Man | 8 | 109 |
| Stuck, feeling | 5 | 68 |
| Subpersonalities | 3 | 44 |
| | 7 | 97 |
| | 28 | 249 |
| Surrender | 6 | 84 |
| | 41 | 327 |

## STUDY INDEX

| Issue | Section | Page |
|---|---|---|
| Symptoms | 7 | 97 |
| Synthesis | 27 | 239 |
| Take up your cross | 21 | 202 |
| Tax collector, Inner | 5 | 68 |
| Temple, Inner | 31 | 269 |
| Temptation to give all up | 38 | 307 |
| Temptation | 2 | 36 |
| Testing the spirit | 43 | 341 |
| Testing | 2 | 36 |
| Theme of your life | 33 | 280 |
| Things | 10 | 120 |
| Things that move your life | 21 | 202 |
| Traders, Inner | 31 | 269 |
| Trial | 2 | 36 |
| Tyranny, Inner | 29 | 258 |
|  | 46 | 355 |
| Unappreciated, feeling | 29 | 258 |
| Unexpected | 26 | 231 |
| Unloved, feeling | 29 | 258 |
| Unsuccessful, feeling | 20 | 191 |
| Vineyard, Inner | 34 | 287 |
| Voice, hidden | 10 | 120 |
| Voice, Inner | 1 | 28 |
|  | 10 | 120 |
| Voice, Negative | 2 | 36 |
| Will | 42 | 336 |
| Witness | 11 | 131 |
| Who am I? | 21 | 202 |
| Who is this, really? | 21 | 202 |
|  | 43 | 341 |
| Woundedness | 5 | 68 |
| Wrong | 17 | 176 |
| Wrong Path | 26 | 231 |

# PART 3

# Walking Out the Gospel: Exercises in Spiritual Psychology

## Introduction

Spiritual Psychology is the term I use for work we do in our minds, our behavior, our attitudes, our emotions—in our souls, to provide a platform or a springboard for us to open to the spiritual life. My opinion is that people who open to the spiritual life without this foundation often do not understand how their soul and mind behavior can color or filter or even censor the activity of the Spirit in their lives, and they then risk unknowingly allowing their inner spiritual gatekeepers or some other influence to control their spiritual lives—and maybe their whole lives. When this happens the result may be sad or tragic.

Training our souls and minds helps us to really hear the Spirit, and to respond with our whole beings to the voice and promptings and leadings of the Spirit. I invite you to participate in the following exercises, either alone, with a friend, or in groups. The exercises are not "required" in any way and are intended to be a supplement to the foregoing text. There may be some benefit in them for you at some time, and the benefit may not be apparent until after you have done them, maybe a long time after. But it is important that you listen and respond to the spiritual leading that is given to you, and that may lead you either to do one of these exercises or not to do them.

Some of the exercises that follow are adaptations of exercises that I learned at The Synthesis Center in Amherst MA and elsewhere, and some are original with me. I would like to express my gratitude to my teachers while I take responsibility for the changes I have made in some of the exercises.

These exercises are not meant to instill ideas, but rather to allow some movement within you, and to elicit some awareness, and to allow you to understand parts of yourself better, so that when you turn to God you do so with a full conscious will.

I invite you to accustom yourself to moving in and out between the Gospel story and these exercises. You may want to make that move often, and allow the Gospel story to become an anchor for your life. If you come back to it often and look for connections between your life and your understanding of the Gospel, you will find both enriched. You may not at first see the connections between some of these exercises and the Gospel, but as you move between the Gospel and the exercises the connections may become apparent.

If you are doing the exercises with another person or in a group, I would suggest the following basic guideline: before proceeding with the exercises or the study of the Gospel together, do an exercise or some prayer to bring all the participants together as a group. It will be helpful if all members of a training-study group agree to a non-judgmental attitude and to confidentiality, and if all members agree that what happens between people in the group stays in the group, so that everyone will feel safe to share of themselves and their lives. This does not mean that such a group should be secretive, for of course the work of the Gospel is meant to be shared, but personal information about others is not. Confidentiality is a way for the group to give permission to each person in the group to be authentic, to be fully themselves in a safe environment. Sharing in such a group is an invitation to the Spirit to be with us, one that the Spirit always answers.

These exercises are intended for use by adults and are meant to be done alone or together with others, or in a group with a spiritual or psychological guide. They are intended for people who are mentally and emotionally healthy, especially if done alone. If you experience any strong or extreme distress while doing any of these exercises, be aware that the exercises may provoke reactions just as Jesus' healings provoked the reactions of spirits within people. If this happens, I urge you to either proceed with care, or get help from an experienced spiritual guide, a practitioner of spiritual healing or spiritual psychology, or a trained psychotherapist. The Gospel shows plainly that some of us experience upheaval and stress during the process of spiritual healing and growth, and it also shows that help is available and that we should accept it when and where it is needed.

If an exercise asks for an inner response but you experience none, do not be alarmed and do not conclude that anything is wrong. All this means is that the exercise does not work for you at this time. Simply go back to the text in Part 2 of the book, and when it seems appropriate, go to another exercise that does work for you. Nothing in this book is "required" or expected; everything that is presented is just to allow helpful possibilities to emerge in your life.

Feel free to adapt the exercises to your needs or to the needs of your group. If you want to, you should always feel totally free to stop doing any exercise for any reason or for no reason, even if you are right in the middle of doing it. Your willingness, intent and receptivity are what allows each exercise to be effective, so feel free to stop whenever you need to. I suggest that any leader of a group doing this work provide explicit permission to all group members to decline to participate in any exercise or to stop participating in any exercise at any time, without judgment of any kind. It is vital that a group respect and honor the needs of each individual.

## Preparation for the Exercises

Before doing each exercise, I strongly recommend that you do a little preparation so that the exercise will be more effective. Here are some suggestions, and you may want to use them or develop your own ways of preparing for the exercises. If you are not comfortable with some of the terms I use, feel free to adapt the terms so that you can go forward comfortably.

Sit erect in a comfortable place with your feet planted flat on the floor. You may want to ring a bell, or strike a singing bowl, say a prayer, or do some other similar action as a call to harmony and to be sign that this is your time to bring your focus to this work. Now, allow all thoughts of other things, other times, other people, to be set aside (in whatever way works for you) as you focus on what you are doing in the exercise now. Take three slow, deep breaths, inhaling all the way and then exhaling with an audible "aaaahhhhhhh." Scan your body and mind for any irritation or tension, and send relaxing thoughts to that part of yourself, and come to a relaxed state before beginning. If you have difficulty setting aside the thoughts that are whirling around in your mind, repeat the previous moves until you feel comfortable and present enough to proceed. As you prepare to start the exercise, move into a receptive or meditative or prayerful state of mind to allow the Holy Spirit to guide you and to inform your responses. Relax, and if you sense any specific expectations,

## EXERCISES IN SPIRITUAL PSYCHOLOGY

allow yourself to release them and come to the exercise with a sense of childlike openness. These exercise are not designed to have specific effects, but to evoke something from within you that you may observe and find useful in some way in your spiritual walk. Some of the exercises have variations for one, two or more people, but one version is not necessarily "better" than another. Sometimes it may be helpful for one person to guide another by reading the procedure for exercise out loud, especially if the exercise asks the participant to close the eyes.

Enjoy what you are doing. If you have been preoccupied with something in life and feel that your preoccupation cannot be set aside, I recommend that you not do any of these exercises until you are able to set your preoccupation aside, at least a little.

When you have finished an exercise, allow a moment of pure silence before doing anything else, including talking. And again, take three slow, deep breaths, inhaling all the way and then exhaling with an audible "aaaahhhhhhh." Be aware that you have been focusing on the exercise and that you are now bringing your focus back on other things, and slowly look around at your surroundings. Realize that the exercise may have an unexpected effect on you, in some way, and end the session with an affirmation or prayer that doing the exercise will be a blessing and have some beneficial effect. Ask for God's guidance, protection and peace.

## Exercise 1a: Repentance (for one person)

## From Section 1 — Change: Conscience and the Presence of the Spirit

Before beginning this exercise, I suggest that you read the "Introduction" and "Preparation for the Exercises" at the beginning of Part III above. This exercise should be done without evaluation, condemnation, self-judgment, comparisons or expectations.

Summary: Find the desire to change within you, express it briefly, acknowledge to yourself that you have expressed this desire, and encourage the part of yourself that desires to change. This exercise should be done in no more than about 30 minutes, as follows (feel free to adapt the exercise to your own needs):

Procedure: Take no more than ten minutes to think, write, talk out loud, pray, or meditate on one (and only one) thought, attitude, habit, behavior or some aspect of your life that you want to be removed from your life, and then speak or write one sentence in the form of, "I desire to turn away from _____," or "I desire that _____ be out of my life," or something similar. What you choose should be something about the *way* that you yourself live, believe, think, feel, react, etc. and not something that is completely outside yourself. Look within yourself and see whether you ever had, or still have, a desire to keep this thing in your life, and release it, "I release any desire I have for _____."

> Example: "I desire to turn away from or stop my tendency to get angry or frustrated about people who call me on the phone when I am in the middle of my work." Or "I desire that my craving for sweets and chocolate whenever I feel stressed out be out of my life, and I release all desire I have for chocolates as a means to relieve my stress."

Choose only *one* thing for each exercise, and don't do this exercise more than once a day.

After you have expressed this desire for repentance— to purge this particular thing from your life— go into an "inner listening" mode, as if one part of you has witnessed your words and heard them clearly and sympathetically, and acknowledges what you have heard: "I hear this part of me say that _____ and that I release all desire for _____. I deeply love and appreciate this part of me."

◆ ◆ ◆

## Exercise 1b: Repentance (for two people)

### From Section 1 — Change: Conscience and the Presence of the Spirit

Before beginning this exercise, I suggest that you read the "Introduction" and "Preparation for the Exercises" at the beginning of Part III above. This exercise should be done without evaluation, condemnation, self-judgment, comparisons or expectations. Both participants should agree that what happens between you will stay between you, unless you both agree otherwise.

Summary: Find the desire to change within you, express it briefly, acknowledge to your self that you have expressed this desire, and encourage the part of yourself that desires to change. This exercise should be done in no more than about 30 minutes, as follows (feel free to adapt the exercise to your own needs):

Procedure: Person A do the exercise as described below, and Person B be a witness—sit quietly and observe Person A without comment or other action; just watch, listen and silently support what Person A is doing. It is important that Person B not interrupt Person A in any way—by speaking, facial expression or distracting body movement. Person A: Take no more than ten minutes to think, write, talk out loud, pray, or meditate on one (and only one) thought, attitude, habit, behavior or some aspect of your life that you want out of your life, and then speak or write one sentence in the form of, "I desire to turn away from _____," or "I desire that

_____ be out of my life," or something similar. What you choose should be something about the *way* that you yourself live, believe, think, feel, react, etc. and not something that is completely outside yourself. Look within yourself and see whether you ever had, or still have, a desire to keep this thing in your life, and release it, "I release any desire I have for _____."

> Example: "I desire to turn away from or stop my tendency to get angry or frustrated about people who call me on the phone when I am in the middle of my work." Or "I desire that my craving for sweets and chocolate whenever I feel stressed out be out of my life, and I release all desire I have for chocolates as a means to relieve my stress."

When Person A has finished the exercise, Person B responds by briefly mirroring back what you have seen and heard, without evaluation (either positive or negative) and without judgment or expectation. Do the mirroring by saying something like, "I hear you say that _____."

Now, Person A, if you feel that Person B has mirrored your repentance accurately, just affirm it, like saying, "Yes, that's it." If you feel that Person B has not quite understood your intention, then saying something like, "No, what I intend to express this: _____."

Afterward, Person B mirror back what you have seen and heard, "I Hear you say that_____." Person A confirm if Person B is expressing it accurately. When it is accurate, then Person B encourage Person A with a statement like, "I deeply love and appreciate this part of you," or something similar and encouraging.

When you have finished, switch roles and repeat the exercise, with Person B doing the exercise and Person A as the witness.

When you have finished the second round, take another five minutes to share your reflections and observations about what has occurred. Again, refrain from evaluation, condemnation, self-judgment, comparisons or expectations.

Choose only *one* thing for each exercise, and don't do this exercise more than once a day.

◆◆◆

EXERCISES IN SPIRITUAL PSYCHOLOGY

## Exercise 2: Presence (for one person)

From Section 1 — Change: Conscience and the Presence of the Spirit

Before beginning this exercise, I suggest that you read the "Introduction" and "Preparation for the Exercises" at the beginning of Part III above. This exercise should be done without evaluation, condemnation, self-judgment, comparisons or expectations.

Summary: This is an exercise to help you to move from repentance to presence, to become aware of what there is in presence, and to allow your awareness to receive the divine presence.

Procedure: Close your eyes if you wish. Recall the aspect you wanted removed from your life in Exercise 1a or 1b. Mentally picture your life as a glass of water, and the aspect you want removed as being particles suspended in the water. Mentally picture yourself filling the glass with clear water (do not pour the old water out), filling the glass to overflowing and continuing to pour clear water into the glass so that the water with the particles overflows the rim until there are no particles left in the glass, only clear water. In your imagination, hold the glass in your hands and contemplate the clear water in the clear glass. Notice how all the colors of your surroundings may be seen in the glass of clear water. Imagine now that *you* are the clear water, and open your eyes. Without turning your head or moving your eyes, notice how many things in your surroundings you can be aware of. Keeping your eyes looking forward but not focused on anything in particular, allow yourself to be aware of everything in your surroundings all at once, as if you had a mental snapshot of your surroundings. Still without focusing on anything in particular, move your awareness to include all of what you hear, see, smell, taste and feel with your sense of touch, all at once, as much as you can without strain or effort. Don't *try* to see or hear or smell anything in particular, just allow yourself to be aware of what you are aware of, and *notice* your awareness. Notice yourself as the "noticer," the witness. Now, imagine that there is also another person standing behind you who is totally invisible to your physical senses, who is doing exactly the same thing that you are doing— being aware of all things present, but for this invisible person you also are in the field of awareness, even though this other person is not in your field of awareness but only imagined. Close your eyes, if you wish, and again imagine the clear glass of clear water, only this time imagine that you are the clear glass of water and that the imagined person behind you holds the glass in his or her hands— securely, lovingly and peacefully, and imagine — picture it, feel it, *allow* it as much as you can — the clear water of deep love and acceptance to flow into you, to fill your glass to overflowing until all of your water is clear. Imagine yourself being held, and allow this awareness and the feeling of being held to just be for a moment. When you are ready, open your eyes, take a couple of breaths, look around, stretch. If you so desire, say a short prayer of thanksgiving.

♦ ♦ ♦

### Exercise 3: Immediacy (for one person)

### From Section 2 — Negative Voices, The Adversary, and the Spiritual Process

Before beginning this exercise, I suggest that you read the "Introduction" and "Preparation for the Exercises" at the beginning of Part III above. This exercise should be done without evaluation, condemnation, self-judgment, comparisons or expectations.

Summary: This is a physical exercise, using awareness and one of your fingers, to heighten consciousness of the "immediacy" of will and decision-making, and to move into the present moment of being, "I am."

Procedure: Hold one of your hands up near your face, and bend one of your fingers. Look at your hand and bend the finger again, allowing a sense of the present moment to be in your awareness as you do this. Notice that you cannot bend it a minute ago, or a minute

## EXERCISES IN SPIRITUAL PSYCHOLOGY

in the future, you can only bend it now. Bend it again, now. Think about the millions of things that must happen for your finger to bend—brain cells firing, nerves connecting, hormones flowing, muscles moving, all right down to the cellular, even the atomic level—and realize that you do not need to know any of this or think about it in order to bend your finger. Stop thinking, and bend it again, *now*. Do you need to know what happens when you decide to bend your finger? Could you possibly know it all? No, you just *decide* and then you *do it*. Feel yourself decide, and hold up your hand, and now *don't* bend your finger. Did you decide? What did you do? Sit quietly for a moment and be aware of your own will. When you decide to do something, after you have made up your mind about what your action will be, do you decide "immediately" or does it take time to decide?

Now be aware of how much your will has no power to decide, even in the moving of your finger. Notice that you do not decide to move the brain cells, the nerves, the hormones, the muscles, the cells or the atoms, yet when you decide to move *your finger*, it moves! Be aware of your power, and be aware of your lack of power.

Bend your finger again, noticing both the power and the lack of power in this small gesture. Is it a miracle that the finger bends? Feel the time, and then feel the reality of *now*. What is closer than this?

Allow yourself to release your thoughts and feelings, such as mentally sending them to sit in a chair across the room for a moment, and allow yourself to move into an awareness of just being, "I am." Nothing more. The thoughts, feelings and sensations will still be there, but allow yourself to focus for a moment on just being, taking it all in at once. Observe. Notice what is going on within you by feeling your body from the inside, then notice what is going on around you. Feel the presence, that these things are happening *now*.

Where is God in the immediacy, the *now* of these happenings? Sit still in the "I am" of the moment, and allow the presence of God to be with you, whether you *feel* it or not.

When you are ready to finish this exercise, do some small motion three times—clap your hands, turn in a circle, bow to the wind, touch a tree or a wall, or blink your eyes.

*Now*, for a moment, reflect on your experience of this exercise. Write down your reflections, if you like.

EXERCISES IN SPIRITUAL PSYCHOLOGY

## Exercise 4a: Qualities (for one person)

## From Section 2 — Negative Voices, The Adversary, and the Spiritual Process

Before beginning this exercise, I suggest that you read the "Introduction" and "Preparation for the Exercises" at the beginning of Part III above. This exercise should be done without evaluation, condemnation, self-judgment, comparisons or expectations.

Summary: Using memory, identify the personal qualities that were involved in a crisis situation in your life, and become aware of how the situation changed the qualities. Identify which of these qualities is important to you now.

Procedure: Take a moment to recall a significant time or event in your life, perhaps a crisis or a challenge of some kind, in which things became difficult for you in some way, or in which you were tested or tempted to go in a "wrong" direction, and then the situation eventually improved, things became better, the testing ended. Allow yourself mentally to briefly scan the series of events and notice how you thought, felt or responded from one time or event to the next. Now, go to the list of qualities in Table A on page 51-52 and pick just one line from the list, with a quality of deficiency, balance and excess. Pick a line of qualities that resonates with you, that you recognize as qualities that played a part in the situation or event that you have chosen to look at. Scan the events that you have chosen to review again, but this time with these qualities in mind. What qualities were visible in you before the event? What did the crisis do to those qualities? Did the crisis move your qualities into extremes, or strengthen your balance? What quality did you see in yourself after the event or time has passed? Which quality do you see in yourself now?

Review the rest of the list in Table A (or alter the list to fit your own situation) to see what other qualities played a part in your chosen significant time, and how they changed. What qualities helped you to get through your crisis? How did the crisis affect your qualities? What qualities are important to you now?

Example: I recall a time when my wife became very gravely ill. I had mostly been very strong and healthy in my life and had never been very sympathetic towards other people in their illnesses. My wife's illness seemed overwhelming to her, and then to me, as we did not know its cause, nor did we understand its nature. Doctors and medical practitioners were mostly ineffective in their attempts to help, and in fact some of their efforts made things worse. The situation went on for years. When it first began I saw myself as a tower of strength and patience. As the illness went on over time and I found that I could not rely on doctors or others to either understand or to help in the way that was needed, I myself became my wife's primary caregiver and caretaker. My strength and patience sometimes evaporated. As we began to understand what was happening and things finally began to improve, my attitude was changed. I look at the Qualities in Table A, and I find myself focusing on the line that contains the qualities of "Angry or resisting, Accepting, and Acquiescing." I did not at the time realize it, but my supposedly "strong, patient" attitude when the crisis started was a cover for my resistance, for I kept a safe emotional distance from what was happening. As we began to become overwhelmed by the circumstances, I found myself shifting over to a passive acquiescence that was equally defensive and distant, although it seemed more peaceful. But my own body began to show symptoms of illness at this time, a sign that I was reacting strongly to what was happening. Eventually, with much help — including the lessons in this Gospel — I came to a place of deep involvement with the process my wife was undergoing, no longer either resisting or acquiescing, but learning God's will and accepting the present for what it is. The crisis, then, burned away some of my "objectivity" but also exposed my own fearfulness and lack of faith, in which I bounced from mindless resistance to mindless acquiescence, and pushed me into learning true acceptance, faith, and a joyfulness in God's provision. After the crisis I was more mindfully accepting of the world as it is, and thus more able to work for healing and change with a spiritual undergirding. The qualities that allowed me to make the change toward acceptance were a willingness to take risks in concert with patience, persistence, and empathy, all of which grew in the process. But now I find that the quality of acceptance is one that I have come to value very highly, for it enables me to better meet reality as it is and therefore live more effectively as well as peacefully.

To take this another step, you may make a collection of pictures, drawings, clippings, sayings, quotes, or other ways to express the qualities that are important to you. You may want to make a collection of pictures such as a collage, or a notebook of sayings, draw some pictures or doodles, or names of people or animals or places that represent the qualities for you, or some other way to gather and display (for yourself or others) some signs or representations of the qualities that are important to you now—qualities that you have or that you admire in others, qualities you once had but have left behind, or qualities that you desire to have.

♦ ♦ ♦

## Exercise 4b: Qualities (for two or three people)

From Section 2 — Negative Voices, The Adversary, and the Spiritual Process

Before beginning this exercise, I suggest that you read the "Introduction" and "Preparation for the Exercises" at the beginning of Part III above. This exercise should be done without evaluation, condemnation, self-judgment, comparisons or expectations. Both participants should agree that what happens between you will stay between you, unless you both agree otherwise.

<u>Summary</u>: This is an opportunity to identify a quality that you desire to be in your life, and to physically make a gesture of invitation to bring the quality into your life. It has been known since ancient times that a ritual gesture of some kind— that is, a symbolic action

that incorporates mind, emotions and body— can be a powerful aid to an intention to co-create a reality in one's life, and is a form of prayer.

Procedure: Person A, imagine the quality you most desire to be in your life now, one that is not present now. Do a walk, a dance, a gesture, some physical representation to symbolize and express this quality in some way. Then, name the quality out loud and indicate in some way that you desire this quality to be yours. Person B, witness and acknowledge Person A without evaluation or judgment of the quality that has been chosen, but with some kind of encouragement, either silent or out loud, with words, gesture, etc. If there are three people, Person C may witness and respond with Person B. Then after Person A has finished, wait a few minutes and change places: Person B express his or her desired quality in some way and Person A, or Persons A and C, witness and acknowledge Person B. If there are three people, then after Person B has finished, allow a few minutes before Person C expresses his or her desired quality in some way.

Remember that acknowledgement and encouragement is not the same as approval or evaluation *of the quality* in any way. Witnesses are acknowledging and encouraging *the person*, not the quality.

When you are finished, share any prayers that come to you in bringing this intention to God.

♦ ♦ ♦

## Exercise 5a: Qualities of a Subpersonality (for one person)

From Section 3 — The Gathering: Spiritual Qualities

Before beginning this exercise, I suggest that you read the "Introduction" and "Preparation for the Exercises" at the beginning of Part III above. This exercise should be done without evaluation, condemnation, self-judgment, comparisons or expectations.

Summary: This is an exercise to identify the qualities of one or more of your own subpersonalities, and to become aware of how qualities are gathered together and how they manifest in your life.

Procedure: Choose one of your own subpersonalities, and with this part of you in mind review each of the 36 lines in Table A on Page 51. Take each line of Table A and look at the qualities listed with your own subpersonality in mind: think of, or write down, the qualities that this part of you manifests most often, and see how they come together to form a subpersonality in your life. Then, over time, choose another subpersonality to review and repeat the procedure. Finally, compare some of your subpersonalities, looking for what qualities change and what qualities remain the same across your life — just to observe your life, to *see* your self.

The following examples follow the exercise only for the first three lines, but you can work with as many lines as seems helpful to you.

Example #1: First I choose to look at my "worker" self — the way I am while at the office in my "day job."

Line 1 - Cynical - Interested - Fanatical. At work I can get pretty cynical at times when I reflect on the behavior of people in business and politics that I am exposed to, but I try to stay interested in my work even though it often happens that my heart is not in it.

Line 2 - Timid - Courageous - Foolhardy. I guess I can be sort of timid at work, in that I don't take risks with the performance of my duties and I am careful to stay within the bounds required by my professional license. On the other hand, I have seen myself be quite courageous maintaining my ethical behavior even under pressure to "cooperate" with demands that would compromise it, and in standing up for people or for what I believe in.

Line 3 - Uncaring - Caring - Worrying. Sometimes I feel really uncaring when my heart is really not in the work I am doing, such as when I am working for a client whose business engages in practices that I am not happy about, or when

I am working for someone I really don't like. But then again, I do care about being honest and fair and I often worry about making technical errors because people rely on the results of my work for construction, environmental cleanup, property management, legal agreement, and other things.

Example #2: Now I will look at my "husband" self — the way I am in relation to my wife.

Line 1 - Cynical - Interested - Fanatical. I regard being a husband as my true "professions," in that I feel that my wife and I together make a whole, so that much of my orientation as a husband colors everything I do in life. My wife and I are sincere and dedicated to each other, so I am always interested and never cynical. I guess that I could be said to tilt a little toward "less interested" at some times and "more interested" at other times. But I never feel fanatic about it and have never had the ancient attitude of "women — can't live with'em and can't live without'em" that many men have had. I have loved being married since the first day, I work at it and have fun with it and enjoy the growing together and toward each other that has happened over the years and decades we have been together. Some men might view my level of involvement with my wife as being fanatic, but I don't. I just enjoy the relationship we have.

Line 2 - Timid - Courageous - Foolhardy. I am not timid with my wife or about how I connect to her, although in the early years of our marriage we fought with each other fairly often and nearly separated once, after we had been married nine years. I reflect on that and see that our fighting was based upon fear of each other in a way, and while I would not have called either of us "timid" I do think that we held ourselves back in an important way, out of fear. But after that near-separation, we both became less afraid— less afraid to be open and honest with each other and more courageous in being able to take risks in becoming different, and feeling confident that changing *toward* each other and *for* each other, out of love, was something that gave great rewards and was worth all the risks. So now, after nearly 30 years together, I feel balanced as a husband and able to be courageous when the need arises.

Line 3 - Uncaring - Caring - Worrying. I have always been very caring as a husband in an overall way. And in the over five years that my wife has gone through recovery from post-traumatic stress disorder and doctor-prescribed drug addiction I have had times when I worried about her to the point of extreme stress, getting myself ill in a variety of ways. We are a very close couple, so I think there is no area of our marriage in which I am totally uncaring, although there are some areas in which I mostly just stay out. And the distance is good for us in some areas. So all in all I feel I am quite well balanced in this are.

Example - Comparing the two subpersonalities:

Line 1 - Cynical - Interested - Fanatical: My wife and reflect that had I developed a professional career in something I loved, my marriage would not have been so good, because when I was younger I tended to completely dive into what I loved to the exclusion of most other things. But since I am less interested in my professional work I easily pour a lot more of my interest into my marriage. So it is interesting to see the contrast and to realize that my lack of interest in one area has produced some surprisingly good results in another area. Now I have been working on writing this book for many years, but since my wife and I share a strong interest in the subject of this book, we notice that the marriage helps the book and the book has helped the marriage.

Line 2 - Timid - Courageous - Foolhardy: I reflect that there is a quality that remains constant across the two subpersonalities, and that is the courage of my convictions. I can be very flexible in many things, but I am quite attached to being ethical and fair. This is one of the qualities that carries over across all of my subpersonalities. On the other hand I do not take some kinds of risks either professionally or in my

> marriage, usually of the kind that would jeopardize something essential.
>
> Line 3 - Uncaring - Caring - Worrying: I think that there is a common quality that manifests in both of these parts of my, which is a sense of personal responsibility. I can become a worrier at work if I feel I am not carrying out my responsibility adequately, whereas at home I worry at times that I am taking care of my wife adequately. So as I write this I see that there is some fear underneath my being a "good guy" — fear of not being good enough or doing well enough. In the week before I wrote this I realized that there are times when I am at work I tend to take other peoples' problems and make them my own, so I am now working to learn the difference between caring and carrying burdens I have no business picking up.

Take some time with your own self-reflection, but don't turn it into self-analysis. Simply observe the qualities that manifest in your life, how they come and go, how they are stronger in some areas than in others, how they may be balanced in some parts of your life and not in others. When you have observed with compassion (as Jesus looked at the rich man, and loved him), you will be more able to make choices for your life.

♦ ♦ ♦

## Exercise 5b: Witnessing (for one person)

From Section 3 — The Gathering: Spiritual Qualities

Before beginning this exercise, I suggest that you read the "Introduction" and "Preparation for the Exercises" at the beginning of Part III above. This exercise should be done without evaluation, condemnation, self-judgment, comparisons or expectations.

# EXERCISES IN SPIRITUAL PSYCHOLOGY

<u>Summary</u>: This is an exercise in "disidentification," in which you will experience the difference between "my thought, or feeling or sensation," and "I, the one who witnesses the fact that there is a thought, a feeling or a sensation." This is an exercise in awareness of pure being— the one whom God has created. Parts of this exercise may be done over a stretch of time— hours or days, if you prefer.

<u>Procedure:</u>

1) Recall a thought you have had in the past hour. Notice how the thought came into your mind, and how it went. Notice that as you recall this thought, you are witnessing or observing the thought, that "you" and "the thought" are not the same thing. Say to yourself or out loud, "Even though I have this thought, that _____, I am not the same as this thought. I *have* this thought, but I *am* more."

2) Now select an emotion that you have experienced recently, and recall it, how it came and went in your experience, how it felt and how it changed. Notice how "you" are not the same as the emotion, for you observe it. Say to yourself or out loud, "Even though I have this _____ emotion, I am not the same as this emotion. I *have* this emotion, but I *am* more."

3) Follow this same procedure with an impulse or a desire that you have experienced.

4) Then again with something you have imagined;

5) Then again with a hunch or an intuition.

6) Finally follow this same procedure with a bodily sensation.

7) When you are done, take some time to be aware of what you have observed, to become aware that you moved your awareness to observe and witness these things. Notice if there is a difference between when you say to yourself, "I think_____," and when you say "I have a thought about _____." Notice if there

402

is a difference between when you say to yourself "I feel _____," and when you say "I have a _____ feeling."

8) See if you can perceive a kind of inner space (presence but not separation) that has come up between *you* and all these things that you think, feel, imagine, desire, intuit, sense. Take a moment to be very still and get a sense of *just being*, beneath or around any specific experience, a sense of just "I am." Feel your "I am" as the space in which all these other things may happen, or not happen.

Feel your own "I am" that God has created before any other part of your life existed— before body, feelings, reactions, thoughts, etc. and that still exists within, underneath, and yet beyond all of the details of your life. Take some time to be still and notice that this "I am" is *always* here and now, even though all the details of life go on and on.

♦ ♦ ♦

## Exercise 5c: The Quality that is Witnessed (for two people)

From Section 3 — The Gathering: Spiritual Qualities

NOTE: This exercise is designed to be practiced after you have done Exercise 5a.

Before beginning this exercise, I suggest that you read the "Introduction" and "Preparation for the Exercises" at the beginning of Part III above. This exercise should be done without evaluation, condemnation, self-judgment, comparisons or expectations. Both participants should agree that what happens between you will stay between you, unless you both agree otherwise.

<u>Summary</u>: This is an opportunity to playfully "get inside yourself" for some self-learning. You will "become" a part of yourself and see what comes out.

Procedure: Person A, go to the list of Qualities in Table A on page 51, and pick one line of qualities—one deficiency, one balanced quality and one excess quality from the same line, for example "Chaotic-Flexible-Rigid." Notice that there is something these three have in common, they are points on a continuum— in the example I gave, chaotic has too little stability, rigid has too much stability, and flexible is the right balance of stability and change.

For this exercise you are to *become* the line of qualities you have chosen, and act out with words, movements, sounds, gestures, etc. how these qualities play a part in your life. Then after you have acted out the quality, move out of the quality and into "I am" and witness the difference between you and your quality, and affirm your being as one who *has* the quality you have just acted out. Person B, witness this presentation, and when it is done, share what you saw that you admire or like or are impressed with in a positive way. Then switch places, and Person B choose a quality set and act them out, and Person A witness and respond at the end. When both are done, thank each other for sharing this experience and take a few minutes to reflect on this time you have shared. Each person, take a moment to sense and appreciate the "I am" of the other person.

Example: (Person A) "I am Jan's flexibility. When Jan is feeling safe and confidant, I can bend (makes a bending gesture) with the situation to fit what is needed. I help his thoughts be open and generous and curious. I help Jan shift his attention (gets up and moves or turns) to whatever is important. But when Jan is feeling stressed, I become rigid and stiff, I shut down his ability to hear anyone (gestures with hands over ears) who doesn't agree with him. I stiffen his body (acts out, getting stiff) so that he gets spasms and pulls muscles, and I make his attention limited so that he focuses on one thing (gestures with hands like blinders) and he can't see other things. Once I got him so rigid that he got preoccupied and he didn't see a car coming, and almost got us killed! When Jan feels scattered, then I become chaotic, I throw (makes a throwing gesture) his emotions (speaking loudly) all over the place, from angry to sad to happy, (acts these out) and he doesn't quite know what's up with himself.

I make his thoughts run from one fragment to another, and I really have a field day when he tries to "multitask," for then his will and his thoughts really plague him and he gets emotionally whacked out. When Jan tries to exercise too much control over his life, then I become rigid. When he doesn't care enough then I become chaotic. When he balances his choices with his awareness of his limits, then I am balanced and this is my true nature as a quality— flexibility." Now as I, Jan, walk out of the role of being "flexibility" and step back into "I am," I find it amusing that this quality in me seems like such a chameleon, sometimes helping me and sometimes hindering me. But I see that this is an illusion, for I am not the quality, and it does not make me. I *have* this quality, and how I respond to events inside me and outside me changes the way this quality expresses itself. I *have* this quality of flexibility, and with some awareness and choices I can express myself very well in this quality. But I *am* more.

♦ ♦ ♦

## Exercise 6: Discerning the Inner Parts of Us that Need Healing (for one person)

From Section 4 — The Work Begins

Before beginning this exercise, I suggest that you read the "Introduction" and "Preparation for the Exercises" at the beginning of Part III above. This exercise should be done without evaluation, condemnation, self-judgment, comparisons or expectations.

<u>Summary</u>: In this exercise you will allow some inner dialogue to come to the surface, to allow yourself to hear or see some of your own inner voices.

<u>Procedure</u>: Take a pen and paper, and on the left side of the paper make a list of ideal qualities. You may use the lists in Table A to

## EXERCISES IN SPIRITUAL PSYCHOLOGY

draw upon if you like, but make the list personal—what qualities are ideal *for you.*

Then, consider each quality, one at a time, and put each one into an "I am" affirmation in the present tense for yourself. We will take "courage" as an example. In this case, your affirmation might be "I am courageous." You may elaborate on the affirmation and say it in different ways several times. Remember to say your affirmation as if it were a present reality, not "I will be" or "I should be" but "I *am.*" This affirmation is meant as an exploration, and you learn most if you do all that you can to say your affirmation with conviction. This is an *affirmation* — *not* an observation! The observation comes next.

As you say your affirmation "I am courageous" out loud, listen inwardly for mental chatter. An inner voice may say, "Yes this is true," or it may say "Well, I am courageous sometimes," or "I try to be courageous," or it may say, "Are you kidding? No way!" or "Courage—that's just macho baloney." Listen for the tone and feeling behind the inner chatter.

Write down the inner chatter on the right side of your paper. If your response to the "I am_____" ideal affirmation is aspiring, or hopeful or emotionally neutral (even "I am not _____, but that's OK"), then you probably have found a part of yourself that is healthy. If your chatter response to the "I am _____" affirmation is arrogant, vengeful, despondent, angry, fearful, hurt, resentful or bitter in some way, or that immediately moves into comparisons with other people, then you may have uncovered a part of yourself that needs healing. Once you become aware of this part of yourself, you may take steps towards self-acceptance and healing. Or you may find that this shows you an issue that you may want to get some help in dealing with.

Don't go through your whole list at one sitting. Come back to it over a period of time, and look at just one ideal at a time. You may do this exercise with someone else as a witness, in which the witness is simply a listener.

◆◆◆

EXERCISES IN SPIRITUAL PSYCHOLOGY

## Exercise 7: Silence (for one person)

From Section 5 — Healing, Forgiveness and Faith

Before beginning this exercise, I suggest that you read the "Introduction" and "Preparation for the Exercises" at the beginning of Part III above. This exercise should be done without evaluation, condemnation, self-judgment, comparisons or expectations.

<u>Summary</u>: This is an exercise in awareness and in the exercise of silence.

<u>Procedure</u>: Sit silently, alert and upright. Take two or three slow, deep breaths, breathing down into your belly, and then relax. Still your thoughts as much as possible, so that you are aware of everything in and around you, but you are not focusing or "thinking" about anything in particular. Be silently aware of the sounds, feelings, sights, the feeling of your body on the chair or floor, the feel of your clothes against your arms, the temperature of the room, try to be aware of everything at once without focusing on any of it for more than a moment. Now allow yourself to become aware that you are aware, and that your awareness is taking in everything that is "now" for you. If a thought about another time or place, plan or event, wish or emotion creeps into your awareness, just become aware of the thought as a present event and let it be without focusing on it, and bring your attention back into the present. Take as much time as feels appropriate for this exercise, up to about fifteen minutes at most.

Now allow one thought to emerge into your awareness: think of what seems to you now to be the greatest blessing, the greatest good thing that has happened in your life in the past week or month. Something that you can pinpoint and say to yourself, silently, "_____ is the greatest blessing in my life now."

End the exercise for now with this thought, and resolve to recall this thought at least once a day for the next week, but without telling anyone about it. Just recall this thought about what is your greatest blessing, and watch and listen inwardly for any thoughts and other awareness that comes to mind as you recall your blessing.

After you have done this for a week — recalling the blessing without speaking about it — then you may, if you like, share your experience with an exercise or prayer partner. If you prefer to remain silent about it, that is all right too. What has the experience of recalling a blessing in silence been like?

♦ ♦ ♦

## Exercise 8: Eating with "Them" (for one person)

From Section 5 — Healing, Forgiveness and Faith

Before beginning this exercise, I suggest that you read the "Introduction" and "Preparation for the Exercises" at the beginning of Part III above. This exercise should be done without evaluation, condemnation, self-judgment, comparisons or expectations.

Summary: This is an exercise in awareness of some inner parts of yourself, and how they relate to each other.

Procedure: Identify one single issue that is of some personal significance and great importance for you—it may be political, social, religious, etc.—in which you clearly believe there is a "right" and a "wrong." Some examples might include issues of abortion, peace and war, sexuality, religious beliefs and practices, political or family issues, personal or ethical behavior or making choices, etc. Choose an issue in which you personally believe that there is a "right," "good," or "true" belief, thought, position or action and that you can or must actively do something about. Get in touch with the part of you that believes in what is right, true or good in this area, and reflect on your understanding of why it is right, true or good, how you came to that understanding, and what results you hope to see in the future about this issue; and also what you are doing or planning to help these hoped-for results become reality. If you like, you can give a name or a nickname to the part of you that you are reflecting

## EXERCISES IN SPIRITUAL PSYCHOLOGY

on, but if not we can refer to it as "the part of you that believes in what is right, true or good."

Now, step back mentally a few steps from this issue and the part of you that believes in what is right, true or good. Take a breath, center, and allow yourself to open to something different.

Identify a part of yourself that clearly does *not* do well in some area. You may want to use Table A as a guide and choose a part of you that exhibits qualities from the far left (deficiency) or far right (excess) columns. This may be a part of yourself that has failed to live up to your expectations, or that has violated a personal rule of conduct, or that is moody or temperamental; perhaps a part of you that has done something that you are not particularly happy about, or a part that you like least about yourself. Choose just one, and allow yourself to be aware of this part of your life, allow yourself to be aware of your own feelings when you call this to mind. Reflect on this for a moment. You can give this part of you a name, or we can call it "the part of you that you like least."

Now again step back mentally. Allow a space between you (your "I am") and this part of you that you like least.

Now, bring both parts of you into awareness— the part that believes in what is right, true or good; and the part that has disappointed or that you like least. Call to mind your reflection on what is right, true or good, and what you are doing or planning to make the hoped-for good results become a reality. Now picture in your mind these plans or actions being carried out, not by the best and strongest part of you, but by the part of you that has failed, disappointed, or that you like least. How does this make you feel? Are you pleased to have the part of you that you like least carrying out plans or actions to bring about these results that are important to you? Are you confident in the results? Would you rather have a different part of you doing this?

Does this exercise heighten the differences between these parts of you? Take some time to pray or meditate, to open yourself to guidance from the Holy Spirit about how these two parts of you relate to each other, and how they fit into your whole self.

Listen within yourself, and allow each of these two parts of you to have a voice for a moment. How does the idealist part of you feel about the part you like least? How does the part of you that you like least feel about the idealist part of you?

You may ask for help in this, from another person or from God. What do you feel is the Spirit's focus and purpose for you in this exercise?

Go back and read the text from the Gospel and the commentary in Section 5 again, and see what it says to you now. How do your inner scribes, Pharisees, tax collectors and sinners fit into this exercise? How shall you invite them all to come together, to sit and eat together with a common purpose? How shall they work together?

Visualize yourself as standing between the two of them, and invite each to come to you with an outstretched hand, and simply accept them as being what and who they are. Ask them each what they need to come to a reconciliation with the other.

Bring this experience to God in the way that seems appropriate for you.

◆ ◆ ◆

## Exercise 9: Gathering Our Twelve (for one person)

### From Section 7 — Mobilization for Service: The Twelve

Before beginning this exercise, I suggest that you read the "Introduction" and "Preparation for the Exercises" at the beginning of Part III above. This exercise should be done without evaluation, condemnation, self-judgment, comparisons or expectations.

<u>Summary</u>: This exercise allows you to identify your own twelve disciple qualities.

<u>Procedure</u>: If you feel a call or an inner prompting to do so, make a list of 12 qualities that will play a primary role in carrying out the work of the Spirit in your life. In this exercise, do not make a list of qualities you would like to have, but look and listen within for qualities that you *do* have. They may not be balanced when you make your list; after all, Jesus called Levi when he was still a tax collector! But your list may include qualities that may serve the

## EXERCISES IN SPIRITUAL PSYCHOLOGY

Spirit when they become balanced, and they may play an important part before they become balanced.

For example, you may choose the quality represented in Table A on page 51 as lethargic-aspiring-ambitious. You may realize that the quality that you actually have now is ambition— a desire to gain something for yourself, like the rich man on page 250 in Section 28. But perhaps you can also see that with some inner work, some change of attitudes and priorities, your ambition may be transformed into aspiration, which is seeking to attain a goal in a spiritual context.

So as you seek to fill your list, you may listen not only for qualities that you currently see at work in your life, but what your current qualities may become. You may find the qualities of the Twelve in Table B on page 104 to be a helpful starting place, and the qualities in Table A on page 51 may also be helpful. Open yourself to become aware of what qualities that the Christ, Jesus within you, may actually see in you, and what qualities will be gathered for the purpose of working together in you.

It may be helpful to start out by making a long list of every possible quality that may be helpful in your journey of spiritual maturation, and then over time select those twelve that will most likely be permanent aspects of your spiritual life. Allow the Spirit to select the twelve if this is possible for you, but if this selection does not emerge from inspiration, then use your best thoughts, insights and intuitions to make your list. The list you make is provisional— allow your experience or your inner guidance to change the list when and where appropriate. Over the coming days or weeks, look over the list. See which qualities are balanced, which have aspects of deficiency or excess. When you see a quality that is out of balance, use a "recognition and choice" exercise (see Exercise 10 below) to come into alignment with the Spirit.

Finally, offer a prayer of praise and thanksgiving to God for these qualities in your life that will carry out the work of the Holy Spirit.

♦ ♦ ♦

# EXERCISES IN SPIRITUAL PSYCHOLOGY

**Exercise 10: Recognition and Choice (for one person)**

From Section 10 — Parables: The Kingdom of God

Before beginning this exercise, I suggest that you read the "Introduction" and "Preparation for the Exercises" at the beginning of Part III above. This exercise should be done without evaluation, condemnation, self-judgment, comparisons or expectations.

Summary: This exercise presents a practical way to allow the Gospel message to work in your life. Jesus' message can be summed up in these words from Section 3: **"The time is ripe, and the Kingdom of God is at hand. Repent and trust the joyous message."** Put differently, it can be expressed like this: Acknowledge and recognize the condition that needs to be renounced, and have faith in the power of God to change your life in the way that is needed. This message is one we are invited to walk out, to make real in concrete ways in our everyday lives, as well as in the overall orientation of our spiritual outlook and commitment. The following "recognition and choice" exercise is one technique for helping you to walk out Jesus' message. It can be used for and adapted to help change a wide variety of circumstances, including thoughts, emotions, habits, behaviors and attitudes.

Procedure: There are three components to this exercise:

1. Recognition Phrase: Verbally acknowledge the existing condition that you wish to turn away from. This is a phrase of recognition and acknowledgement only—not of desire, judgment, evaluation or method. The recognition phrase should include an acknowledgement of your own personal emotional connection to this existing condition, in a way that resonates deeply within you, so that you can physically feel that when you speak the phrase you are really "putting your finger on it." The phrase should sum up your "gut connection" to what is happening in this area of your life. For example, "I feel a craving for chocolate when I am under

# EXERCISES IN SPIRITUAL PSYCHOLOGY

stress." The recognition phrase is just that —recognition of a present reality, and no more.

2. <u>Choice Phrase</u>: Verbally express the condition that you choose to replace the existing condition. The new condition you choose should be specifically a transformation of the existing condition that you are turning away from, not something unrelated to it. For example, if your existing condition phrase is "I have a craving for chocolate," the condition you choose is not something like "I choose world peace," or something unrelated to your craving for chocolate. Your choice phrase needs to involve a healing or transformation of the existing condition, such as "I choose to be relaxed and free of all cravings." Again, as with the "recognition" phrase, the "choice phrase" should zero in on what is personally meaningful to you; it should have some emotional resonance with where you want to be in relation to your situation. The "choice phrase" should be expressed in positive language such as "I choose to be_____" or "I choose that _____ be the case for me now." Avoid negative language like "I choose not to crave chocolate." Make your choice in the affirmative and in the present tense. A better approach, using the example given, might be "I choose to be free of cravings and have a healthy relationship with food." The recognition phrase is often used in the form of "Even though_____," and the Choice phrase begins with "I choose_____." So to fill in the example I used above, a complete recognition and choice exercise might be "Even though I feel a craving for chocolate, I choose to be free of cravings and have a healthy relationship with food."

3. <u>Involve the Imagination and the Body:</u> Create or select a way to involve your imagination and your body in the process of both recognition and choice. This is an essential part of the process, because without the participation of imagination and the body the recognition and choice would be merely verbal or intellectual and will not involve your whole personhood, and so they will have less chance of

## EXERCISES IN SPIRITUAL PSYCHOLOGY

being effective. Involving mind and body, awareness and imagination and will together in the process of recognition and choice brings great power to the process.

a. One way to involve the body in the recognition and choice process is to use the energy tapping techniques (called "Emotional Freedom Techniques") developed by Gary Craig and others. This is a method that allows the mind to communicate with the body by means of certain acupressure meridian points in the hands, head and upper torso. Tapping on these points with the fingers while doing the recognition and choice phrases provides a powerful means for involving your whole person in this process. I personally have found that this method has provided great benefits that were not available any other way. Information on the basic uses of this technique is available from books and the internet.

b. Another method of involving your imagination in the process is to mentally see yourself in the existing situation, and then make a shift to mentally call up a picture of yourself in your chosen ideal situation. Imagine yourself in the "choice" circumstances, and picture it to yourself in as much detail as possible, and as vividly as possible. This is one way to walk out Jesus' instruction to "trust that you have received all that you pray and ask." When you picture your choice as already accomplished, you lay the inner groundwork for your choice to become reality.

c. It may be most helpful to combine methods that use imagination and bodily responses to gain the maximum benefit. One way would be to use the imaginative pictures while doing the meridian tapping, first picturing yourself as things are, and then picturing yourself as you choose to be as you tap and use the verbal phrases.

EXERCISES IN SPIRITUAL PSYCHOLOGY

    d. Recognition and Choice may be combined with imagination and physical activity in other ways to support inner and outer change. Recent scientific research has confirmed that intelligence, memory, emotional awareness and decision-making are not limited to the "conscious self" and the brain, but are distributed throughout the heart and other organs and systems in the body. To follow Jesus, to repent and trust the joyous message and walk in his footsteps, we cannot merely *think* the process, but we must recruit our feelings, memory, imagination, and bodily energy into the work. The Spirit works throughout whole personhood, not just with our thoughts, and many people have felt unhappy that their resolve to change has not been successful, not realizing that more than thought is needed for inner change. Different forms of the Recognition and Choice exercise may become an essential part of your transformation. Feel free to create new methods that work for you.

4. After you have worked with Recognition and Choice in the mind, imagination and body, surrender the entire process to God and, after contemplating this surrender for a moment, release it from your attention— let it go.

♦ ♦ ♦

## Exercise 11: Inner Child (for two people)

From Section 12 — The Work of Faith: Life and Healing

Before beginning this exercise, I suggest that you read the "Introduction" and "Preparation for the Exercises" at the beginning of Part III above. This exercise should be done without evaluation, condemnation, self-judgment, comparisons or expectations. Both participants should agree that what happens between you will stay between you, unless you both agree otherwise.

<u>Summary</u>: In this exercise you will simply become directly aware of an "inner child" part of yourself, and discover what that part of you needs most right now.

<u>Procedure</u>: Person A: Bring to mind an inner child of your own; that is, yourself at an earlier age, in your memory and awareness. Go mentally into that part of yourself, to identify yourself as that part of yourself. Either speak as if you are the child, or listen and watch inwardly and report out loud what the inner child says, thinks, feels or does. Tell Person B briefly who you are, what age you are, what location you are in imaginatively or in memory, saying what the inner child says. Person B: listen and acknowledge the presence of the child, and ask the child what he or she needs most *right now*. Person A: as the child, and if you wish to do so and are able to do so, answer Person B's question, but if you do not answer that is OK. Person B: Allow and give permission if the child does not wish to answer; or if the child does answer, say it back, mirror what was said back to the child to make sure you have heard what needed to be said. Person A may make corrections if any are needed. Person B now just receives what the child in Person A has shared, be present and appreciate it. Acknowledge what has been shared, and thank Person A for sharing, and suggest that Person A now disidentify from the inner child and come back into the present moment as his/her adult self. Person A, take a couple of deep breaths and slowly come into your normal awareness, become aware of your surroundings in the present.

Acknowledge the need that your inner child has shared. Make some notes if you need to. Do not follow up on the matter of meeting the needs at this time, but simply acknowledge what has come up and thank the inner child for the sharing. If it is appropriate, you may make a mental or physical note to consider the follow up at a specific later time.

When you are ready, switch roles and repeat the exercise. When the second round is over, share any reflections or appreciation as desired. If appropriate or as needed, lift your inner children and their needs up in prayer as you are led to do so. If the exercise brings up any difficult thoughts or feelings for either participant or seems to have any lingering negative effect, you may want to consider getting help from someone who is trained to assist you to deal with such responses.

♦ ♦ ♦

**Exercise 12: Becoming Aware of Blessings (for one or two persons)**

From Section 20 — Spiritual Resources, Part 2

Before beginning this exercise, I suggest that you read the "Introduction" and "Preparation for the Exercises" at the beginning of Part III above. This exercise should be done without evaluation, condemnation, self-judgment, comparisons or expectations. If two persons participate, both participants should agree that what happens between you will stay between you, unless you both agree otherwise.

Summary: This exercise is to allow you to review your day with an emphasis on what blessings have occurred.

Procedure: Now or at the end of the day, take up to a half hour and recall the blessings — the good things and events— that have occurred or appeared in your life during this day. You may want to explore the blessings a little— how they occurred, what aspects and connections they have, how you are aware of them, and so on, with the intent of filling out your awareness of them. Make any exploration brief and do not go into details except those that seem spiritually significant. Make no comparisons or judgments, no evaluations or expectations, but rather just allow the blessings to come to your awareness, look at them simply.

Then give thanks for them, and give them back to their Source, knowing that God works all things for good.

If two participate, first one person do the exercise and the second person just listen and be present. Then change roles and repeat.

## Exercise 13:  Trust and Awareness (for two people)

## From Section 23 — Faith

Before beginning this exercise, I suggest that you read the "Introduction" and "Preparation for the Exercises" at the beginning of Part III above. This exercise should be done without evaluation, condemnation, self-judgment, comparisons or expectations. Both participants should agree that what happens between you will stay between you, unless you both agree otherwise.

Summary: In this exercise one person will become "blind" and the other person will become a guide, so that the first person will experience a short journey without the sense of vision, and allow the other senses to come alive. The purpose of this exercise is that the "blind" person will have the opportunity to trust another as a guide, and the guide will have the opportunity to provide guidance and accept trust.

Procedure:  Person A put on a blindfold so that you cannot see anything at all. Person A is to remain mostly silent through most of the exercise, except if speaking is necessary. Person B is to lead Person A on a walk through whatever building you are in, or outside, into a park, along a sidewalk, in places where it is safe to do this. The journey should not be taken near traffic or in crowded areas. You may stop and sit down together, or stand for a moment. Person B should guide Person A in every way that is needed, letting Person A know what is coming, such as when you are going through a doorway or coming to a step or curb, whatever is necessary to help Person A walk along with you safely. Person B should offer a hand or an arm so that Person A has physical guidance. Person B should not describe where you are going more than is necessary for Person A to walk along safely, not tell Person A in detail what he or she is experiencing, but suggest at various times that Person A stop and touch something (like a wall or a tree) by guiding Person A's hand to the thing to be touched; or listen to something, smell something, or be aware of something like the breeze. Person A, notice your sensations, feelings and thoughts as you go along. Person B, your purpose is to allow Person A to experience a short journey without sight. Do not lead Person A where it is difficult and make sure you have Person A's agreement before you proceed at every step. Yet you want to allow Person A to have a new or unique experience, if this is possible. Person A, you should help Person B guide you by telling Person B what you need in order to experience what Person B is leading you through. Person A, your purpose is to learn how to trust this process, and to say or do whatever you need to make it easier and safer for you to trust, and to be aware of what you are experiencing. Have fun with this exercise and allow something new to happen. Make the journey last about 15 to 20 minutes and end more or less where you started. Create whatever variations in this exercise that will make it most fruitful for you.

Reverse roles and repeat the exercise. When the second round is finished, take some time to share what the experience was like.

♦ ♦ ♦

**Exercise 14a: Inner Marriage (for one person)**

From Section 27 — Wholeness

Before beginning this exercise, I suggest that you read the "Introduction" and "Preparation for the Exercises" at the beginning of Part III above. This exercise should be done without evaluation, condemnation, self-judgment, comparisons or expectations.

Summary: In this exercise you will call into awareness the seemingly opposed qualities in your life that in fact work in close cooperation.

Procedure: Refer to the list of qualities in Table C on Page 246 for starters, or choose other qualities that are not in the Table. Are there any qualities from the left column and the right column that are "married" within you? For example, are you both intuitive and reasoning? or sensitive and resilient? playful and purposeful? Find some qualities that embody the synthesis within you, and draw on other qualities that are not on the list to get a better picture of how seemingly opposite qualities are joined within you to make you whole.

> Example: Albert Einstein used dreams and images to visualize concepts, and then used logical and mathematical skills to translate his visualizations into formulas and principles, using both intuitive and reasoning qualities to produce understanding that could not be expressed without drawing on both intuitive and rational sides of his being.

Look for qualities within yourself that function as a team even though they seem to be unalike. Feel the joining within yourself and be present to the oneness that this joining expresses in you. If you like, do some symbolic action to express both of the apparently "opposite" qualities, and allow the two sides to come into an appreciation for each other, and feel them coming together. See if there is some symbolic activity that you can do that involves both qualities working together or in tandem, or imagine them working together. Reflect on your experience. You may wish to speak or write about these reflections.

♦ ♦ ♦

## Exercise 14b: Building Inner Marriage (for one person)

From Section 27 — Wholeness

Before beginning this exercise, I suggest that you read the "Introduction" and "Preparation for the Exercises" at the beginning of Part III above. This exercise should be done without evaluation, condemnation, self-judgment, comparisons or expectations.

Summary: In this exercise you will identify one or two extreme qualities in your life that seem opposed, and visualize them coming into an inner synthesis or marriage.

## EXERCISES IN SPIRITUAL PSYCHOLOGY

Procedure: Turn to the list in Table D on page 248. Scan the columns on the far left and the far right for one quality that you have, but would prefer not to have—a quality that you would be happier or better without. Be specific, give yourself an example. Now, instead of seeing yourself with the "undesirable" quality, visualize that quality as being transformed, balanced, moving toward the center of the list. The quality on the far left would move toward the second left, or the quality on the far right would move toward the second right.

> Example: If you see yourself as "obsessive" about something in your life, visualize that obsessive behavior transforming into "contemplative." If you see part of yourself as "judgmental" about something, visualize this part of yourself becoming "discriminating." Recall a situation in your life in which you acted out the extreme quality, and visualize the circumstances changing as a result of your own quality transforming from an extreme quality to a healthy yin or yang quality. Mentally replay the situation so that your desired quality comes into play and the outcome is different.

How does your life change when the quality changes? What would enable you to make this change? Are there obstacles to the change? What step can you take to start this process?

Look across the line from the quality that you chose for transformation at its "opposite" at the other end.

> Example: If you notice that in a particular area of your life you tend to behave in an obsessive way (a Yin quality), and you have chosen to see your obsessiveness transform into healthy contemplative behavior, look across the line at the Yang side to see whether you also have some behavior or attitudes that are very frenetic, the opposite extreme. Look for areas in which you seem to bounce from one extreme feeling to its opposite. One extreme yin quality can often be balanced by an extreme yang quality, so that when you begin to balance the one it is also important to balance the other. If

you are learning to balance your sense of being obsessive in one area, you may find it very useful to locate an area where you are frenetic and work to balance this also. Then your inner marriage, which may be very stormy when obsessiveness in one area is married to frenetic activity in another area, becomes tranquil and productive as a healthy contemplative attitude about some things in life is balanced by an active approach to other things.

Visualize the deep synthesis or inner marriage of the qualities. The synthesis will be characterized by your awareness of both qualities operating together, instead of *either* one *or* the other alone.

Find the qualities that are most significant to you and explore the range of qualities in your life. Try mentally replaying some situations with the desired quality and watch for changed outcomes.

♦ ♦ ♦

## Exercise 15: Asking (for two persons)

## From Section 30 — Faith, Part 2

Before beginning this exercise, I suggest that you read the "Introduction" and "Preparation for the Exercises" at the beginning of Part III above. This exercise should be done without evaluation, condemnation, self-judgment, comparisons or expectations.

Summary: The purpose of this exercise to allow the Spirit to guide you in a significant direction, (not to rehearse what you want to happen at the moment), to allow your mind to become aware of the desires of your heart, and to allow your heart to open to the deep leading of the Spirit, and to bring awareness of this leading into consciousness.

Procedure: After a moment in which both participants become still and centered, opening for guidance, and come into silence and stillness, Person A asks Person B: "What do you want? What do you deeply desire?" Person B, rather than *thinking* of what you want or desire, take a moment to *observe* a desire that is already there in you and allow a response to form itself deep in your heart, then allow that response to rise into awareness in some way, and then express that response—in words, in gestures or movement, or whatever way is most appropriate to what you have been given. If you do not feel you have been given any particular response, simply express a desire that you feel within you in whatever way seems appropriate. Person B, Allow yourself to respond to the question without judging, and remember that your response does not have to be an *answer*. It may be a question, or something else. When your response has finished, return to stillness.

Person A, witness Person B's response without comment, and return to stillness. After a moment, ask the same question again, "What do you want? What do you deeply desire?" Person B, go within and allow yourself to go to a deeper level within yourself, and if that happens, observe what emerges. Allow the response to come forward again as before, and repeat the process. Both people, repeat the process a third time if a response if forthcoming, and if there is none then accept that as it is. When there is no more response, change roles: Person B ask the questions, Person A respond.

When both persons have concluded the process, share reflections as this seems appropriate, share appreciation and thanks to each other and to the Spirit who guides this process, and to God.

◆◆◆

## Exercise 16: Prayer (for one person)

From Section 32 — Spiritual Power, Part 3

Before beginning this exercise, I suggest that you read the "Introduction" and "Preparation for the Exercises" at the beginning of Part III above. This exercise should be done without evaluation, condemnation, self-judgment, comparisons or expectations.

Summary: This is an exercise in one kind of prayer

## EXERCISES IN SPIRITUAL PSYCHOLOGY

<u>Procedure</u>: Allow a situation or a person for whom you feel called to pray to arise in your awareness. This is different from choosing what to pray for. Choose to come into a close relationship with God, and then choose to allow the Holy Spirit to show you who or what to pray for. Once you have been given a prayer subject, just hold this person or situation in the mind for some time, sensing the being of your subject and living connections between your subject and others. Become aware of the connections, the relationship, between your prayer subject and yourself. Are you at ease about every aspect of your subject and of your relationship to it? Are you at ease about yourself as you contemplate it? Do not try to change anything here, just be aware. Do not judge your subject or yourself, for it is not necessarily better to be at ease about it. Just notice your thoughts, your feelings, your responses.

Ask within yourself whether you need to give or receive forgiveness about any aspect of your prayer subject or your relationship with him, her or it, or about any other matter or person in which unforgiveness stands between you and your prayer. If you need to do so, then give and receive forgiveness in every way that you can, and ask God's blessings on the forgiveness to flow out and flow in as needed. Rest for a time, and contemplate yourself and the other as being forgiven, and give thanks to God for this.

Now, return to your prayer subject, and to your connection to this person or situation. Ask the Holy Spirit to show you what response is best for the situation—what is best for all, for everyone involved and every thing that is involved. Ask God to give you an intention, a desire of the heart, about your prayer subject—what shall you ask for, what shall you desire, what is best for all? Allow this desire to form in your awareness. Ask God to make this desire a reality, not for your sake or for some other's sake, but for all. See the realization of your prayer in your mind's eye, visualize it in as much living detail as possible. Praise and give thanks to God.

Slowly allow yourself to come out of your "prayer mode" and back into normal awareness. Allow yourself to feel as if the results of your prayer have already occurred in some way, "immediately," knowing that the manifestation of your prayer may take some time in the world. Accept it as "done," and if possible act as if it is now a fact. See how it is best for everyone involved.

# AFTERWORD

AFTERWORD

# The Author and the Work:
# A Believer in Search of a Faith

For different reasons many of us have the disposition or need to believe in something larger than ourselves. Perhaps it is "hardwired" into us. For most people in Europe and the Americas, as well as for many others in the world, that "something larger" has been presented to us, and to our parents and grandparents, in some form of Christianity. Our culture and history are saturated with Christian thought and influence, so that even those who reject Christianity are affected by it.

Still, there are questions around historical facts that have troubled both Christians and non-Christians for nearly two thousand years: why has Jesus Christ, the Prince of Peace, been invoked in the cause of arguments, schisms, murders, persecutions, massacres, wars, genocide? Why has Jesus, who taught love and forgiveness, been cited by people who judge, separate, condemn, despise, punish, enslave, hate, avenge? Why is God, whom Jesus taught to be a loving Father, said by many Christians to be wrathful and willing to condemn people to eternal (unending) torment?

Is Christianity something morally neutral, like a hammer or a law of physics that is available equally to the builder and the destroyer to do with as they please? Historically, this has seemed to be so, as saintly Christians have helped, healed, taught, built, loved and shared their spiritual riches; while at other times and places Christians have done horrible things that they have justified by some teaching in the name of Jesus.

But Christianity is different from a hammer and from a law of physics, for Christianity has a specific purpose— its object is to save people. Yet this is exactly why its history is so troubling. While many are saved, why are many others condemned, persecuted, tortured and killed in the name of Christ? Why, historically, have some Christians announced that they were saving the very people they were killing?

The answer given by many — that those who are condemned, persecuted, killed have not made the choice to embrace Christianity or its vision of God (or the correct *version* of Christianity) — is not sufficient or satisfactory, for it suggests that there is a condition under which condemnation, persecution or killing are acceptable to

## AFTERWORD

Christians, even if these actions are "regretted." It suggests that the God in whom Christians trust either approves of such atrocities or is powerless to prevent them. I believe that a Christianity that is ultimately willing to exclude such "unbelievers" or "apostates" from its purpose of salvation has in fact abandoned its purpose, and it then becomes a neutral tool, available to anyone to either build or destroy, depending upon how broadly or narrowly the term "unbelievers" is defined. How Christianity is then used becomes a matter of preference, policy or politics, bending to suit the purpose of the moment, just as the findings of "science" have been manipulated in our times to alternately support or condemn certain practices or products, like gambling, tobacco or drugs.

The result of Christianity's abandoned purpose is that in our time, people are leaving Christianity in the millions, while others who remain Christians struggle to reconcile themselves with a faith that is apparently so flexible that it can be used to justify and support totally opposite positions and actions. Some who remain Christians are trying to remedy things by removing this flexibility, yet the faith of some of these has become inflexibly hard-hearted, judgmental, excluding and condemning, dividing "us" from "them" in a permanent partition as they abandon Jesus' compassion for all in favor of "salvation" and "righteousness" for the few.

I wrestled with these questions 45 years ago as a teenager, and decided then that they were not worth the effort. I rejected Christianity, religion, God and "all that" completely, in favor of what I thought was "reason" and practicality, and got on with my life. As it happened, my life took several turns for the worse and went from loneliness to aimlessness, to addiction, to disease.

I found myself on death's doorstep in a cancer ward at the age of 29. Or rather, I *was* found there. A spontaneous, deep personal spiritual experience, while alone in my hospital bed, had the effect of immediately evaporating my atheism and my materialism. Whether I was immediately healed of cancer is unclear, for I continued chemotherapy. Yet even though one of my doctors had given me only a 10% chance of survival, when he did exploratory surgery three months later to search for remaining signs of cancer, none was found and none returned.

While my atheism and materialism gave way in the light of healing experience to an awareness of spiritual life and relationship with God, my experience did not occur within the framework of any religion, or even any specific religious beliefs, ideas or practices. Mine was an encounter, not a realization. I had no name for the One whom I encountered — "God" is a term I use now, but did not use then. I remained aware of the questions I had about Christianity—in fact I was far more aware of its misuses and abuses than I was of any truth or benefit connected with it.

My spiritual encounter and healing had the effect of leading me to want to help others, first in the hospital while I was still a patient, then later in my daily life. Within a year of my healing, an opportunity presented itself, as my terminally ill father suddenly became homeless. In an echo of my spiritual experience in the hospital, I was led by an inner prompting to make the decision to take him into my apartment and care for him. This work only deepened my commitment to learn how to love, how to care, how to help.

After his death a year and a half later, the inspiration descended again, with the result that I decided to enter the ministry, for that seemed to me the most appropriate way for me to live a life of helping people. To prepare for this life I entered Divinity School, where I studied for a year and began to get a more balanced view of Christian history, thought, and practice. Nonetheless, my closer study of the New Testament actually heightened and sharpened my questions about Christianity, for I found in black and white some of the language that I thought had been historically used to justify evil actions in the name of Christ.

I did not pursue these questions in Divinity School, for I felt a stronger call (again, in response to an inner voice that I now knew came from beyond myself) to pursue a different kind of ministry—marriage. I soon found myself unable to support my new family as a divinity student, and so left graduate school and returned to the working world. My involvement with Christianity continued, though, for my wife was a "born again" Christian. My love and respect for my wife quickly ran headlong into my historic distrust of Christianity, and the next 20 years were marked by the joyful and difficult process of our seeking life and truth together, learning to respect our differences while maintaining our individual integrity and sense of spiritual truth.

This exploration was enhanced as I began several years of study and training in psychosynthesis, a spiritually-oriented approach to

# AFTERWORD

psychology, twenty years after leaving Divinity School. Psychosynthesis is grounded in a basic acceptance of spiritual life without endorsing any particular religion or spiritual path. It uses an inclusive "both/and" approach to many issues of spirituality, psychology and human relations that stands in contrast to the exclusive "either/or" approach that is adopted by many philosophers, theologians, and psychologists. One aspect of psychosynthesis is that its synthetic approach attempts to transcend personal and social conflict by inclusion of people, perceptions and issues, rather than resolve conflict by means of excluding people, viewpoints or issues. The synthetic approach allows one to include disparate viewpoints, thoughts, feelings in a holistic approach to people and issues without needing to choose to exclude what is "wrong," and also without the need to "compromise." Synthesis does not simply "fill the barrel" with whatever is there, but searches for ways to allow the Spirit to create something new in the process of bringing people, ideas, feelings, attitudes and practices together. This perspective allowed me to begin to reevaluate personal and intellectual issues in a new light.

Upon leaving Divinity School I had felt a great disappointment in abandoning my plans for a "professional" ministry and in not completing my studies. However, I also became aware of now feeling an extreme reluctance to enter a church or read the Bible. This continued throughout the following years as I devoted myself to the practical affairs of earning a living, supporting my family, raising two stepsons. The tension I felt toward Christianity began to abate only after 20 years of living with and loving a person whose Christian faith was an integral part of her life. She and I finally began a Bible study together, choosing to read the Gospel According to Matthew, and to share our reactions, thoughts, reflections, leadings.

Suddenly I found myself reading all my marginal notes from Divinity School, recalling both inspiration and objections. Our study together was enjoyable, and was a watershed in our relationship, for we were able to overcome some spiritual obstacles that had remained between us. After we had finished studying Matthew together, I was left perplexed; for we had encountered so much that was wonderful, yet the old questions rose up again as I compared some of the words of Jesus with what I know of the history of

# AFTERWORD

Christianity—schism, crusades, sectarian wars, conquests, forced conversions, slavery, the Inquisition, and the long and tortured tales of Christians' rejection of dissent, challenge, difference, apostasy, heresy or unbelief, and their often violent behavior toward people who do not subscribe to their own beliefs and doctrines.

I asked, "Is Christianity like a forest, where I can naturally expect to find both hummingbirds and rattlesnakes?" I think the answer to that question is, "yes," for Christianity is a phenomenon in the world, and those who call themselves "Christian" may be like beautiful birds or poisonous snakes.

But I no longer believe that Jesus taught much of what Christianity has become. This belief began to take root in me as I began my second Bible study with my wife, on the Gospel According to Mark. After Matthew, the Gospel of Mark seemed lean and sparse; but I also noticed as I read that my troubled feeling lifted as I studied Mark. Was this because so much seemed to be "missing" in Mark? And then the question descended upon me, in a wonderful flash of inspiration: what if the things that seem to be "missing" in Mark are not supposed to be there in the first place? I began to recount some of the "missing" elements— no "genealogy of Jesus," no story of the birth in Bethlehem, no wise men, no flight into Egypt, no tirade against Pharisees and Sadducees by John the Baptist, no dramatic confrontation between Jesus and the devil, no Sermon on the Mountain or Sermon on the Plain, no beatitudes, no "Lord's Prayer," no quotes in fulfillment of old prophecies of Isaiah, no division of sheep and goats, no weeping and wailing and gnashing of teeth in the outer darkness, and so much more. Why, then, is there so little in Mark?

Many people take the gospels to be the "good news" of the story of Jesus: his birth, life, ministry, death and resurrection, and for many people the *belief* in this *story*—belief in Jesus, in the truth and significance of this story—*is* salvation. The four gospels are generally held by many Christians to show different aspects of the Christ story, each presenting important elements of the faith. Nearly everything in the Gospel of Mark can also be found in Matthew or Luke, where the story is much more detailed, and for many people more inspiring.

I wondered about this. If the purpose of the Gospel was to tell the story of Jesus, then Mark doesn't seem to do it very well. But

## AFTERWORD

then I asked myself, what if the purpose of Mark is something else? What purpose could be served by leaving out so much detail?

In a teaching situation, there are several ways to work with students. One way would be to be for the teacher to explain the lesson, and then to help the students absorb the lesson by asking questions about the lesson and comparing the students' answers with the correct answers. The students may learn the lesson more thoroughly by learning the correct answers to the questions.

Another way might be quite different. The teacher would present a lesson that would have a direct, personal impact on each student. The teacher would explain the issues and present the questions, but because the lessons are designed to have a personal impact the teacher would have to work with each student individually, because the answers to the questions would be highly individual. Each student would have to examine his or her own life to see how the lesson was to be applied.

A text book for the first type of learning would probably contain lessons, questions and answers. The text for the second type of learning would contain lessons and questions, but no answers.

It seemed to me that the first type of learning is exemplified in the Gospels of Matthew, Luke and John, which are full of "answers" (and quite differing ones at that), whereas the second type of learning is analogous to what is presented in the Gospel of Mark. Mark tells about John the Baptist, but does not relate much of what John said; it tells of Jesus in the wilderness, but not what was said; it tells us that Jesus went up the mountain, but not what he said there; it tells of his resurrection, but nothing of what actually happened after the empty tomb was found. I was led to believe that the writer of the Gospel According to Mark is not really telling a story, for he leaves most of the details out. He appears instead to be describing the outlines of a story. Upon examination, it seemed to me that the details of the story that are included serve a particular purpose, of highlighting themes of importance and emphasizing key points, yet not giving "answers." So I concluded that the Gospel of Mark is not a story book, but a spiritual study book; not a text for the public, but a handbook for teachers and self-motivated students.

As I studied this Gospel more, I also came to the conclusion that Mark is remarkable in another respect: many of the elements that Christians argue or fight over—the "elect," the "sheep and the

## AFTERWORD

goats," faith versus works, eternal hell and punishment, condemnation, judgment, destruction—are not present in the Gospel of Mark. Most of us read Matthew before we read Mark, and then we consider Mark in the light of what is presented in the other three Gospels. For some of us, this makes Mark seem inadequate by comparison. I suspect that most of us "fill in" the gaps that seem to be missing in Mark with information we get from other New Testament books, but this not only fills in "information," it also colors our reading of Mark and injects interpretations that do not belong in Mark.

What if Mark is *the* original Gospel, perhaps written by an aide to Peter as the tradition suggests— what if the original Gospel is intended to be sparing of details so that the Gospel *process* would take hold in the lives of readers and students? It is widely held that Mark is, in fact, the earliest Gospel. Why should we accept the hypothesis that the later books have more truth in them?

It is well established and reported in ancient times that from the earliest days after the death of Jesus there were arguments and disagreements about what Jesus said and did, about the meaning and significance of his life and death. The Gospel According to Mark actually records such events while Jesus was still alive, such as the episode when John tells how the Twelve ordered someone to stop healing in the name of Jesus, because he was not one of them! It is no surprise, then, that the writings we now have show numerous inconsistencies, even contradictions, for the competing factions among the Christians not only wrote their own books but also altered the ones they received to fit their own doctrines, and pronounced only certain books "authoritative." In one such case, an ending was tacked onto the Gospel of Mark (Chapter 16 verses 9-20) that was more satisfying to the writer, but was not at all consistent with the message and purpose of the original Gospel.

If we take the Gospel of Mark by itself and read it without filling in the "blanks" by reference to other New Testament writings, but take Mark entirely by itself, we arrive at a startlingly different view of Jesus, his words, life and death. If we then read Matthew, Luke and John in the light of Mark, then the other three also appear in a totally different light— they seem to be designed to persuade us to accept answers and explanations, and to adopt a viewpoint that was missing in Mark. For some of us, the things that the other gospels added to Mark are wonderful, and for some of us, they are the

## AFTERWORD

difference between Christ and "the church," and not so wonderful at all. For me, the difference between the Gospels of Matthew and Mark is partially summed up in the contrasting approaches to people that I discovered when I began to study psychosynthesis. Matthew is full of "either/or" thinking, separating sheep from goats, and excluding the "goats," while Mark shows Jesus as a welcoming presence who heals and invites all. My approach to the Gospel of Mark could be viewed as an application of some of the principles of psychosynthesis to the interpretation of the Gospel. The practical and spiritual benefits of this approach to the Gospel have been manifest in my life ever since I embarked on it.

What I discern in Mark's Gospel is a core teaching, a foundation of the Christian spiritual life upon which other teachings have been built. But I am not happy with the "house" that has been built in the history of Christian churches, which are structures that often claim precisely the kind of "authority" that Jesus himself cheerfully punctured. So in my reading of Mark I have removed the house, in a manner of speaking, so that we can see the foundation more clearly. Perhaps we can rebuild the house so that it rests more securely on its foundation.

I believe that in this foundation I have found the teaching of Jesus that answers my questions, for the condemnation, judgment, wrath and punishment are not found in this foundation. Seeing a foundation of love and power, I believe we may build a strong spiritual house on it.

Jan Kuniholm

# AFTERWORD

Many years before this was written, the author's mother, the late Virginia Flint Kuniholm (1914-2004), experienced a low point in her life, when it seemed as though she was "covered with dirt" and life was not worth living. At a point when she felt she could not go on, she experienced a vision of Jesus, who held out his arms to her and offered her an alternative to her misery, saying, "Take My Joy." She felt an infusion of joy and well-being from within, felt truly *delivered*. A few hours later she felt that, as an artist, she simply had to draw something of what she had experienced, but she had no drawing paper in the house. So she found some faded blank newsprint and quickly sketched the One she saw. Later she had this sketch printed and gave copies to whomever asked for many years, and "Take My Joy" became her ministry, as copies of her vision went all over the world.

At the time of her vision, her son wanted nothing to do with her "religion." How things change. He hopes that the present work is an extension, in a way, of her ministry; for first there is vision, and later, after the vision leaves, there is the work and the walk that is Life.

**TAKE MY JOY!**

CPSIA information can be obtained
at www.ICGtesting.com
Printed in the USA
EDOW031001190313
948ED